In Search for a Theology Capable of Mourning

In Search for a Theology Capable of Mourning

Observations and Interpretations after the Shoah

H. Martin Rumscheidt

Foreword by
Richard L. Rubenstein

WIPF & STOCK · Eugene, Oregon

IN SEARCH FOR A THEOLOGY CAPABLE OF MOURNING
Observations and Interpretations after the Shoah

Copyright © 2017 H. Martin Rumscheidt. All rights reserved. Except for brief quotations in critical publications or reviews, no part of this book may be reproduced in any manner without prior written permission from the publisher. Write: Permissions, Wipf and Stock Publishers, 199 W. 8th Ave., Suite 3, Eugene, OR 97401.

Wipf & Stock
An Imprint of Wipf and Stock Publishers
199 W. 8th Ave., Suite 3
Eugene, OR 97401

www.wipfandstock.com

PAPERBACK ISBN: 978-1-5326-1900-7
HARDCOVER ISBN: 978-1-4982-4499-2
EBOOK ISBN: 978-1-4982-4498-5

Manufactured in the U.S.A.

Contents

Foreword by Richard L. Rubenstein | vii
Preface | xv
Acknowledgments | xix
Author's Note | xxi

I: Salutes to My Mentors

1. Dear Karl Barth | 3
2. The Freedom of God and the Freedom of Christians | 5
3. "Socialists May Be Christians; Christians Must Be Socialists!" Karl Barth Was! | 19
4. The Dire Situation of the Protestant Church: An Illustration of Transition in Karl Barth's Theology | 32
5. Josef Lukl Hromádka: Theology in Solidarity with the Wretched of the Earth | 48
6. The Political Worship of God: The Example of Beyers Naudé | 61
7. To Helmut Gollwitzer on His Eightieth Birthday, December 29, 1988 | 72
8. Something About Bonhoeffer | 76
9. Discipleship between Conflicting Commandments: Dietrich Bonhoeffer in the Conspiracy against Hitler | 84
10. A Calling in a Higher Sense: Dorothee Soelle's Theopoetics | 95
11. The Gift of Hospitality | 114

II: Quaestiones Disputatae

12. To Intervene or Not to Intervene: Is That the Question? | 119
13. Dying as an Act of Defiance | 133
14. Failing the Promise of Nuremberg, or How the Germans' Inability to Mourn Blocked Reconciliation | 143
15. Since Auschwitz Everyone Should Know That Things Worse Than War Are Possible | 155

III: After the Shoah

16. Poetry, Theology and Ethics: A Study in Paul Celan | 167
17. The Light of the Torah and the Children of "Hitler's Willing Executioners" | 181
18. Teaching the Next Generation: The Son of a Perpetrator Reflects | 189
19. White-Collar Crimes Against Humanity: The IG Farben Auschwitz Story | 195
20. Professional Ethics after Auschwitz | 208
21. Children of Perpetrators: The Generations after Auschwitz | 218
22. Rebuilding Christian Faith after Auschwitz: An Autobiographical Reflection of a Perpetrator's Son | 231

Bibliography | 245

Foreword

My Friend Martin Rumscheidt

I FIRST MET MARTIN Rumscheidt when I came to Toronto to participate in a dialogue with Professor Emil Fackenheim on the subject of Jewish theology after the Holocaust not long after the Arab-Israeli War of 1967. I later learned that Martin was born in 1935 in Leuna, Germany, a small town near Leipzig that was destined to play a major role in both World War I and II.

Our story really begins with Martin's father, who was born in 1900 and was conscripted into the German armed forces in 1918. After military service, he pursued university studies and received a PhD in chemistry in 1927. He was hired immediately by IG Farben, the giant German chemical and pharmaceutical conglomerate, as a researcher in the company's Leuna factory.[1] During World War II, he was sent to oversee factories in western Europe, where there was considerably less abuse of workers than in eastern Europe. There were also far fewer Jews, if any, among the workers.

During World War I, the factories of BASF, Germany's largest chemical firm, were located within easy range of French military aviation. The factories produced ammonia, a product necessary for the production of both fertilizers and explosives. A second factory site was constructed at Leuna in central Germany. In the first World War, Leuna was beyond the reach of French aircraft. In World War II, Leuna was the object of very heavy bombing. Today, BASF's Leuna site is one of the corporation's largest.[2]

At the end of the nineteenth century, there had been widespread apprehension that the world was running out of fertilizer. If the trend continued, millions were likely to die of starvation. In 1898, a British scientist, Sir William Crookes, warned that unless crop yields were increased through the use of nitrogen fertilizers, the world's population would soon outstrip

---

1. Martin Rumscheidt, "White-Collar Crimes Against Humanity: The I.G. Farben Auschwitz Story," lecture presented at the University of Bridgeport, April 16, 2014.

2. https://en.wikipedia.org/wiki/BASF.

its food production. Though the atmosphere is composed of about eighty percent nitrogen by volume, this nitrogen is unavailable to plants unless it is first "fixed" in the form of a water-soluble compound, such as ammonia.

Fortunately, a solution to the shortage of "fixed" ammonia was found by two scientists, Fritz Haber (1861–1934), a converted Jew, and Carl Bosch (1874–1940).[3] Their work was supported by BASF. In September 1913, BASF's first industrial-scale ammonia plant began production. It literally produced chemical ammonia and, hence fertilizer, "out of thin air."[4] Both Haber and Bosch were awarded the Nobel Prize for their crucially important discovery.

On December 2, 1925, six major German chemical and pharmaceutical corporations, including BASF, Bayer, and Hoechst, merged into one giant conglomerate, IG Farben. At the beginning of World War II, Farben was reckoned to be one of the world's largest corporations. Incidentally, four of the men on Farben's original supervisory board (*Aufsichtsrat*) were either Jewish or of Jewish descent, as were approximately twenty percent of the professional staff.[5]

I mention these details to remind readers that, although IG Farben became a criminally destructive organization under Hitler, BASF, one of IG Farben's most important units, supplied the resources that made the Haber-Bosch process possible. Moreover, according to Thomas Hager, the author of *The Alchemy of Air*, the Haber-Bosch process was *"the most important discovery ever made."* See if you can think of another that ranks with it, in terms of life-and-death importance for the largest number of people. Put simply, *"the discovery is keeping alive nearly half the people on earth."*[6]

Nevertheless, of all the terrible abuse perpetrated during the Holocaust, few, if any, were worse than those perpetrated by IG Auschwitz, one of IG Farben's major wartime business investments.[7]

---

3. See *Encyclopedia Britannic*, Article, "Fritz Haber: German Chemist," https://www.britannica.com/biography/Fritz-Haber, ref261496. See also Thomas Hager, *The Alchemy of Air*.

4. See https://www.basf.com/us/en/company/news-and-media/science-around-us/fertilizer-out-of-thin-air.html.

5. There is a copy of a very good painting of the original IG Farben supervisory board (1926) at File: IGFarbenGoetterrat.jpg. There is an accompanying file listing the original members of the IG Farben supervisory board. The Jewish board members were Arthur and Karl von Weinberg, Franz Oppenheim, and Ernst von Simpson. Both Arthur and Karl von Weinberg were killed in the Holocaust because of their Jewish descent.

6. Hager, xi, italics added.

7. Rubenstein, *The Cunning of History*, 48–67.

During World War II, Germany faced a severe labor shortage at a time when German military and civilian needs for buna, synthetic rubber, were rapidly expanding. After several meetings between IG Farben executives and Economy Ministry officials, it was decided to locate several new plants in the Polish town of Oświęcim, known by its German name, Auschwitz. By February 1941, IG Farben's decision to locate its new enterprise at Auschwitz appeared to have been a highly profitable venture, as indeed it was meant to be. IG Farben invested a total of 700 million Reichsmark in IG Auschwitz. In 1974, that investment was estimated to be the equivalent to one billion.[8] Today, such an investment would in all probability be worth more than twice that amount.

The Auschwitz location had good supplies of water, coal, and almost cost-free labor. Moreover, Heinrich Himmler, head of the SS, assured IG Farben's leadership that the SS would place at its disposal all available skilled prison labor held at Auschwitz. In effect, IG Farben was guaranteed a steady supply of death-camp prisoners who could be and were worked to death. The prisoners understood that they would remain alive only as long as they kept up their work schedules. No other incentive was needed. Given the combination of harsh work schedules and near-starvation diets, few, if any, prisoners could survive for more than two or three months. Since the supply of prisoners was constantly being replenished by the SS, an almost inexhaustible supply of prison labor was available at IG Auschwitz.

Martin Rumscheidt has written that I was unknown to him in 1967 when, at Emil Fackenheim's suggestion, he came to hear the dialogue between Emil and me at Toronto's Congregation Beth Tzedek. Apparently, something of what I said made a deeper impression on him than I realized at the time. Martin wrote about it in my *Festschrift*:

> I knew that evening that Rubenstein had irrevocably altered what I had hitherto expected or even wanted my vocation of theology to become *After Auschwitz*—a phrase which . . . ineluctably moved me toward what Carole Etzler sings of in her song, "Sometimes I wish my eyes hadn't been opened, sometimes I wish, I could no longer see." In a manner of speaking, I can say that I wished I had not met this man, the relationship to whom I have come to call friendship. He made me see, or perhaps more accurately, hear: a bellowing silence. Six million Jews dead, gone; I never knew you, but how present you are to me in the silence of my parents.[9]

---

8. Ibid., 61.
9. Rubenstein and Berenbaum, eds., *What Kind of God?*, 51.

I was surprised when I first read Martin's words. I did not think I had that kind of influence. I had occasionally met a few German students and scholars, some of whom became very important to me. In addition to Martin, two professors were especially important, Klaus Rohmann, whose book, originally his doctoral dissertation, explored my work and that of Harvey Cox.[10] Klaus and I became and remain good friends. Another German academic who was important to me as was Paul Tillich, whose course on classical German philosophy I consider the best and the most important course I *attended* at Harvard. Note my words, I did not write that it was the best course I *took* at Harvard. I took no exams. I wrote no papers. By the time I became aware of Tillich's importance, I had completed my course requirements and had submitted a thesis proposal that was eventually published as *The Religious Imagination*.

Of the Jewish theologians at work on Holocaust theology at the time, Emil Fackenheim was among those for whom over time, I developed great respect. I first contributed to the debate on God and the Holocaust in *After Auschwitz*.[11] My fully developed views were published in an essay, "God after the Death of God," and went through several formulations and reflected the strong influence of the great Jewish mystical teacher, Rabbi Isaac Luria of Safad (1534–1572) in what is now Israel, as well as Hegel and Paul Tillich.[12]

Emil was working on the same problem at about the same time, but from a very different perspective. I confess that I did not fully understand Emil until I read Martin Rumscheidt's Foreword to Henry Knight's book, *Celebrating Holy Week in a Post Holocaust World*.[13] One of Emil's most important teachings, perhaps his most important, was that a "614th commandment" had been given at Auschwitz, namely, "Thou shalt not hand Hitler posthumous victories." To despair of the God of Israel is to continue Hitler's work for him."[14]

According to Moses Maimonides, arguably the greatest Jewish religious authority of the Middle Ages, traditional Jewish law contains 613 commandments (*mitzvot*). It was Emil who taught that after Auschwitz, a 614th commandment was given. Probably no passage by a contemporary

---

10. Rohmann, *Vollendung im Nichts?*

11. Rubenstein, "The Dean and the Chosen People" in *After Auschwitz*, 1-13.

12. Ibid., *Morality and Eros*, 183–96 and *After Auschwitz*, 293–302; on Luria, see Scholem, *Major Trends in Jewish Mysticism*, 21; on Hegel, see *The Phenomenology of Mind*, 81. For further documentation, see the full notes to the chapter, "God After the Death of God" in *After Auschwitz*, 2nd ed.

13. vii–xii.

14. Fackenheim, *To Mend the World*, 213.

Jewish religious thinker became as well-known as Emil's statement about a "614th commandment." It struck a deep chord in Jews of every social level.

Emil understood that after the Holocaust committed Jews were not interested in exploring the theologically problematic aspects of their own tradition. Too much had been destroyed. They wanted to build, if possible, and for many the 614th commandment pointed the way.

I often saw Martin at meetings of the annual Conference on the Church and the Holocaust, an institution founded in 1970 by two Protestant theologians, Franklin Littell and Hubert Locke. Martin spoke for both of us when he wrote:

> For years the Annual Scholars Conference on the Churches and the Holocaust . . . was almost the only place in North America where critical discussion and exchange was possible, allowing for reexamination of one's conclusions, questions, and proposals, and for developing a post-Holocaust, biblical hermeneutics.[15]

Martin also taught me that there was a way of understanding Emil's idea of a 614th commandment that was new to me. After the Six Day War, there was a discernible increase in hostility toward Israel within the United Church of Canada, the church with which Martin is affiliated as a minister, as well as many other Christian religious institutions. To the surprise of most observers, the Israeli victory was unexpected and, for many, unwelcome.[16]

Israel's wholly unexpected victory was marked by increased hostility of some important Christian groups towards Israel. I believe that the hostility was compounded by the fact the victory took place in *the Holy Land*. I am also convinced that the roots of this antagonism go back to the very earliest days of the early church. Moreover, unlike many of his colleagues in the United Church of Canada, Martin understood that faulting Israel for effectively defending itself in the Six Day War was, perhaps unknowingly, an attempt to give Hitler a posthumous victory.

Unlike many in his church, Martin Rumscheidt had come to understand that leaders like Gamal Abdul Nasser and his allies in the Arab world had every intention of keeping their promise to destroy Israel, if they could. Had they succeeded, Hitler would have achieved his "posthumous victory." Undoubtedly, Martin's Protestant and Catholic colleagues would deny that they were seeking to bring about the utter destruction of Israel.

Martin had been trained in the classical methods of understanding the New Testament, which contains a number of passages that he has

---

15. Knight, viii.
16. See Oren, *Six Days of War*. This is a highly praised account of the war.

characterized quite rightly as "anti-Judaistic and anti-Semitic" and they are the kind of passages that have served as justification for the worst kinds of anti-Jewish behavior. Moreover, Martin was rooted in the Protestant Reformation and its nonnegotiable principle of *sola scriptura*, namely, that scripture alone is the supreme authority in all matters of doctrine and practice. Such passages have been employed to incite or justify anti-Semitic movements and behavior.

Clearly, Martin took Emil Fackenheim's 614th commandment seriously but he also tells us of the relationship with Sally, a Jewish woman when he was a student at McGill University. He spoke of it in a lecture that he gave on April 16, 2014 to the faculty and students of the University of Bridgeport's College of Public and International Affairs. It was undoubtedly one of the most memorable lectures we had heard in recent years. In his UB address, Martin told us, "I grew up in a devout Christian home." In the same lecture, he said that he learned the "anti-Semitic stuff" from his teacher, "a Nazi, who wore his brown shirt and swastika armband fairly regularly." He also relates that when the family emigrated to Canada, he met a number of Jews, especially among his fellow students at McGill University and, to use Martin's own words, he had "a wonderful relationship with a Jewish woman." He wanted to bring Sally home to meet his parents, but when he asked his parents for permission to bring her to the family New Year's Eve party, his father replied, *"Du bringst uns doch keine Jüdin ins Haus!"* ("You are not bringing a Jewish woman into our house, are you?") Reflecting on his father's response years later, Martin reports, "That day, fifteen years after the end of the Nazi years, I discovered that anti-Semitism is a poison that has longevity. I wondered whether I also had it lurking inside me still." He tells us that "The relationship with Sally ended because I feared that I could possibly hurt her badly were it to erupt from me when I held her in my arms. I carry the hurt of the break with her still this day."

Quite naturally, as Martin learned about the Holocaust, he was curious about the involvement, if any, of his father, a senior executive of one of the world's largest and most important corporations, IG Farben, and its successor corporations. Normally, everything about his life, religion, home, education, reflects what can be described as creative orderliness, discipline, and structure. There was, however, one issue about which he could do nothing: He was born in Nazi Germany in 1935 and was ten years old when the war ended in Germany's total defeat. A number of IG Farben senior executives, colleagues of Martin's father, were arrested and held for trial. As we shall see, these included Walter Dürrfeld who was a friend of his father's, before, during, and after the war. Martin describes his feelings at the end of the war:

When the first IG Farben trial opened in the summer of 1947, I felt that a sense of apprehension about that trial had descended on my parents. I was too young at the time, only 12 years old, to discern the real underlying reasons for that. What I do remember, however, is that there was fear that Father might also be indicted and tried. And then when the news came later that fall that Father would not be tried, how utterly relieved Mother was. I can now conclude only that there were reasons for the apprehension, that is to say, that my parents knew what IG Farben had been involved in. When I later raised the subject of the 1947/1948 trial with Father and, in particular, the eight-year prison sentence imposed on Walter Dürrfeld, (he was released after only three years!) he retorted that what Nuremberg manifested was nothing but a political act that arose directly out of the war psychosis and which outraged any sense of justice; it was "victors' justice."[17]

Much that had given order and structure to Martin's life had been called into question. I believe that what saved him emotionally and intellectually was at least in part, his religious vocation and the doors it opened from people of many backgrounds. Had he chosen a scientific career, the range of issues, ideas, and people available to him would, I believe, have been narrower. Whatever he learned about the Holocaust and his church, Martin had the ability to remain faithful both to his church and his personal identity. It was not simple. The issues were not restricted to his parents, friends, or the Church. Martin understood that the issues involved went far beyond mass murder. Unlike war, which ends sooner or later in the defeat of one side by the other and is normally followed by an attempt on the part of the victors to permit the defeated side some kind of restricted existence, if only servitude and domination, the Holocaust was different: the Nazi objective was *universal extermination* of the victim-people.

Summing up, I first met Martin Rumscheidt in 1967. Over time, the relationship grew from that of an acquaintance I met at a lecture to one of friendship, high regard, and profound respect. I marvel at the problems he had to overcome. What an extraordinarily painful confession to admit, "My people, my church, my family, we did the 'worse,' we were complicit in the extermination of Jews, we were murderers."[18] Writing about Martin, I would have hesitated a long time, even if familiar with all of the evidence before making such a declaration, and perhaps out of friendship, I might have

17. Rumscheidt, "White Collar Crimes Against Humanity," lecture presented at the University of Bridgeport, April 16, 2014.

18. Ibid.

been tempted to remain silent. Not so, Martin. In a quiet, dignified way, he confronted the truth about a painful upbringing. He could easily have declared, "I was so young when it all happened. I had nothing to do with it" and, of course, he would have spoken the truth, but it would not have been a *healing truth*. By his utter honesty and frankness, above all, with himself, Martin has achieved that healing for himself and for us.

—Richard L. Rubenstein

Preface

THE PIECES GATHERED IN this collection derive from my now over fifty-year-long confrontation with the problematic legacy of my native land, my parents, and of the church of which I was part and still am today. I have had to face that legacy particularly in my choice of vocation, in theology. Over the years, the dilemma grew ever shaper: abandon the theological endeavor altogether because of its structural inflexibility or seek to "repair" it. On my journey I have had the company of many who were similarly burdened by the catastrophe that the name *Auschwitz* identifies and who had also experienced Dietrich Bonhoeffer's analysis: ". . . it seems to be over: the great dying out of Christianity seems to be here."[1] I interpret that assertion in light of the Shoah and in agreement with Arthur A. Cohen's assessment of it: "[The Shoah] is, at one and the same time, a destructive event that uniquely occurred . . . as well as a reality that endures and continues to make assaultive claim upon subjective, impassioned, even unconscious awareness."[2] The Shoah marks my being as a native of the Germany ruled by Hitler, it colors my being as a child of a father who, through his employment in the IG Farben conglomerate and, in particular, its program of "extermination through labor" at Auschwitz-Monowitz, is complicit in the Holocaust. And it assaults my theological existence, not only in my vocation but also in my personal identity.

The essays gathered in this book address phases of my journey in the search for a theology that is capable of taking up the labor of mourning. I seek a theological existence that is committed to confessing its enmeshment in the "destructive event" and to engage without flinching in the task of answering Bonhoeffer's question in *After Ten Years* whether it was "still of any use."[3] My understanding of his question is that he had concluded that it is the very reality of God itself that we have failed and that we experience now our

1. Dietrich Bonhoeffer, *Ecumenical, Academic, and Pastoral Work*, 55.

2. Arthur A. Cohen, *The Tremendum*, 40. I owe this reference to my colleague Henry F. Knight, at Keene state College, Keene, NH.

3. Bonhoeffer, *Letters and Papers from Prison*, 37–52.

own inadequacy before that reality. He was equally certain that the strength of theology does not derive from its self-consciousness but from its ability to be self-critical and self-corrective. My notion of reparable "theology capable of mourning" is that it can affirm its inadequacy and thereby do justice to the reality of God and at the same time to the reality of life in all its fullness.

The collection includes material intended from the outset for publication in journals and *Festschriften* and collective works with specific themes and a number that were addresses at conferences or occasions where I had been invited to speak. In the latter of these I have deliberately kept their format, especially the personal tone and substance of the occasion because of the singular importance of the group or organization who had invited me to describe my progress in addressing my "after Auschwitz" personal and theological existence. In several essays I retell what, for the lack of a better word, I call "my story." I chose not to avoid such repetition because I do not want to lose the emotional component which energizes the theological search I am engaged in. Having read the story once or twice, the reader may skip it and pick up where it leaves off. For me, the incident in Philadelphia when a survivor of the Birkenau extermination camp gave me the commandment "to speak" determined my willingness to retain such repetition. Several texts include material quoted from sources published in German. Most of them that are part of the chapters in this book are my own translations; I have provided revised translations of some other German-language material that had already been published in English in order to render the original German more accurately in my judgment.

I owe immeasurable gratitude to many persons for their unflagging willingness to "keep on keeping on" with me on this unmapped and unfinished journey. Without their patience, their commitment to keeping me focused, and their often necessary and appropriate critique, I would not have been able to enter ever more deeply into that "valley of the shadow of death." I thank Barbara Rumscheidt, my partner-in-marriage (*requiescat in pace*) and our children Peter, Robert, and Heidi, and Nancy Lukens, my partner-in-marriage now. I treasure the solidarity of several German colleagues who share in bearing the burden of the legacy that weighs upon them as it does on me: Eberhard Busch, Helmut Gollwitzer, Friedrich-Wilhelm Marquardt, Luise Schottroff, Jürgen Ebach, Bertold Klappert, Andreas Pangritz, Dieter Schellong, Martin Stöhr, and Klaus Wengst. In North America, I received the truly undeserved support of Jewish women and men who have given me the gift friendship: Susannah Heschel, Marilyn Nefsky, Marcie Sachs Littell, Leonard Grob, Henry Knight, David Patterson. To my copy-editor, Jeremy Townsend, I owe immeasurable gratitude for rendering the manuscript amenable to up-to-date computer technology.

I dedicate this book to two Rabbis who like "older brothers" watched over me and helped me not to lose faith in the journey: Rabbi Emil Fackenheim (of blessed memory) and Rabbi Richard Rubenstein.

Acknowledgments

THE AUTHOR GRATEFULLY ACKNOWLEDGES publishers' permission to include the following:

"Josef Hromádka: Theology in Solidarity with the Wretched of the Earth," originally published in German "Die Theologie Hromádkas auf dem Weg zur Kirche der kleinen Leute," in *Theologia Viatorum*, vol. 32, and used by permission.

"Discipleship Between Conflicting Commandments: Bonhoeffer in the Conspiracy Against Hitler," originally published in *Analecta Bruxellensia, Europe Between Wars; Bonhoeffer. The Struggle for Peace and the Cultural Heritage. A Salute to Jurgen Wiersma*, vol.13, Tomson, P.J.; Reijnen, A.M., eds., used by permission by Shaker Verlag GmbH.

"To Intervene or Not to Intervene: Is That the Question?" This was originally published in *The Conrad Grebel Review* 28, no. 3 (Fall 2010), 57–72, and is reprinted with permission of the publisher.

"Poetry, Theology, and Ethics: A Study in Paul Celan," originally published in *Between Ethics and Aesthetics: Crossing the Boundaries*, Dorota Glowacka and Stephen Boos, eds., used by permission of State University of New York Press. 2002. State University of New York. All rights reserved.

"A Calling in a Higher Sense: Dorothee Soelle's Theopoetics" was originally published in *The Theology of Dorothee Soelle*, Sarah K. Pinnock, ed., Trinity Press International, used by permission of the publisher.

"'Socialists May Be Christians; Christians Must Be Socialists!' Karl Barth Was!" originally published in *Toronto Journal of Theology*, vol.17, no.1, used by permission of the publishers.

"The Dire Situation of the Protestant Church," originally published as "The Need of the Evangelical Church: An Illustration of Transition in Karl Barth's

Theology," in *Journal of Theology in Southern Africa*, no.57, 1986, used by permission of the publisher.

"The Political Worship of God: The Example of Beyers Naudé," originally published in *The Legacy of Beyers Naudé*, used by permission of The Beyers Naudé Centre Series on Public Theology, Stellenbosch University, vol. 1, 2005.

"To Helmut Gollwitzer on His Eightieth Birthday December 29, 1988," originally published in German ". . . die dir nahestehen, prüfst du; wie ein Vater hältst du ihr Erinnern wach," in *Junge Kirche*, vol. 49, no. 12, used by permission of the publisher.

"The Light of the Torah and the Children of 'Hitler's Willing Executioners,'" originally published in German "Das Licht der Tora und die Kinder von 'Hitlers willigen Vollstreckern," in *Wendung nach Jerusalem. Friedrich-Wilhelm Marquardts Theologie im Gespräch*, © 1999, Gütersloher Verlagshaus, Gütersloh, in der Verlagsgruppe Random House, used by permission of the publisher.

"Dear Karl Barth," originally published in *National-Zeitung Basel*, Nr. 145, Monday, May 10, 1976, used by permission of the Karl Barth Archive, Basel.

"Professional Ethics After Auschwitz" originally published in *The Century of Genocide*, Daniel J. Curran, Richard Libovitz, and Marsha Sachs Littell, eds., used by permission of Merion Westfield Press International.

"Children of Perpetrators: The Generations after Auschwitz," originally published in *What Kind of God. Essays in Honor of Richard L. Rubenstein*, edited by Betty Rogers Rubenstein and Michael Berenbaum, Copyright ©1995.Used by permission of Rowman & Littlefield Publishing Group. All rights reserved.

"Dying as an Act of Defiance," is an edited version of "Dying in the Death Camps as Acts of Defiance," in *Facing Death: Confronting Mortality in the Holocaust and Ourselves*," edited and Introduced by Sarah K. Pinnock, Seattle: University of Washington Press, 2017. Used by permission.

Author's Note

THE FOLLOWING ADDRESSES HAVE not been previously published.

"The Freedom of God and the Freedom of Christians" delivered at Luther Seminary, St. Paul, MN, June 23, 1994.

"Something About Bonhoeffer" delivered at Bridgeport University, Bridgeport, CT, October 13, 2006.

"The Gift of Hospitality" Convocation Address and the reception of the degree of Doctor of Divinity, *honoris causa,* Atlantic School of Theology, Halifax, NS, May 4, 2013.

"Failing the Promise of Nuremberg" delivered at the Annual Scholars Conference on the Holocaust and the Churches, Cleveland, OH, March 12, 2007.

"Since Auschwitz Everyone Should Know that Things Worse Than War Are Possible" delivered at the Annual Scholars Conference on the Holocaust and the Churches, Kean University, Union NJ, March 4, 2002.

"Teaching the Next Generation: The Son of a Perpetrator Reflects" delivered at Monroe Community College, Rochester, NY, May 4, 2005.

"White-Collar Crimes Against Humanity: The IG Farben Auschwitz Story" delivered at Bridgeport University, Bridgeport, CT, April 16, 2014.

"Rebuilding Christian Faith" delivered at the Holocaust Education Center, Westchester, NY, March 21, 2003.

I: Salutes to My Mentors

1.

Dear Karl Barth

TODAY, THE TENTH OF May 1976, you would celebrate your ninetieth birthday. In memory of you and to thank you once again for your important contribution to theology and the church, I write this letter to you even though some people may think it a bit odd seeing that you have not been among us since your death in December 1968.

    I know quite well that your expressions of gratitude on the occasion of jubilees in your life—I think in particular of 1966, your eightieth birthday—gave you little pleasure. When at the end of my student-days in Basel I said good-bye to you and tried to tell you how profoundly your thinking, your manner of teaching, and your openness to others, your *Mitmenschlichkeit,* had touched me, you responded quite briefly: Freely you have received, freely give now! Of course, that is true, but you know, Herr Professor—oops! I forgot that you have left your doctor's hat at heaven's wardrobe—Herr Barth, for us down here who are still theologians and who know that the very existence of Christianity as such is at issue, it is just that every now and then we have to express our gratitude to those who have shown us the way to go and who keep us on track. You were not thrilled when you were declared to be a great theologian. Did you not once call the linking of those two words a square circle? So be it then; but you were a great teacher and still are today. There is a lot of uncertainty in our guild these days; there are even some who think that this can change only when we rediscover a right method with which to do theology. For others to whom the subject of theology is more determinative, your way of always starting from the beginning with the Bible and the story told there of the loving God who is in search of the human being is a constant encouragement also to begin always from the beginning. For that you are to be unambiguously and heartily thanked.

    Perhaps, where you are now with Mozart, Calvin, Schleiermacher and—as you once wrote me—Harnack, where there surely is no more uncertainty, this may sound so human, all too human. Perhaps there is a chuckle on your face now, as there was so often in your seminars and classes.

But it was the secret of your ability to chuckle about quirks of theology and church that helped us also to strive in joyful expectation of the ultimate word and with courage and patience toward that goal and to look to it that things down here are well looked after.

Whether there is theology in heaven I do not know. But thanks to you it is at times a happy science here and that is why, Herr Barth, I greet you and remain most respectfully your pupil.

—Martin Rumscheidt, Halifax, Canada

2.

The Freedom of God and the Freedom of Christians

THE YEAR 1933 PROVIDES the perspective from which this topic will be discussed. Chancellor Adolf Hitler and his party, The National-Socialist Workers Party, were rapidly turning Germany into a totalitarian state. It became apparent that the churches, too, were freely willing to accommodate themselves to the ideology and power of that state. Karl Barth raised the question in a public address whether Christians were even free to bind themselves in the manner Hitler and his party demanded of them. The address "Reformation als Entscheidung" ("Reformation as a Decision") describes a wholly different, a resisting freedom: it is an act of separation, decision and bondedness, according to Barth.

An overview of the year 1933 will precede what Barth believes are the theological implications of that year; in the concluding section, I will try to make some theological observations.

1. The Year 1993

For Karl Barth—and not only for him—that year called forth numerous reactions and demanded decisions; it became necessary to take a stand which in some instances meant that a decision once taken was irreversible. What did he think about the events happening in Germany? Already in December 1931 it was clear to him what the phenomenon of "fascism" meant theologically. In December of that year, he wrote in the newspaper *Zofinger Zentralblatt*: ". . . with its deep-rooted, dogmatic ideas about the one thing, national reality, its appeal to foundations which are no foundations at all, and its emergence as sheer power," fascism is a religion. Is Christianity aware, he asked, that it can expect nothing but acute opposition from that religion? Or will it in the face of it succumb to great temptation to conform to it?[1] In a retrospect many years later, he said: "... when the year 1933 came, I had no doubts where I had to stand and where not.... Simply because I saw that the good people of Germany had begun to worship a false God ... I reacted instinctively. I no longer had to consider that this had to be rejected."[2] The Quarterly *Foreign Affairs* published an article in which Barth said: "Rauschning was right when he identified the real esoteric of National Socialism as pure, consistent nihilism which in the last resort was completely destructive and hostile to the spirit." And so it was clear that "from the beginning the National Socialist policy on religion and the church could only be aimed at the eradication of Christian belief and its expression. But again, it could only move towards this goal ... step by step, indirectly and in a variety of guises."[3] Eberhard Busch explains how Barth assessed the church and its disposition at that time: "... the church was not equipped to deal with an 'opposition which had taken a hitherto unfamiliar shape' and indeed that it was even incapable of recognizing the National Socialist state as an opposition. It transpired that 'over the centuries the Protestant church had been in fact "assimilated" as a result of all kinds of other less ostentatious and aggressive alien pressure to such a degree that it simply could not repudiate, promptly and confidently, the crude assumption that the church, its message and life could be "assimilated" into the National Socialist state.'"[4]

Barth's resistance against this adversary, against this creeping obsequiousness of the church vis-à-vis the religion of Nazi-fascism, is apparent theologically in three separate documents from the year 1933. On March 10 and 12, he addressed audiences in Denmark on the subject: "Das erste Gebot als theologisches Axiom" ("The First Commandment as an Axiom of Theology"); the second is the hotly debated "Theologische Existenz heute" ("Theological Existence Today") written in one sitting in the evening hours of June 24 and the early morning hours of June 25, and, thirdly, "Reformation als Entscheidung" ("Reformation as a Decision"), an address delivered in Berlin on October 30.[5] Barth attacked a specific form of the assimilation: the conjoining of God's revelation with other matters. "In it he detected a danger of having 'other Gods' than God in every theological attempt to connect 'the concept of revelation with other authorities which for some reason are thought to be important' (such as human 'existence,' 'order,' 'state,' 'people'

1. Busch, *Karl Barth*, 18.
2. Barth, *Letzte Zeugnisse*, 43–44.
3. Busch, 223.
4. Ibid.
5. "The First Commandment as Theological Axiom." See also Barth, *Theologische Fragen und Antworten*, 127–43.

and so on) 'by means of the momentous little word and.'" And he challenged Christians at last to say farewell 'to all and every kind of natural theology, and dare to trust only in the God who has revealed himself in Jesus Christ.'"[6] In his lectures of the summer that year he dug up the Disputation of Berne of 1528, citing its important first thesis as an admonition to his audiences and the church out there in the new Germany. "The holy Christian Church, whose only head is Christ, is born of the Word of God, and abides in the same, and listens not to the voice of a stranger."[7] In the church "outside" the call of the German Christian Movement to accommodate themselves to the state and the will of Hitler was proclaimed unmistakably and was heard. On Pentecost Sunday 1933, a book was published, edited by Walter Künneth and Helmut Schreiner, entitled *Die Nation vor Gott* (*The Nation before God*). They wrote the following in the foreword:

> The epoch-making events of the first months of this year have given Germany a new face. The German will to preserve itself that the Treaty of Versailles could not destroy has broken through into political form in a mighty national movement under the leadership of Adolf Hitler and the blessing of the ageing President of the Reich. In continuation with the glorious traditions of Prussian-German history, borne by the best of the people's strengths, a new Reich of German Nation is in the making. It is to rise up in a struggle against subversion inside and threats from the outside; this labor calls all who love Germany to join the National Front.
>
> This book, too, begun at a time when swastikas did not yet wave over the land, cannot pursue any other goal in this hour of national awakening than to take part in building the new Reich. This book grows out of the fundamental conviction that the great work of national renewal can be carried out beneficially only when it is connected to the eternal forces over which people and state have no power as such, when it is done in obedience to God's ordinances and measured against the inexorable truth of God. *Thus, the German nation in its changed destiny stands before God.* As it happened so often in its history, it will be crucial for the future of the Reich whether the demand that comes to our people from God's revelation, is heard or not. The following presentations seek to contribute to this inner contemplation of our self, which inescapably leads to an encounter with God, as well as to the question of the existence of political formation.

---

6. Busch, 224.
7. Ibid., 225.

> *At the heart of the matter is the theological word of the church to the innermost questions of the national rebirth.* In face of the truth of the revelation in Christ this ecclesial-theological word knows itself to be unconditionally responsible as it is for the life of the nation to which this word is spoken in the bonds of deepest love and common destiny. The state that arises from the natural base of the people and its becoming a nation in the Reich today needs more than ever a church and an evangelical proclamation that speaks, bound by the authority of God, with power from above. It is a pressing task of the present time to clarify and advance further from a position rooted in faith and beyond the political level the pending questions of national and people's politics, and on that basis create an interaction of all participants. The aim is not that consensus is reached in each and every subject; what is essential is that every discussion is guided by the joyous good will towards the nation and by the understanding of the unique task of the church among the totality of the people. *The service of truth is the decisive service the nation is waiting for and which the church and theology are called upon to provide.*
>
> *The nation before God!* This momentous question of destiny compels us—in the midst of the passionate agitation of the day and the urgency of action—not to avoid but resolutely to face it.[8]

During the night of June 24 to 25, 1933, Barth composed his still provocative pamphlet *Theologische Existenz heute*. In my view, his retaliatory punch is contained in the repeatedly falsely understood sentence: "The decisive thing I am trying to say today is simply that, as I have ever before and as if nothing had happened, I strive—perhaps in slightly louder tones, but without direct references—to do theology and nothing but theology."[9] In the fall of 1985, Eberhard Busch presented lectures at Atlantic School of Theology and other universities in North America; in them he showed persuasively that this sentence has to be understood as follows: The event the German Christian Movement people were so vociferously heralding is *theologically speaking* utterly a "nothing" in the sense of Jeremiah 10:3: *Denn der Heiden Satzungen sind lauter Nichts* (Luther's German translation), a sham (NRSV), a delusion (The Tanakh), *un pur néant* (Bible de Jérusalem). It was quite clear for Barth at least that it would be pure idolatry to look upon the event of Hitler's accession to power and its consequences as something of theological import. "The church preaches the Gospel in all nations

---

8. Künneth and Schreiner, *Die Nation vor Gott*, vii–ix.
9. Barth, *Theologische Existenz heute*, 26.

of the world. It preaches it too *in* the Third Reich but not *under* and in *its* spirit."[10] The US American periodical *The Christian Century* published some autobiographical sketches by Barth in 1938 under the title "How My Mind Has Changed." "In the first number of *Theologische Existenz heute*, I had nothing new to say but only what I had always been trying to say, namely that we cannot have any other gods next to God, that the Holy Spirit of the Scriptures suffices to lead the church to the truth, that the grace of Jesus Christ suffices for the forgiveness of our sins and for the order of our lives. It is only that I had to say this all of a sudden in a situation in which just this could no longer be in the manner of an academic theory but, without my wanting and turning it into a call, a challenge, a combat mission, a confession which in the end it did become. The consistent repetition of this teaching, together with its simultaneous intensification in this new space, became quite by itself praxis, decision, action."[11] Barth's "declaration" was a clear declaration of combat because the freedom of the Gospel was at stake and with that the Gospel itself. That is why for Barth the freedom of Christians in the Third Reich was anchored in the testimony, in the confession that concretizes itself in praxis, decision and action.

Later that year, on September 6, at a meeting of the Synod of Prussia, a law was approved that included the infamous Aryan Paragraph; three weeks later, the demand of the German Christians for a *Reichsbischof*, a supreme bishop for the Protestant Church of all Germany, was met with the appointment of Ludwig Müller. Participating in the life of such a church would have been for Barth a radical justification of rampant idolatry, of heresy. On October 18, he withdrew from the journal *Zwischen den Zeiten*; in explaining that move he wrote:

> Some time during this summer I read . . . in *Deutsche Volkstum* Gogarten's acceptance of Staple's theological dictum that for us the law of God is identical with the law of the German people. . . . In his remarks Gogarten has taken over the fundamental principle of the German Christians. . . . When we appeared to be fighting together at the beginning of the 1920s, I always thought that it was against what can now be seen in concentrated form in the mentality and attitude of the German Christians. I cannot see anything in German Christianity but the last, fullest and worst monstrosity of Neo-Protestantism. . . . I

---

10. Ibid., 59. It is fascinating that this formulation by Barth and the depiction of the Protestant church in the former German Democratic Republic say much the same even though different words are used in the latter: "We seek to be church not alongside, not against, but in Socialism."

11. Barth, *Der Götze wackelt*, 187–88.

regard Stapel's maxim about the law of God as being an utter betrayal of the gospel.[12]

The dimension of praxis, decision and action, has clearly moved into the core of Barth's resistance and his theological understanding of the freedom of the Gospel and of human beings. On the eve of Reformation Day, he is in Berlin where he was to deliver an address as part of the celebration of the Reformation and of Luther's 450th birthday. "Anyone who wants to celebrate Luther today must have a sword in his hand,"[13] he wrote in a special issue of the series *Theologische Existenz heute* for this anniversary. For it takes a sword to make the necessary incision that leads to the separation in which actual decisions for or against become real. Barth's address had the loaded title: "Reformation als Entscheidung,"—"Reformation as Decision."

2. The Reformation Day Address in Berlin

I regard that address to be an important part of Barth's call into resistance and of his own work in it; it certainly is not a manifest of ecclesial politics. Even though the occasion for it was a Luther-jubilee, it would be a mistake to think that Barth wanted to replicate a position of "Here I stand and I can do no other." He never gave in to such pathos. The critical point of the address is *decision*. But in this context, decision means the acceptance of the decision God effected long ago, on the one hand, and that we cannot longer delay our acceptance of it, on the other. A *theological* decision of this kind is often a *political* one at the same time. For what Stapel's does is to render the praxis, the decision and the action that is based in the decision God has made to be God for us, into a betrayal of the Gospel; it creates a *status confessionis*.

Barth outlines theologically what founded the church anew in the sixteenth century. He lays aside several of the conventional explanations and goes back to one that circulated soon after Luther's death. It says that someone was among us—a prophet like Elijah or John the Baptist—who received his theology a priory, that is through revelation; it was someone in whose work the purity of the prophetic-apostolic teaching was reflected. For something like that alone can found the church and found it anew; something else does not found the church. A Christian church that strays from the teaching of the prophets and apostles does not build up the church; it is heresy, false

---

12. Busch, 229–30.
13. Ibid., 231.

teaching. When the church is founded anew, it returns to itself from heresy and the voice of the prophets and apostles is heard anew in it.

> What was the manner of this prophetic-apostolic speaking? The answer is simply this: The Reformers' thinking and speaking was like that of the prophets and apostles that came out of a decision just taken and that desired in essence to be nothing other than the announcement of and responsibility for that decision. A decision was made where for once an end has been made to our human "balanced" examination and consideration of various possibilities, to our searching for their potential higher unity, to our supposed familiarity with such a unity. Instead, what we face is a judgment, a *choice to be made*, a certain pull and a setting aside, to super- and to subordinate. To decide means to divest oneself in one's freedom of one's freedom. Those who have decided have *bound* themselves.
>
> A friendly and protective dusk or a genteel superiority has been left behind where we can still do this or that. Having left and stepped down into the plain light of day we now must say Yes *or* No, have to do this *or* that, stand here *or* there. The Reformers were decision-bound people. They had left the place where they still had many possibilities open to them. And that is why their teaching had only *one* dimension, only *one* concern, only *one* intent. It was partly an appeal to all who desired to decide with them, partly responsibility for the substance of this decision over against those who did not desire to decide with them, and partly communication with those who had already decided with them. . . . The teaching of the Reformation does precisely not come from some lofty place. It does not make comparisons, does not deliberate or discuss. Instead it announces, explains, disputes. . . . This is what it has in common with the prophets' and apostles' proclamation. . . . Reformation is decision and the church of the Reformation is there and only there where there is decision.[14]

But how does such a decision come about? Is it to be presented and to be understood as the result of the doctrine of the Word of God and the Christian truths being taught properly? Hardly! Even the purest teaching cannot found the Christian life. All articles of faith can become empty articles. Any kind of orthodoxy can stand on clay feet as any other pious zeal for God and hide the fact that pure doctrine can never be the beginning but only

---

14. Barth, *Der Götze wackelt*, 75–76.

the result of the Christian life, only the proper and simple expression of Christian action. Only *to the extent* that the church already lives in faith, already in acknowledgement of the decision God has made will the church find the appropriate, plain expression of its decision. If the church does *not* stand there, if that decision either still lies before it or it thinks that it already lies behind it, it will only find whatever form of orthodoxy offensive and do away with it as a bizarre and useless form of faith.[15]

There are different forms of decision. All decisions humans make, including those we deem important and serious, with the exception of one, are reversible or can be corrected over the course of time. Many who yesterday declared solemnly that they firmly decided to take their stand here or there, will be found somewhere completely different tomorrow. It is comforting to know that even for our noblest decisions today there is a tomorrow where a little or also everything may change. For in every decision, with the exception of one, we seize *our* possibilities, devote our energy to it and bind ourselves on the basis of our own decision. Thus, the loss of our freedom that we have laid on ourselves by our own decision is, in fact the triumph of our freedom. As long as we have time, we can in our un-relinquished freedom bind ourselves today differently from yesterday and tomorrow differently from today. A decision that cannot be revoked, that is, a decision in which we are irrevocably bound and our freedom is truly annulled, would correspondingly have to be one that would not let us have time to reverse it. Such a decision, with the exception of self-imposed death, is the decision for Christian faith. For in *that* decision we bind ourselves irrevocably: there is no possibility to do something else later or even to think about it once again. Should we be bound differently or not quite as rigorously then the decision was not one for Christian faith. In *that* decision, we lay aside our freedom to make a different decision at a later time. There is no more time to turn away from faith. For that decision is a decision for God in whose hands lies our time (Psalm 31:15). We can do much that differs from faith; what we cannot do is to have faith *and* presume that we continue to be free not to have faith. In the decision for faith we have been bound and every subsequent decision can only be either a repetition or a confirmation of that decision. The decisions of the Reformers were characterized by irreversibility. Barth demonstrates this in his address in terms of some of their teachings.

Doctrine as such is not what gives rise to Christian life or leads to the decision for faith; this point has to be upheld. But doctrine is the critical compass for the decision. The Reformers' teaching of Holy Scripture shows that:

---

15. Winzeler, *Widerstehene Theologie*, 438.

> God is to be found by human beings where it has pleased the Holy One to look for us. That means we will not find God where we think we can find Him/Her with the help of our means: not in the sphere of our own possibilities whatever names we have for them, such as reason or experience, nature or history, the universe within our outside us. Not where our wisdom makes us believe we can talk about the Holy One, but where She, in Her wisdom, has spoken to us. And God has spoken to us, once and for all. Scripture, and it alone, witnesses to what is phrased in the perfect tense: *Deus dixit,* God has spoken. That is why Christian proclamation cannot and must not be philosophy in any sense whatever, that is, a development of some form of the world and of life we have shaped ourselves. Christian proclamation is bound to and as interpretation of the Scriptures. Any other teaching has no right to be in the church; it has no promise. This Reformation doctrine of Holy Scripture is plain right away to anyone who understands that it speaks out of the definite, once for all decision. It says that since God has sought us in the miracle of His condescension in Jesus Christ . . . all our efforts to find God through our own abilities have become not only pointless but have been shown to be impossible in themselves.[16]

The doctrine of the justification of sinful human beings by faith alone ought not to be perceived as a final option for creating a new life, if not by their own actions, but with help of their religion or ability to believe. Justification means: "precisely because we, using our own freedom, cannot do within the sphere of our possibilities what in the eyes of God is right, namely that we can look for our righteousness only where God has given and offered it to us. . . . Believing means: deciding for God as our Lord. . . . Everything depends on us understanding clearly that this all comes from the decision that has been made. . . . No longer can one even think of another goodness than that of God because of that decision."[17]

The ever so frowned-upon doctrine of predestination the Reformers taught is about the simple understanding that

> . . . the decision for Christian faith in the event of the divine condescension, in the mercy of God made known, is indeed a human decision but precisely not one of the decisions humans make in and on the basis of their freedom. It differs from all other decisions in that it is the decision for God as Lord in which the freedom of human beings is sacrificed in it.

---

16. Barth, *Der Götze wackelt,* 78.
17. Ibid., 79.

> That makes the decision to be a serious, grave, necessary and incontrovertible decision. But who makes such a decision for God? They who truly do so, that is, they who believe, will never invoke their freedom for doing so. For this is what Christian faith says about itself: that it rests on an utterly unmerited and incomprehensible choice by the One in whom it believes. Christian faith asserts that humans are not free to believe or not to believe whereas God is free to be merciful as well as to be hardened according to Her pleasure. . . . They who think *about* faith will never arrive at the result this doctrine wants to proclaim; they who think *from* faith will.[18]

I called Karl Barth's address elsewhere his assault on "theological Liberalism";[19] the adversary who had to be resisted that October day in 1933 was the liberal Neo-Protestant position of the German Christian Faith Movement. That it had made a decision was utterly plain: for God *and* Führer, people's law *and* Decalogue, nation *and* Gospel, etc. A particular freedom was also defended in that decision. Barth describes it as follows:

> One thinks and speaks in good faith from a premise wholly different from that of the Reformers, no longer from the decision taken but from the exploration and comparison, from the higher unity of two possibilities of which Christian faith was just only one, strongly and honestly emphasized perhaps, but nonetheless just one possibility. Faith was not relinquished but one had regained one's freedom over against it. One's Freedom! Liberalism after all? . . . Liberalism in the church looks like this: one chooses faith, one has reasons to do so, with sincerity and conviction, but one chooses it as one of one's own possibilities. One confesses this faith but one does not want to overlook the many other possibilities besides it that could be chosen in the same freedom. One basically still has time for it or has it once again. Of course, one wishes to serve God and only God, but one wants to do so again from that lofty standpoint from which serving Mammon appears as a serious option. Precisely because one seeks to serve God also, one's own freedom triumphs, a freedom in which one occupies the middle on principle. This middle is endorsed. There is time for comparing, for assessing, in short, time for oneself.
>
> And in this fundamental condition of time-for-oneself and one's possibilities one wants to understand and confess the

---

18. Ibid., 80.
19. Rumscheidt, *Adolf von Harnack*, 33–36.

Christian faith, explain and proclaim it. But this means: one understands and confesses, explains and proclaims this faith in connection with the understanding of oneself and of one's possibilities for which one happens to have time or, to be precise, that one is "modern." Christian faith has to be understood in relation to morality, people used to say once, later in relation to reason, and later still in relation to humanity or culture and today—as we all know—in relation to national custom, tradition and the state. As a child of this or that age, as someone partaking in its history and spirit, or sharing its characteristic opinions and convictions, one affirmed this or that view of the human being and taking it to be the only correct view at that time. And faith, of course, *must* at all costs be in relation to the human being *thus* defined. Otherwise—according to what is so lamented these days—on would be suspended "in a vacuum." What has quietly become peculiarly assured and important is that faith *has to be* a moral or a reasonable, a humanistic and nowadays a "folkish" (völkisch), a people's faith. . . . The question, to put it bluntly, is: What is more certain and more necessary in such times: the *relation* of faith to morality, reason, humanity, culture, national custom and state, in short, to the human being in whatever self-invented determination,—or faith *itself*?[20]

Let us close the circle. What manifested itself in 1933 in church and society was, interpreted theologically, a very acute form, including its disfigurations, of the autonomy of the powerful human being (perhaps that should more accurately be "the powerful male"?) whose freedom ultimately defines itself as "determination of the self" and "domination by the self." Barth had subjected that view to incisive critique even before 1933; now he changed from critique to resistance, to praxis, decision, and action.

3. Concluding Observations

Later in his life, Barth spoke of God as *"der in Freiheit Liebende"*—the "One who loves in freedom"; God's creature is freely chosen by God in an act of election in which God binds Herself freely to the creature. Freely bound: not in the sense that God is bound now and not at some other time but in the sense of a covenant and a covenant-bond in which God's faithfulness is constant. The freedom of Christians is analogous to God's freedom: on the basis of a similar—*but not equal*—free decision for God as Lord, that is, for the God who, in the covenant made with the creature, is bound to the creature

---

20. Barth, *Der Götze wackelt*, 82–83.

as her or his Lord. Christians are bound in an irreversible way that is not unlike how God in freedom is bound. And in this bond there is no tolerance of other gods next to this God. This "Adonai" is God next to whom there is no other Lord God. Hence no "God and . . ." and no "Yes today but tomorrow maybe No." No freedom to bind oneself today and to call it off tomorrow; no freedom for God *and* something, someone else. Paradoxically, the freedom of Christians consists also in having decided freely to bind themselves to God as the Lord of lords; they have released themselves from choosing other such covenantal bonds.

The parallelism of the abrogation with theological liberalism in the understanding of freedom between Barth and Bonhoeffer is surely no coincidence. In his lectures on *Creation and Fall: A Theological Exposition of Genesis 1-3* in the Winter semester of 1932/33, Bonhoeffer also set freedom and binding in relation. Bonhoeffer said:

> To say that in humankind God creates the image of God on earth means that humankind is like the Creator in that it is free. To be sure, it is free only through God's creation, through the Word of God. . . . For in the language of the Bible freedom is not something that people have for themselves but something they have for others. No one is free "in herself" or "in himself"—free as it were in a vacuum. . . . Freedom . . . is a relation and nothing else. Being free means "being-free-for-the-other" because the other has bound him/herself to me . . . [I]t is the message of the gospel itself that God's freedom has bound itself to us . . . that God wills not to be free for God's self but for humankind . . . we can think of freedom only as a "being free for . . ."[21]

Thus, freedom is real only in solidarity, in being-for-the-other in such a way that she/he may find liberation. (Liberation for solidarity therefore means solidarity for the liberation of the other.) And that is why in freedom the corporative always has priority over the individual. What Barth noticed from the very beginning was that everything Hitler and his retinue packed into their concepts of *Volk* and *Nation* was nothing more than an exclusivist and inward-looking so-called solidarity that eliminated all "others" who could then expect from the Third Reich not freedom but only servitude under a false "lord." If I understand Barth here correctly, he developed a dialectic of freedom in this address. When we human beings, living as we do in a conditioned world,—it is conditioned in that God is its creator—make a conditioned decision—conditioned because the number of available options is limited—we at the same time surrender something else like or

---

21. Bonhoeffer, *Creation and Fall*, 62–63.

similar to what we have opted for. It is an illusion to believe that we human beings actualize ourselves in our limited decisions as God does in Her decisions. Striving for that illusion is what theology calls "the fall." The concrete praxis of freedom always and of necessity includes the sphere of un-freedom which is the reality of what lies beyond the scope of our choosing. The decision for freedom *in the sense of liberty*—the knowledge of the boundary or the center that may not be crossed or entered, namely the affirmation of the Creator's priority over the creature, rules out that we remain free to be for whom or what as we choose. When we confess that we stand before God we can no longer decide to be for this or that in addition. Committing oneself to participate in a concrete project that in the exercise of solidarity contributes to the liberation (the "liberty") of our fellow humans renders other commitments and concomitant decisions impossible. But the necessity to surrender other options is in fact *not* a negation of freedom but a condition of its concrete praxis. The will to freedom of choice that opposes this condition is, as Bonhoeffer puts it in the lectures mentioned earlier, the will to *sicut deus,* the will to be like God. God alone exists without preconditions; God alone has freedom (in the sense of "liberty") and, therefore, the possibility for the all-embracing act of freedom; God alone is at the center of every act of freedom. And that is why every attempt humans make to lay hold of that divine prerogative, to take their place at the center, is sin itself. The only true freedom of the creature lies in the affirmation of its "ex-centricity" and of the other's sovereign freedom. For the boundary that is set by the other's sovereign freedom is what gives every limited act of freedom its value. What theology calls original sin is the refusal to affirm this structural limitation of our freedom in our *actions* and instead insist that in ourselves we are our own horizon or that at least we can determine it in and through our decisions, that, in other words, nothing is impossible for us.

I believe that on the basis of this dialectic Karl Barth could see right away that the being and doing of the National Socialists and German Christians was not simply a kind of nihilism or a nadir of liberal Christianity but also blasphemy and contempt of humanity that had to be opposed with every means possible. It was not surprising that Christians and churches found it hard to be confronted with such theology.

But why did that "God and *Volk*," "God and the German nation" not disappear when Hitlerite Germany came to its end? Why does that carry on today in the various forms of "God and . . ." that are rampant on every continent? Or in different words: Why when "hyphen theologies" lead so readily into deceptive thinking do people cling inveterately to the little but big word "and"? Why "God and the free market" or "God and the traditional family" and the like? Why are there churches that defend patriarchy in the invocation of God? Or why is there a "Christian Heritage Foundation," "Christian schools"? Why "God and America?"

I leave it that and conclude with reference to the title of a book by a Swiss author, Jean Ziegler. In 1992, the German edition of a book he and Uriel da Costa had written appeared and is entitled *Marx, Wir brauchen Dich. Warum man die Welt verändern muß.* (Marx, We Need You. Why the World Has to Be Changed.) The questions I just raised and others make me exclaim: Karl Barth, we need you for the world needs to be changed!

3.

"Socialists May Be Christians; Christians Must Be Socialists!" Karl Barth Was!

I

THE TITLE OF MY essay includes a statement by a Christian in Germany who wished to specify how he understood his personal theological existence. Adolf Grimme spoke those words in 1946, in the aftermath of Germany's defeat in World War II. Hunger was widespread, material deprivation extensive and untold human tragedy weighed down a people dehumanized by the idolatry of National Socialism. A collective shouldering of the burden of reconstructing Germany gave the word "socialism" a powerful appeal. Whether it was infused with a Christian or a Marxist meaning was secondary to the vision of freeing this concept from the Nazis' barbaric distortion of it. Grimme belonged to the tradition known as "Religious Socialism"; it landed him in prison during the Hitler years. He envisioned the overturning of those social conditions that are based in capitalistic private ownership. In that aim, he was as unequivocal as Hermann Kutter, the Swiss Religious Socialist of the early part of the twentieth century, who, in 1903, had published his manifesto *Sie müssen!* (They Must!). Grimme's imperative "must" is derived from that work and expresses precisely what Kutter's conclusion had been: Christians must be Socialists. It is historically illuminating that in 1946 the reaction of Christians to Grimme was quite mild. Kutter, on the other hand, reaped anger. Today, in the context of the Christian church's and the Western theological guild's accommodation with neo-liberal capitalism, professing that as a Christian one must be a Socialist is met with the same anger.

Grimme was on the left wing of Germany's post-war Social Democrats and shared extensively in Europe's Christian-Marxist dialogue, which the Warsaw Pact invasion of Czechoslovakia in 1968 brought to an abrupt halt. He knew well that only fundamentalist Marxists insist on the radical incompatibility of the same person being a Socialist *and* a Christian.

However, he was not so sure that it is only fundamentalist Christians who would assert a similarly radical incompatibility of being Christian and Socialist. He believed that when a Marxist becomes a Christian it does not automatically mean that Marxist convictions and the program for social revolution are abandoned. But it does mean that the ambition to replace religion with the Weltanschauung of atheism is stifled and that the methods of revolutionary labor are corrected by the humanism of the gospel. That Socialists may be Christians says that the Socialists' revolution is compatible with Christian existence. What is also implied is the breakdown of the hitherto asserted or assumed axiom that Marxism is obligatory atheism. In Grimme's view, adherence to or acceptance of that axiom prevents any form of union of Marxism and Christianity from being more than a mere marriage of convenience between two distinct entities. But he knew of Christians and Socialists taking such alliance seriously as an expression of the convergence of each other's orientations, as manifested in France, Italy, Spain, and Latin America. This experience made him agree with Roger Garaudy's declaration at the first Christian-Marxist dialogue of the Paulus Gesellschaft in Salzburg in 1965, that "[the] future of humanity cannot be established against or without the people of religious faith nor will the future of humanity be able to be built up against or without the Communists."[1] Given the existence of such alliances, however besieged, feeble and temporarily visible in the West, the readiness of Christians and Socialists to join together from their diverse positions and to pursue a common political goal did not suggest to Grimme that Socialists had to become, nor that they not be, Christians. They may be Christians without being regarded as second-rate Socialists or inferior Christians.

But the second part of Grimme's dictum is qualitatively different. The word "must" seems to suggest that Christians *as Christians*, that is to say, in the name of Jesus Christ, are bound to a certain political program that is not rooted in Christian soil. Was Grimme naïve? Was he advocating a Christian faith that falls short of or tries to reverse the profound Reformation conviction of the freedom of the Christian? Christian faith, according to that teaching, does not *commit* one to any particular Weltanschauung, social order, or program. When any such conceptions become the substance of evangelism, the gospel is degraded into law. Grimme had himself witnessed the Confessing Church's repudiation of the German Christians' affirmation that "Christians must be National Socialists" and hailed that repudiation as a solid testimony to the freedom of the gospel.

---

1. Gollwitzer, *Umkehr*, 14.

Christians "must" nothing! No imperative, no compulsion or coercion to a prescribed conduct governs the Christian's relationship to God, the Reformers taught. If it is possible to free Luther's vehemence against "the law" from his anti-Judaism, his powerful assertion of the freedom of the Christian can be interpreted, as he himself did, in the brief sentence: *volo omnia quae vult deus*—desire all that God desires. "A Christian is a free sovereign over all things and subject to no one; a Christian is a helpful servant of all things and subject to everyone."[2] This perceptive insight into the Christian dialectics of autonomy and heteronomy suggests that the Christ-centered relationship between God and human beings makes the followers of Jesus fellow knowers and lovers of God's will. It is their joy to be God's fellow workers: *volo omnia quae vult deus*. This is the disciples' autonomy, which the gospel asserts over against the heteronomy of the "musts" imposed on humans by the principalities and powers, the sovereigns of *this* world where we humans are in bondage to conditions, proscriptions, ideologies, and so-called "ways of life."

But the Reformers also attested to a heteronomy of the Christian, which Grimme takes up in his imperative. It is, of course, a *voluntary* submission to such heteronomy: *volo omnia quae vult deus*, a heteronomy that resides in the love for and of God's will. The disciples of Jesus to whom God's will is made known by and in Jesus Christ desire the welfare of all whom Christ has revealed to be their sisters and brothers by seeking to serve their lives. But the disciples always find themselves with their sisters and brothers in concrete arrangements of social relationships that have specific structures and orders. As soon as they seek to serve the welfare of their fellow humans, the disciples come face to face with the power of those structures and orders. In other words, they face capitalistic private ownership, globalized economies, the reality of racist class-society etc., in all of which different decisions are made in relation to the dignity, viability, and significance of the life of society's diverse members. The moment the disciples enter into serving their sisters and brothers, they enter into participation in the manner the social order is perceived, planned and implemented—in a word: politics. Their perspective in this service is to change class-society by determining that there be equal justice for all of society's diverse members, that all have concretely the same chance to develop their lives and those of their descendants, that the strong help the weak. Production is to serve all members of society rather than to enable the privileged minority to cream off whatever of the social product they have the means to acquire. In relation to the goal envisaged for our human community, which is also the criterion for

---

2. Luther, *Martin Luther*, 269.

the critique of existing orders of society, the will of God leaves no choice to the followers of Jesus: "Christians must be Socialists," as Grimme puts it. He did not mean this as something that was an open choice, one among several possible alternatives facing the Christian. The decision for Christ is one that rules out such open options: Socialist is what the Christian must be. It has the quality of Luther's famous assertion, "here I stand, I can do no other." The gospel testifies to what the life is that God wills. Its testimony signals the orientation in which, under the conditions of every age, the best possible can be achieved for the demolition of social deprivation and privilege. The "how" of this is, of course, a matter of reason.

II

On February 14, 1915, Karl Barth addressed a group of Swiss Social Democrats in Zofingen on the topic of "War, Socialism and Christianity."[3] In that speech, delivered around the time he joined the Swiss Social Democratic Party, he said the following: "True Christians must become Socialists (if they intend to be serious about the reformation of Christianity). True Socialists must be Christians (if they are concerned about the reformation of Socialism)."[4] Barth signals clearly that both Socialism and Christianity are in dire need of reformation. Just weeks earlier, Germany's intellectuals had published a manifesto that demonstrated how deeply they had given in to nationalist madness. Most of his theological mentors were among them. In addition, Europe's Christian churches had blessed the embrace of the course that developed into mass-slaughter. The Socialist parties had supported war-credits. Everywhere in Europe, they were proud that, as Karl Bröger, the worker poet from Nuremberg put it: Fatherland "your poorest sons were also your most faithful."[5] When Christians become Socialists and Socialists Christians, the reformation that both urgently need could come about, Barth maintained in face of that delirious delusion the war demonstrated itself to be.

In the opinion of the majority of the people who study Karl Barth, the reformation that Christianity needs was advocated by him increasingly

---

3. Professor Friedrich-Wilhelm Marquardt refers to this address in a talk he gave in early December 1971 to a colloquium of doctoral students at the Free University of Berlin on Karl Barth's so-called "Socialist speeches." To date those speeches have not yet been published in the magnificent *Karl Barth Gesamtausgabe*, except those he delivered before 1915; these may be found in vol. 22: *Vorträge und kleinere Arbeiten*, Hans-Anton Drewes and Hinrich Stoevesandt, eds.

4. Marquardt, *Verwegenheiten*, 473.

5. Gollwitzer, *Umkehr*, 24.

through determined and unfettered listening to the biblical message, together with subsequent reflection on and concrete witnessing to it. And a good many of those who followed, and still follow, him in this endeavor hold that he minimized, if not altogether wrote off, the significance of Socialism for the reformation of Christianity. It is my view that Barth was consistent throughout his life in his insistence that an integral, inseparable component of Christian theological existence was what he later called "the political worship of God." The witness-action of the Christian community, through which it interprets what it teaches, is always and irrevocably a political one. Barth's 1946 "*Christengemeinde und Bürgergemeinde*," (The Christian Community and the Civil Community) affirms, in my opinion, the claim that the less frequent appeals to Socialism on his part, in what we may loosely call his "middle period," is no evidence that his conviction about Socialism as the concrete political praxis appropriate to Christians had weakened. I share the view of Helmut Gollwitzer and Friedrich-Wilhelm Marquardt in Germany, and George Hunsinger in the United States, that Barth's infrequent overt references to Socialism between the late twenties and the mid-forties of the twentieth century has more to do with the prevailing manifestations of Socialism itself, in particular its Stalinist disfiguration and subversion of democracy. I quote from that 1946 essay: "The Christian community stands in the political sphere as such and, hence, necessarily in the engagement and labor for social justice. And in choosing between the diverse Socialist possibilities (Social-Liberalism? Unionism? Syndicalism? Free Trade? Moderate or radical Marxism?) it will always choose the one from which it should expect the greatest measure of social justice (leaving all other considerations on one side). . . . Christian political distinctions, judgments, choices, wishes and engagements tend on the whole towards the formation of state, which, if it is not actually realized in the so-called 'democracies,' is at any rate more or less honestly clearly intended and desired."[6] Without a determined move in this direction on the part of Christians and the church there would be for Barth no genuine reformation of Christianity *and*, as he asserted three decades earlier, of Socialism. I do not claim that Socialism is in his view what advances the determined and unfettered listening to the Bible and the subsequent reflection on it; what I am saying is that in the necessary and concrete witness that Christians give to the biblical message, Socialism assists in leading the church out of the clutches of middle-class, bourgeois interests, out of its classism, its complicity in imperialism, its tradition of individualistic interpretation of the Bible and its false inwardness that has rendered faith so unproductive. It is my conviction that for Barth Socialism

---

6. Barth, *Against the Stream*, 36 and 44. (Translation altered.)

is the movement for the church's liberation from religion and for service in and to the community, for "the welfare of the city" (Jer. 29:7). Did not Bonhoeffer sum it up when he said that Jesus had not given us a religion but a community here on earth?

III

Let us step back for a moment and look at Barth the Safenwil pastor and those forty-three manuscripts from the period of October 1911 to November 1919, the texts Marquardt refers to as "Socialist Speeches." That material covers four major areas of concern: the internal problems of the Social Democratic Party, the First World War, the world's political situation at the time and, finally, the relation of religion and Socialism. For example, in the crucial years 1917 to 1919, Barth spoke of the General Strike of Switzerland in 1918 and the course of the Bolshevik Revolution. In relation to the latter, he spent a number of weeks reading and interpreting every section of the first Soviet constitution to his fellow Safenwilers. He had become what many church adjudicators worry about to this day in connection with their social-activist or leftist theology students and clergy: he combined his Sunday preaching with weekday political agitation. I quote at some length from his speech of December 7, 1915, on "Religion and Socialism."

> I became and am now a Socialist in a very simple manner. Because I want to believe in God and God's reign, I take my stand where I see something of God's reign breaking in. Do not think that in so doing I have fashioned for myself an ideal image of Socialism. I believe that I see the errors of Socialism and of its advocates quite clearly. But more clearly still I see in the basic ideas and essential aims of Socialism a revelation of God that I must acknowledge before you all and in which I must rejoice. The new society that rests on the foundations of commonality and justice, instead of on those of the law of the jungle and on caprice, on the new order of labor in the sense of a common activity of all for all, instead of the order of exploitation through the selfishness of individuals, on the new relationship of human beings as human beings beyond the barriers of class and nation . . . and finally on the road to those aims: simple fraternity and solidarity, at first among the poor and disenfranchised of all countries—all these new factors that Socialism brings into political and economic life I must acknowledge as something new from God. . . . Despite its imperfection, about which one may calmly and openly speak, Socialism is one of the most

> cheering signs of the fact that God's reign is not immobile but that God is at work. That is why I may not and cannot stand indifferently before it . . . [I must take my stand with it] from a sense of duty that tells me: this is where you belong if you are serious about God. By means of my membership in the Social Democratic Party I think that I am able very simply to attest at a very important juncture that God is to be given glory and honor. . . . You may have religion and join another political party or none at all. If I were concerned with religion alone, I would probably be among those unaffiliated with any party or perhaps even join the Liberal-Conservatives. But I cannot find God's reign wherever money is ever and again taken to be the measure of all values, where one's country is timorously and in petty ways elevated above humanity, where one always believes more strongly in what is now than in what is to come.[7]

A year earlier, on February 1, 1914, speaking on "Gospel and Socialism," he said

> How did I come to bring the gospel and Socialism into conjunction? I was brought up not to judge human beings according to what they're worth in money and to regard others' material hardship as a serious problem to be addressed. As a student, I came to know the satiated indifference of the bourgeois circles and, in Geneva, I came to know poverty. At that time, I still viewed social hardship as a fact of nature and all that faith had to do was to place a strong but impractical hope beneath that hardship. Calvin's idea of God's commonwealth here on earth was something new to me and helped me to understand that Jesus spoke of God's reign as a condition of complete love of God and love of neighbor. [Since coming to know Socialism,] I have come to regard the socialistic demands as an important piece of the application of the gospel. But I also believe that those demands cannot become reality without the gospel.[8]

Then there is a sixty-one-page dossier of statistical material Barth had gathered on factors affecting workers. Here he engages in straight empirical analysis. According to Marquardt, the material Barth had gathered, including newspaper clippings from union newspapers and other media, is remarkably wide ranging. Barth's conclusive analysis is unambiguous. Was not all this the epitome and the practical aim of a thoroughly materialistic view of reality? he wondered. "As long as this economic principle of

---

7. Marquardt, *Verwegenheiten*, 472–3.
8. Barth, *Gesamtausgabe*, 730–31.

efficiency is in the service of 'the system,' that is, of capitalistic production, all rationalization [of work] does not serve general progress but only the maximization of the shareholders' profit; it also continues to suppress the workers morally and politically who, through personal isolation and the loss of their ability to reflect and to feel, are bereft of the consciousness of solidarity. This in turn means the break-up of the working class, the defusion of its will to resist and of the proletariat's drive to organize itself."[9] No exact dates are available for this dossier but its composition coincides with Barth's joining the Social Democratic Party in early 1915; it was the still radical socialistic and not yet revisionist Social Democracy of the Second International; the leftist, Communist wing had not yet left the party. On July 21, 1914, just a few days before the outbreak of World War I, watching how European Social Democrats mounted no little opposition to an inevitability that was even embraced as a positive necessity, Barth writes, "Not practical questions now but the question of God. For it is God from whom we expect more, for which reason we address more critically what is now and affirm more energetically the ideal."[10]

Barth's terms "expectation, longing, better world, believing in what is to come, ideal," which we then come to find in the second edition of his *Römerbrief*, are appearing with greater frequency and urgency throughout those eight years. As *theological* terms, they are exemplary expressions for and within social-political reality. He uses them to free the Socialist vision from the incursions into that ideal of what is now. Here again is Barth's urging that Socialism reform itself by becoming truly radical. This is also, of course, where Barth's famous dictum is rooted: *totaliter aliter* (wholly other). "Wholly other is the coming revolutionized world in comparison to the existing capitalist one. And when God is called 'the wholly other,' it is in this radical, social sense."[11]

On June 9, 1919, speaking on "The Christian Life," he said:

> The reign of God is the reign of *God*. We cannot picture radically enough the transition from the analogies of the divine to the reality of the divine. The schema of development, of progress has failed us.... The new Jerusalem has not the least to do with the new Switzerland and the revolutionary future state; it comes to earth in God's great freedom when the hour has come. The order of creation will then be wholly reordered. Only God can break the barriers that stand against the perfecting

---

9. Marquardt, *Verwegenheiten*, 476.
10. Ibid., 480.
11. Ibid., 487.

of currently existing conditions. . . . But we need not be at all afraid that the view on this completely new turn in the history of God's deeds will rob us of the courage and the power for what is to be done today, here and now. . . . The power of the beyond is the power of the here and now. The *spes futurae vitae*, the hope in the life to come, is the secret lever of all worldly development and revolution. It may reassure or else upset you when I state that in view of these considerations I am truly glad to be a Social Democrat. . . . We have enough pure world citizens, we also have enough enthusiastic fighters, enough people who long for the heaven that is above in pure light. And all of them are right in their own way. But we have too few people who understand that God's reign is all at once and one in the other *regnum naturae, regnum gratiae* and *regnum gloriae*, the reign of nature, of grace and of glory. Were we such people and stood in this central understanding of the ways of God, which is the true understanding of life, we would be disciples of the resurrection of Jesus and have no need of Christian ethics. . . . Whoso have ears to hear, let them hear![12]

IV

In seeking to understand what in his Gifford Lectures of 1937 Karl Barth plainly called "the political worship of God,"[13] I draw on the work of Helmut Gollwitzer, Friedrich-Wilhelm Marquardt and Eberhard Busch. Gollwitzer addressed the question of the reign of God and Socialism in Karl Barth in an extensive essay, published in 1972 in the series *Theologische Existenz heute*; George Hunsinger made a fine translation of it.[14] Gollwitzer skillfully demonstrates how Barth's declaration, "I do not speak of God because I am a minister; I am a minister because I *must* speak of God,"[15] is integrally related to his conviction that *because* he is a minister who *must* speak of God he *must* be in the forefront of the class-struggle *if he is to be serious at all about God*. The way Gollwitzer develops that integration shows clearly what I have already mentioned, namely that the visions held by both Christianity and Socialism of what is to be and is to come are in mutual need of each other lest both be sullied by the world as it exists now, namely

---

12. Ibid.

13. Barth, *Gotteserkenntnis*, 203. It is not at all clear why the translators chose to render *der politische Gottesdienst* into English as "the state's service of God."

14. Hunsinger, *Karl Barth and Radical Politics*.

15. Busch, *Karl Barth*, 61. (Translation altered.)

the capitalist one. This mutual dependency provides an understanding of what *Barth* understood by Socialism, an understanding not to be found in dictionaries or the phenomenology of political scientists, economists, politicians or bourgeois Christianity.

I speak of *dependency*, not of *identification*. I regard it as the fateful flaw in the diverse critiques of Barth, especially on the part of "evangelicals," on the one hand, and "scientific, academic" theologians of the Western middle class, on the other, that they have not paid sufficient attention to the difference between "dependency" and "identification" in connection with Christianity, or the reign of God, and Socialism in Barth. It is said too readily that a *political* motivation is at work in him rather than a *theological* one. One can gauge the measure of that flaw in how Barth's dictum of June 1933 is interpreted: "I intend to do theology, and nothing but theology, as if nothing had happened."[16]

The Social Democrats' failure in the face of World War I and Lenin's development of the Socialist vision into a centralized party program had deeply disappointed Barth. One may compare his disappointment to the disillusionment of Socialists in many parts of the world with the reality of Socialism (*der real-existierende Sozialismus*) as it presented itself in the countries of the former Warsaw Pact, on the one hand, and with the readiness of Social Democratic parties in the countries of the still existing North Atlantic Treaty Organization to make pact with nuclear weapons, CIA-machinated insurrections, and brutal, militarily sustained sanctions, such as the one against Iraq, on the other. As a result, Barth did rethink his earliest, daring sense of the identity of God's reign and Socialism. He knew, of course, that the Socialism of God is infinitely superior to the Socialism we humans fashion. He also knew that this did not exclude, but in fact, included our hard labor for the revolutionary overturning of the present, God-denying orders of society in favor of those that correspond more to the Socialism of God. From father and son Blumhardt he had learned that the ways of God seek bodily realization on earth. They had learned it from the gospel, and our toil for such orders was for Barth the practical form of the *analogia fidei* that shapes his work.

> It is one thing to recognize the identity of God's reign and Socialism and quite another to identify our Socialism (as an idea, a movement and a finally accomplished condition) with the reign of God. In the first instance, we follow the movement of

---

16. Barth, *Theological Existence*, 9. On that dictum, see the careful study by Eberhard Busch, "'Doing theology as if nothing had happened'—The freedom of theology and the question of its involvement in politics," 459–71.

the gospel, serving, believing and obeying its promise. In the second instance, we exploit God for our purposes and then we have—thinking that we were revolutionary—simply turned over a new page of the churches' and religions' old sins, the commodification of God in the service of our interests, a new page of bourgeois Cultural Protestantism, with the result that instead of liberation there is new enslavement of human beings. The warning against turning the divine identity of God's reign and Socialism into the identification of our work with the work of God, the warning against these preposterous identifications, fills the second edition of [Barth's] *Römerbrief*.... This warning alone is what the broader public took notice of ... and, therefore, mistook it as his renunciation of his social-revolutionary activity before.[17]

I am persuaded by Gollwitzer's interpretation of the relatively few high-profile references to Socialism in the "middle period" of Barth's life:

He is—a lot like Karl Marx—a man of solidity, a fundamental thinker and worker; the rambling talk of the world improvers who were then passing as Socialists was just as abhorrent to him as the theological liberalism which called itself Christian but which stemmed more from the humanistic *Zeitgeist*.... A Socialism of theologians that lacked a solid theological foundation was to him paramount to fooling around. A church that [toyed with such a "Socialism"] would fail to provide both the world and Socialism with the very thing that is to be brought into both by the church and only by the church. He had now discovered something of that very thing by laying himself open to the Bible and doing it in a way he had not learned from his liberal teachers: by laying himself open to the radical contents of the biblical writings, precisely in their strangeness, without premises conditioned by modern culture.... To find and lay a solid foundation for Christian thought and action—that was what a professor of theology had to be about now, that was his *political* task.[18]

V

I return to Hermann Kutter's "Sie müssen!" Grimme's "Socialists may be Christians but Christians must be Socialists" and Barth's "true Christians

---

17. Gollwitzer, *Auch das Denken darf dienen*, 328–29.
18. Ibid., 330.

must become Socialists and true Socialists must be Christians." These "musts" have a particular quality that I embrace. Let us make note of the following features. With this imperative Kutter, Grimme, and Barth do not face Socialists from an outsider position, somehow chiding them for their atheism and calling on them to repent for it. They are not suggesting that it is as a result of atheism that Socialism is in need of reformation. All three speak *as* Socialists *to* Socialists because with them these three Christians are troubled about and by the condition of the Socialist movement, a movement that in their view (but not only in theirs!) Western human society needs so urgently. But all three also share with fellow Christians a deep concern for and over the condition of the Christian church, a movement and community that in their view (but not only in theirs!) that same society needs equally urgently. They asked their fellow-Christians what would help the Christian church and its reformation, and they answered: We must be Socialists so that this reformation may begin. In like manner, they asked their Socialist comrades what would help the Socialist movement and its reformation and they answered: We must be Christians so that this reformation may begin. Their "must" has the quality of a mutual exhortation and not that of a demand or command.

Barth speaks as a Socialist who listens to the Bible and who, listening to its testimony, has discovered how little we humans can protect ourselves, in our political labors especially, against the dangers of resignation and fanaticism, arrogance and cowardice, against the threat of our mind's obscurantism when it is left to its own devices or becomes encrusted in hardened traditions, dogmatism or opportunism. It was as easy at his time as it is now for those who stay away from the efforts to revolutionize social orders to pillory the shortcomings of such a radical undertaking. Barth's "must" is addressed to people who are committed to the renewal of the human order, a renewal that needs people who are genuine Socialists and genuine Christians in one. Gollwitzer puts it like this,

> The shortcomings [of Socialism] which caused it to need reformation may have resulted precisely from the fact that it had no Christian Socialists, no Socialist Christians. Those shortcomings, cited self-righteously by Christians on the outside, are the responsibility of those very Christians. But if Socialism is a movement that a society mired in the disorder of class-conflict badly needs, then those Christians who were absent from the Socialist movement were also absent from the society that suffered hardship; they failed to take their stand at the place in society where they were needed. If they, instead of calling on Socialists to repent, became themselves ready to repent, then they

would take their stand at that place. And they will discern that it is the gospel itself which, on account of its inherent orientation, makes them responsible for the advancement and the fate of the Socialist movement. Their own *metanoia* will be the opportunity for the Socialist movement to renew itself. The reformation of Christianity and the reformation of Socialism are one and the same reformation. This daring conviction of the young Socialist minister has lost none of its relevance. . . . It is a conviction that trusts the promise that the little company of Christians will become effective as salt and light far beyond its confines if only it dares to go actively into the world into which it has been sent.[19]

Barth's "must" becomes immediately invalid when the word Socialism is identified with specific programs such as we came to know in the *real existierenden Sozialismus* of the Soviet bloc countries. Indeed, such identification puts Christians under a yoke and the freedom of Christians is lost. Barth's "must" makes no such identification. He has seen something else that helped him, and that helps us also, to expect more from God than from globalization, to face more critically what is now, particularly when it calls itself "liberty," and to affirm more vividly what is to come.

---

19. Gollwitzer, *Umkehr*, 27–28.

4.

The Dire Situation of the Protestant Church

An Illustration of Transition in Karl Barth's Theology

THERE IS A STIMULATING tension in the discussion about Karl Barth's theology these days. It is about the hermeneutical approach to a theology whose *Sitz im Leben* was the parish and the academy, rural-industrial Safenwil and the urban, though not cosmopolitan, Göttingen, Münster, Bonn and Basel, the labor-union, the political party and the church. Like Tertullian in the second century C.E., numerous recent interpreters of Barth ask: What has Jerusalem to do with Athens? and wonder what his activities in the labor-union and political party have to do with those in the church.

Without going into detail, I would like to illustrate the matter by citing the comments of two interpreters about the famous statement: "as for my part, I intend to do theology, and nothing but theology, as if nothing had happened," from his important pamphlet *Theological Existence Today*, written in June 1933. In the currently topical preoccupation with questions of peace, development in the Two-Thirds World, ecology, etc., Christians reflect deeply on how they are to speak and act in relation to such matters in the name of the One they confess in faith. Professor Klaus Scholder remarked that Barth's doing theology as if nothing had happened was a positive undertaking and that Barth meant to declare what had been a basic stance of his thought all along, namely that theology had to abjure politics, that it needed to be non-political in principle. Professor Helmut Gollwitzer countered that interpretation by saying that what Barth said had been entirely bound to the specific context of Germany in 1933, and that he fairly soon thereafter adhered to the intention no longer and engaged in doing theology which constantly had a political reference. (These opposing positions remind one of G.K. Chesterton's account of his stroll along a residential street where he heard two people from opposite sides of the street shouting about something in loud voices, but with seemingly little understanding; Chesterton observed that, clearly, the two were speaking from different premises.)

This has something to do with the exploration of transition in the thought of Barth. If one lives in the house of *Geistesgeschichte* à la Dilthey, one will presumably draw a Barthian trajectory from his theological liberalism in the Harnack-Herrmann mold to a Kierkegaardian *diastasis* of God, world and humankind, on to an Anselmian analogy of faith in which, in an ever-deepening penetration into the mystery of Jesus Christ, one finally sees a theology of the humanity of God. That *is* a fine trajectory; it tells of what is there in fact and moves along much that "is worthy of all acceptation" for its beauty and constructiveness. And it is worthwhile to explore where, in this perspective, the points of transition occur and under what circumstances Barth shed, for example, his liberal cocoon and started to soar with dialectical wings with his friends around *Zwischen den Zeiten*. Or, what leads to his leaving the "school of Kierkegaard" (as he put it in 1963 during his visit to København) for that of Anselm and writing the book, which he later remarked, had been written with the greatest satisfaction?

But what if one does not see things through the glasses of *Geistesgeschichte*, what if "ideas don't fall from the skies" (to borrow George Casalis's phrase)? What if it is true that the material conditions of human existence, of the daily preoccupation with securing individual and communal survival, are what give rise to phenomena of the human spirit?

At this point I need to introduce a concept which not only is apropos to this point but which is also of importance for the interpretation of Barth I have made my own. It is *Sehnsucht,* profound longing, in the sense which the late Max Horkheimer gave the term in his study *Die Sehnsucht nach dem ganz Anderen. Die Sehnsucht nach dem Absoluten;* (Yearning for the Wholly Other. Yearning for the Absolute); interestingly, this is Horkheimer's definition of theology. (I shall deal with the meaning later.)

Returning to the glasses through which to see things of the spirit, what if it is the material conditions of personal and communal life that elicit this specific *Sehnsucht* for peace, an ecologically sound world, a new humanity? What, for example, if the sigh *veni creator spiritus*, with which Barth ended his address "The Need and Promise of Christian Preaching" (of July 25, 1922) did arise from the specific material conditions of a Europe which had lived through war and revolution, and where human misery and deprivation were still prevalent? Then what leads to transitions in theology? Barth talked about that clearly. He recounted his experience in the early days of the First World War of reading in the papers the manifesto of ninety-three German intellectuals in support of the precipitous war-policy of Kaiser Wilhelm II. Every one of his revered teachers, with one exception, had signed it. He recalled asking how he could possibly go on accepting their so-called "firm conclusions" on exegesis, their hermeneutic, and even their piety, if they were ready to speak as Christians in support of a war their ruler had started. For Barth, the lights had gone out all over Europe in more ways than one. It was for him a time when foundations collapsed, the "tools of his trade" were shown not only to be blunted but dangerous for the very thing he wanted to be about and do. His work in the parish and in the civil community had no basis any more. Could one say, therefore, that it was the war which caused the transition from liberal to radical theology? I see that conclusion to be too general, albeit not without truth. The truth is masked here since the explanation thinks of transition as a shift, caused by a material condition, from one theoretical construct to another in which there is a better *explanation* of what is going on and how one might act with better prospects of success. However, for Barth theology was not a theoretical construct, an endeavor to find and formulate better concepts, but a basis for social action. He said in an interview, on April 26, 1956, that he "decided for theology, because [he] felt a need for a better basis for [his] social action."[1]

It was Barth's social engagement in Safenwil and its labor-problems and his experience of total disillusionment with the theological tradition in which he stood which, when reflected upon in light of the Gospel and then confronted by that Gospel Sunday by Sunday and crying out for a theology without clay feet, caused the first major transition in his theology.

I shall develop my picture of the transition in Barth's theology in the early thirties on this basis. His theological development is, as I see it, not moved by an ongoing quest for a more appropriate theology *per se*, even though that *may* in fact also have happened in the process; it is moved, rather, by that profound longing already referred to and what happens to it in the crucible of Barth's daily experience.

What specifically is this *Sehnsucht*? In an insightful paper, Professor Dieter Schellong makes the following helpful observation.[2] Talking about the sociopolitical and intellectual roots of Barth's theology, he referred to the peculiarly colorful socialism of a number of critical intellectuals before, during and immediately after the First War. He names, in particular, Ernst Bloch, Antonio Gramsci, and György Lukács. Like Barth, they were all born around the middle of the 1880s and, prior to the War, they had already beheld the imminence of collapse and the vision of something new: first a new

---

1. Hunsinger, *Karl Barth and Radical Politics*, 203.
2. Schellong, "On Reading Karl Barth from the Left" in *Radical Politics*, 139–56.

human being and, from there, a new humanity. Their early works were all published around the same time, between 1919 and the early 1920s. Barth had access to their ideas, if not their writings, through his associations with the very exciting Zurich of the day where, partially due to the neutrality of Switzerland, a variety of intellectuals, dissidents, critics, revolutionaries, artists, etc., had gathered. Barth's contact with this company was provided through his relation with the Swiss Kutter and Ragaz, the leading Religious Socialists of the time. It was the time when he worked on, and eventually published his "twilight of humanity" in the first and, three years later, the second, thoroughly revised, edition of the commentary on *Romans*. According to Adorno it was not the famous twenties which brought the intellectual and artistic turning-point but, rather, this earlier period up to the beginning of that decade. By the time Heidegger published his *Being and Time* in 1927, the instigators of genuinely creative unrest had already gone further in order to come out of that unrest into a new formation. Barth had moved into dogmatics so as to find a better basis for a new formation, his vision and praxis of something new. It must be added here that Heidegger and others of those who, in the twenties, set about "renewing" things—the so-called "revolutionaries" of that time—not only generalized what they had learned from their predecessors but also neutralized it. The "revolution" of those twenties in many ways suppressed the visions of the earlier thinkers and allowed their work to lapse into obscurity; when the National Socialists came to power, they made sure that what those "revolutionaries" were proposing was suppressed. In my view, the twenties were, at best, a revolt of the bourgeoisie against what the intellectuals a decade earlier had proclaimed. I fail to see how a real renewal of humanity and society can be accomplished on the basis of the work on which the Nazis were able to build their own revolution of nihilism.

To return to our argument, what is this unrest, the profound longing for a wholly other? Schellong states that that generation was grasped by an indeterminate historical consciousness that bourgeois society was on the brink of collapse, and that these thinkers were profoundly moved by this *Sehnsucht*, as Lukács and Thomas Mann actually called it, this profound longing in the face of a world radically dissociated from the bourgeoisie. Most of these intellectuals were socialists but their tendency towards socialism was an expression of their longing for the different, the better which not only needed to come about but which had announced itself in the foreboding of the imminent collapse. The socialism which established itself in Soviet Russia after the 1917 revolution could not satisfy this longing in a real way. What had been spoken of as the new human being, the new humanity in view of the demise of the bourgeoisie and the horror of war, just was not what came to expression in post-revolutionary Russia and, later, in Weimar Germany. Even something anarchistic, syndicalistic and spontaneous marked these intellectual socialists, they still entered into cooperation with the political party of the Socialists for they were seeking a vanguard which would inwardly permeate the whole, whether this vanguard was now a band of poets or intellectuals, such as the famous Patmos Circle or the group around the journal *Die Kreatur* or, in Barth's case, the church. To be noted is their new understanding of the church as the vanguard of the radical change of everything in the light of the Gospel.

At the heart of Barth's theology there is this questioning seeking, this *Sehnsucht* for the wholly other, for it is a theology which, even though insisting on the primacy of God's revelation, does not proceed from a *possessing* of God; it comes from a position of "waiting in action," to use the felicitous phrase of the younger Blumhardt. Here one discerns well the intriguing dialectic of Barth's theology, this feature which is so important to an understanding of his periodic transitions to a better way of acting in society: in his political engagement, in his actions, it is his theological reflections which cause his waiting, while it is exactly that waiting which stimulates the action. In specific historical situations, such as the deepening marriage of the German Evangelical Church with National Socialism in the early thirties, this dialectic of waiting in action leads to a better way of speaking of God, which is precisely identical with a better basis for social action as beheld in the vision for a different world manifest in *Sehnsucht*. Even the later volumes of the *Church Dogmatics* with its copiously developed Christology produce what the earlier Barth considered to be the only thing possible: a prolegomenon to Christology, that is, a reconsideration of the conditions under which one may speak of Christ as the one who is the object of *Sehnsucht*, of hope and prayer. For Barth, Christology itself is highly dialectical, for it is both the iconoclasm of everything that is and seeks to remain so, and the vision of the new to come. Speaking theologically, Christology is no less *and* no more than the clarification of the conditions under which they who wait for Christ and serve him can speak about him for whom they wait and act, with strained patience ("revolutionary patience," Dorothee Soelle calls it) toward that which he has promised.

The theological definition of the church, which emerges from this discussion, is as follows: The church is they who wait for Christ and serve him by waiting for and straining toward him and what he promised in *guter Hoffnung* (in good hope, to use the happy German expression to describe expecting parents). It was such waiting and straining people who waited in action, whom Barth was seeking to be the vanguard that would inwardly permeate the whole. In 1911, a week before Christmas, the young parson, barely five months after his induction into the parish of Safenwil, put the matter as follows:

> And now to my socialist friends who are present: I have said that Jesus wanted what you want, that he wanted to help those who are least, that he wanted to establish the commonwealth of God upon this earth, that he wanted to abolish self-seeking property, that he wanted to make persons into comrades. *Real* socialism is real Christianity in our time. . . . He wanted what you want as you *act* to attain it. There you have the difference between Jesus and yourselves. He wanted what you want, but he *acted* in the way you have heard [a moment ago]. . . . Jesus says to you quite simply that you should carry out your program, that you should *enact* what you *want*. Then you will be Christians and real human beings.[3]

It is apparent from the sermons Barth preached in Safenwil that, according to him, Jesus did not want war, bourgeois self-seeking property (also known as "private property") in any of its economic, spiritual and political power dimensions, the helplessness and hopelessness of the least, etc. To enact what *Sehnsucht*, focused now specifically on the One who promised to come again and reign in *God's* commonwealth, *wants*—as my argument stipulates—demands a new theology. In terms of the dialectic of waiting and acting, what was needed was a theology in which it was *this* Jesus for and upon whom the church waited, and it was *God's* will rather than our wishes, which comprised its action. The substance of such a theology would be a new church, an *ecclesia semper reformanda*, the vanguard that would enact God's will and, in so doing, would through active waiting and waiting action become and be the bearer of change in the world and society.

We can now turn to the address: "*Die Not der evangelischen Kirche*," which I translate as "The Dire Situation of the Protestant Church." It was delivered in Berlin on January 31, 1931, and repeated two weeks later on consecutive days in Bremen and Hamburg. The formal question is about what it may tell us of transition in Barth's theology; the material question is about the better basis for the social action Barth was engaged in at that time. Drawing on the point just made, the question would be about the better basis for the kind of church needed for witnessing to Christ concretely in face of dangers from a people bent on turning to a radical rightist politics, economics and national philosophy. How does a church act and how does it not act when it is an evangelical, a protestant church, a church of the Gospel? How should the church think of and portray itself if it is the church

---

3. Ibid., 36–37.

under the promises of God? Or, when does a line have to be drawn, in word and deed, against the ideologies of false masters?

The Context of Barth's Address

Many Germans believed that the experience of the First World War, particularly the defeat in 1918 and the subsequent revolution in 1919, were the womb of a new German nationalism. A conservative revolution swept the country; an observer said that a genuine attempt was underway "to put back into daily practice all those elementary laws and values without which a people loses its relationship to nature and God and becomes incapable of establishing genuine order."[4] This sense of new German-ness gave rise to a synthesis of God and *Volk,* God and *Volkstum;* people spoke of God and Germany in a manner that conferred on Germany an extraordinary sense of election and on God an extraordinary relation to Germans. God became a national deity in light of 1918–1919. The late Karl Kupisch drew some helpful distinctions which provide clues to Barth's reaction to this civil religiousness and his own experience in face of it. Kupisch says there were the ecclesial administrators who favored the German-National People's Party and there were ordinary people in the pews who voted for the various democratic factions; there were the administrators' projections, statistics and visions, and there was the actual life of the church which looked different for a long while after the War; there were well-paid and coddled clergy and there were members of parishes who suffered materially and badly so. And there were those who accepted and propagated Germany's nationalism, populism, and its religion with its inclination toward militarism and there were those who went along only to prevent the worse. There were theologians and pastors who truly believed that Bishop Otto Dibelius's proudly proclaimed slogan: This is the century of the church! was truth. Given the German propensity to desire and follow authority-figures and given this kind of hierarchical self-understanding, it is not surprising that the church could count on its clergy and with them erect an ideological edifice in which nationalism was the cornerstone. And so the church entered upon a lively building program, launched an extensive news media network and even established a bank— all recognizable features of the bourgeoisie's way of settling in. The bank, by the way, was called *Evangelische Zentralbank*; it invited investors to save the evangelical way: *spare evangelisch!* The church had become a visible and public power structure.[5] In 1930, the press-service of the church published

4. Winzeler, *Widerstehende Theologie,* 117.
5. Ibid., 118.

an assessment of its success over the past years, calling an *Erfolgsmeldung*. "It has become clear that the religious idea is more deeply rooted in the German folk-soul than was visible on the outside. The sacred 'nevertheless' has prevailed. What we call the empirical church has achieved success both in its steadfastness and elasticity. The leadership of the church in the last decade has been masterful. . . . We may not be out of the woods yet, but we are over the hurdle."[6]

This sort of language always aroused Barth's ire; the humor, scorn and bitingly sharp criticism of his Basel ancestry would come out. He replied shortly thereafter in the pages of *Zwischen den Zeiten:*

> Disregarding professorial cumbersomeness, circumspection and care, I will be blunt and assert that wherever such language is used, a dangerous conspiracy against the substance of the church of the Gospel is present. A conspiracy more dangerous than anything Soviet atheism could mount and accomplish against "Christianity!" And in such language we, the people of the church, are presented to the working class, the intelligentsia and to other countries, without being able to defend ourselves. I am sick and tired about keeping quiet. For if such stuff is allowed to be declared among us without opposition, if that is what we have to listen to and believe, then the church is dead at its very core. If they who now speak of the Protestant (*evangelische*) church and hold office in it and turning the church into this, then it is time to tell everyone that the church is done for and that the people are being deceived. A church like that is forsaken by God and anyone who leads it in that direction betrays the church (and not only the church!) . . . The church cannot engage in propaganda, seek its self-fulfillment, build itself up and praise itself. When, therefore, *this* church says "Jesus Christ," one not only hears but, indeed, must hear only the church's sense of itself of having arrived in glory and of feeling quite secure; no one should be surprised that its invocation of him is no more than whistling in the wind. The talk we hear completely misses the real needs of real people; it is as if there were no housing-crisis and no unemployment in Germany.[7]

In Barth's view, such a church cannot possibly be the vanguard of the change from within simply because it is bent on incorporating into itself what exists in the sphere of those powers it wants a share of. And such a wish is usually achieved by blessing those powers. Barth's critique, his scorn

6. Ibid., 119.
7. Ibid., 119–20.

is filled not only with anxiety about the church but also with his own recognition that a different way was still needed to deal with such a church and move it to a new praxis.

His speech in Berlin, Hamburg, and Bremen was a sociological and theological analysis of the church that uses such pompous language. He called this phenomenon "the flight into visibility" where the substance of the church that bears the name of Jesus Christ is lost. But there still is another "Protestant (*evangelische*)" church in Germany, quite different from that "empirical" church. Barth seems to have been thinking of the pacifist wing of Protestantism and of the religious Socialists.

The Address

A brief summary of the text must suffice. There is something compulsive in the very nature of the "*evangelische*" church. It has in it promise, blessing, and glory. It is something to be affirmed which, when this is done, affirms the Protestant church. But there is something in the existence of the church that cannot be affirmed, something that has to be resisted and met with protest. The former is a heavy burden to bear even though it is full of hope; to deny the burden or the get rid of it is to fall into the latter. The church that calls itself "The Evangelical Church of Germany" has fallen into the latter condition.

By nature, the church is church under the cross; wherever it is not under the cross it is not *evangelisch*. *Tertium non datur!* The Protestant Church came into being when people recognized that to be such a church meant to be outside the church. They recognized and confessed that the crucified Christ is himself outside the church and was out there with them. This is how the Reformation gave rise to the Protestant Church. To be where Christ is as the crucified one is to be the evangelical church. But *crucified*—not a Christ who has shed that death like an old garment, a Christ who is a king in a manner different from how he was king before Pilate, a Christ of cosmic vitality and power, a mighty organizing principle of a continuously visible institution of glory. An evangelical church is a church of sinners, of people rejected by God, with no claim on salvation, alive only in forgiveness. It is a church whose people live by faith alone, who have no other revelation next to the free and present act of God. An evangelical church can serve only *God*; yes, it does so by showing love to others but not by *serving* them. It cannot serve itself either. It can *serve* only God. It is, therefore, not the continuation or representation or embodiment of the revelation and reconciliation of Christ. It cannot ascribe to itself what it can only give witness to. The evangelical church knows that what it lives by, if it lives at all, and what it offers, if it has anything to offer at all, is God's promise of the commonwealth to come. This promise is the church's only through prayer and in hope. It is a church "in need." It lacks a continuous, haveable, fulfilled and complete knowledge; it lacks synthesis. *Wir sind Bettler, das ist wahr*—we are beggars, that is true. It is bad when there is *Sehnsucht*, there is instead synthesis to be filled with things one no longer needs to pray and hope for because one *has, possesses* them.

Protestant church exists "as a human community in the midst of other human communities, a community whose peculiar activity consists in remaining steadfast in confronting those communities with the crucified Christ as the utterly exclusive order and origin of the salvation of humankind. [It exists] to be and to signify nothing but the witness, given in simple obedience, of and to the confrontation of the crucified Christ and the world."[8] If the evangelical church exists in that form, then there is no dire situation. But there is one when the church is ashamed of the Gospel which it boasts to be proclaiming. For then it does not accept the compulsion mentioned above. And then there must be protest. According to Barth, the flight *into* visibility is what characterizes being ashamed of the Gospel.

For the sake of the purity of God's work there has to be flight *from* the church's visibility; it is required for protecting that work against ugliness. The divine must not be materialized; the church must not be institutionalized and expect nothing from its people but purity. But, by nature and necessity an evangelical church lives in concreteness and humanness and, hence, in weakness, temptation and the need for forgiveness. "One cannot desire Christ but not the neighbor in whom he comes, not desire the questionable community of his believers, the clergy and the consistory and take all seriously."[9]

There is flight *into* visibility, not the visibility *of the church* but just crude visibility. It is such visibility that Barth identifies as the most blatant misery of the church in Germany at that time of rushing toward the right. That rushing is as apparent in the world as it is in the church; the use in both of shibboleths like history, fate, reality, sociological necessity, community, *Gestalt,* order, factuality, etc., makes that plain. In their usage, the church shows its longing—its *Sehnsucht*—for public visibility. Its wish to be acting for the public weal is its wish to be seen by people and be shown deference by them. To ask what is to be visible is to be told: the Gospel, which the church *has*, is to be made visible. But that only raises the question of what

---

8. Barth, *Zwischen den Zeiten*, 100.
9. Ibid., 105.

to have the Gospel means. Does the church have the Gospel in its pocket, in its head or conscience? There is no evidence at this time, says Barth, to believe the ecclesial spokespeople even sense that the Gospel is "ours" by faith, prayer, and in spirit instead of in contemplation, possession and in the flesh. There are no signs, he says, of a church that is even remotely embarrassed that it does not believe Martin Luther's often-sung hymn *Aus tiefer Not schrei ich zu Dir* (Out of deep anguish I cry to Thee).

Whenever the church focuses its attention on its existence as such, it is unavoidable that the question of its life becomes one of power. The church in Germany in the 1930s said that it needed *Lebensraum*—a term also used by the Nazis, but in a different sense. It has the Gospel but now it needs power which, at that time, meant concretely the certainty that the state supported it, that it had influence in the state, in society, in school and in public morality, that it had the attention of the masses and their allegiance. This kind of church, according to Barth, is a "me-too-church." Other, strange names and entities take up the space where one name and entity may rightly be. Who still seriously and realistically looks first for the commonwealth of God? Instead Barth said:

> As I see it, what is presented in the average sermon as the Gospel, the invocation of the Bible and all that pathos for Martin Luther notwithstanding, is mysticism spiced with a pinch of moralism, or moralism spiced with a pinch of mysticism and not the word of the cross as the Reformers understood it. What the average preacher has to say these days is meant for the decent and, with God's help, hopefully ever improving human being rather than for the lost human who finds salvation in Christ alone. It is about a commonwealth of God in us, already present among us, to be built upon by us, and certainly not about a commonwealth and a salvation which only comes to us. In biblical terminology: it is an ideology of the elevated middle class that comes to expression in sermons. Its content is utterly different from that of the doctrine on which our evangelical church rests.[10]

To all intents and purposes, that flight into visibility is the will to power; it is a death wish at the heart of the church.

(There is a remarkable postscript to the address, a five-page response by Barth to a rebuttal by Bishop Otto Dibelius delivered in the same hall in Berlin one week later. Barth replied that there was absolutely no relation between what he had said and the Bishop's so-called response. He said that every single word of the Bishop was thoroughly Laodicean—an

---

10. Ibid., 114–15.

allusion to Revelation 3:14ff, especially v. 17, which Barth cites; "I am so rich and secure that I want for nothing." "Does the Bishop not notice that there are people who struggle not to despair over the German Evangelical Church because they almost no longer hear the Word of Christ there but almost always alien, hostile paganism? And why is that so? Because of this foul wind of wretched self-satisfaction and self-assurance that floats like poison-gas, from nearly every sermon and declaration."[11] There must be no false peace; it is either this or that and not both or a clever middle in-between. *Tertium non datur.)*

Transition

Barth's address signals a transition in his theology. As in the early days of World War I, it was a political crisis that compelled him to rethink the conceptual basis of his theology. And again, he was seeking a better basis for his social and political action and he offered resistance to a church gone awry in its alliance with a capricious ideology. The basis for political action had to be subject to unconditional norms rather than what narrow Germanic nationalism offered in its interests of power.

The indicators of transition are the four terms I have already mentioned: the church as vanguard of change, *Sehnsucht*, the commonwealth of God, and bourgeoisie. Clearly, Barth's ecclesiological concern is not a theoretical conception of the church, but its praxis as the church of the Crucified. Bishop Dibelius had understood Barth even though he completely misunderstood him: it is not the nature but the existence of the church that was at issue, the existence of a church whose nature is to be evangelical, to be an *ecclesia crucis*. No *ecclesia gloriae* can be such a church, especially if the glory is derived from alliances with the ideologies of power. The German middle-class had entered into alliance with the anti-republican, right-wing conservatives whose aim it was to pursue a specific glory for Germany, such as "to make Germany great again," the hegemony of what was defined as the truly German *Kultur*, its racial, male-dominated and chauvinistic ideals. This was, of course, the glory the National Socialist Party of Adolf Hitler propagated publicly before Barth delivered this address. For him it was all an experience of *déja vu*, except that it now was both more banal and more vicious. As he attacked the embourgeoisement of church and theology in his Safenwil days and the liberalism that had nurtured them, he now attacked the elevated middle-classism and its predestinarian nationalism that were moving the church more and more

11. Ibid., 120 and 121.

to the right and producing all those German evangelical *Bindestrich Theologien* (hyphenated theologies) in which whatever deep-seated sentiment became revelatory of the Divine One.

Such a church cannot be, because it does not will to be, a vanguard for change from within; it is, to put the matter simply, a church in *Gleichschaltung*, a homogenized church with the clout of power. For Barth, the Gospel told another story about the church. It is to be the instrumentality of Jesus Christ to announce and be part of bringing about the all-changing *world-reality* known as the commonwealth of God. But now, the church had begun to listen to the language of the thousand-year commonwealth (known then as *Reich*) of the master-race and accepted the praxis of those who expressed their deep longing for such a world and "meet and right and worthy of all acceptance." Barth is on the lookout for a theology that can provide a better basis for the social action, for the resistance that has to be offered to that praxis. It is not a *theologia perennis* that he seeks but the genuinely unconditional in Christian faith which, if given courageous witness to, will undercut the idolatry in church and society.

Barth was among the first to recognize that German nationalism was a religion with its own sources of revelation, its priesthood, hierarchy, commandments, rites and faithfulness. He also saw that it had its specific *Sehnsucht*, its vanguard of change, its commonwealth or *Reich;* where he spoke of embourgeoisement as the creeping alienation of the church and the people, German nationalists spoke of the "red Front," the "communistification" of the race. Sound analysis was needed, clear interpretation and proposals for action. As the two editions of the commentary on *Romans* were such an analysis, interpretation, and action-proposal indicating the new direction Barth was exploring for theology and church, so this address and the work he produced around that time are analysis, interpretation, and action-proposal.

Let me back up briefly. In 1914–1915, Karl Barth moved away from liberal theology. He declared that:

> It is one thing to live in the world of relativities and to become completely satisfied with aesthetic good pleasure at how wonderful it all is, it is quite another to live in the world of relativities with a constant disquiet and longing (*Sehnsucht*) for something better which is to come, for the absolute goal of human social life beyond all temporal necessities. [To adopt liberal politics] would be to forego a deeper understanding of the cause of

social evil and to accommodate oneself to a world of wars and capitalism.[12]

What is present already in that statement is what Dietrich Bonhoeffer in a letter to Barth came to call "violet theology" in reference to the theology of bishop Dibelius, the substance of which Barth attacked in 1931 as the wretched smugness of *habemus ecclesiam, habemus evangelium*, of possessing church and Gospel. To adopt German-nationalistic politics would be to accommodate oneself to a world of war and to racism, homophobia, to the feeling of being supermen, etc. The revulsion at the intellectuals' support for or alliance with the Emperor was there again that year as well as the stunned recognition that theology itself was a silent, and often not so silent, pillar and flying buttress. Barth recognized that his own theological reflection was still not quite capable of sustaining the better and needed social action for the time.

How did he come to see that? What experience lay behind it? Biography cites three items to be named here. The first is from something Barth had written for a local newspaper in Switzerland:

> Fascism [is] a religion with deep-rooted dogmatic ideas about one thing: national reality; it appeals to foundations which are no foundations at all and emerges as sheer power. Moreover, it [is] a religion from which Christianity can expect only opposition and, in face of which, Christians have an even greater temptation, namely to conform to it.[13]

The second is from reminiscences recorded in 1962:

> I followed the efforts of a few thoughtful people, the small groups of people of good will who took the "Weimar Republic" and its constitution seriously and wanted to build up a German social democracy.... I also saw and heard so-called "German nationals" of the time—in my memory the most undesirable of God's creatures whom I ever met. They have learned nothing and forgotten nothing and torpedoed absolutely every attempt to achieve the best that was possible on that basis. With the inflammatory speeches they probably made the greatest contribution towards filling to the uttermost a cup of wrath which was then poured out on the German nation over the next two decades.[14]

---

12. Hunsinger, *Radical Politics*, 198–99.
13. Busch, *Karl Barth*, 218.
14. Ibid., 189.

The third is of a different genre; it is not a reflection of Barth's on a specific phenomenon he observed but a direct experience of powerlessness and abandonment. In October 1931, there erupted what became known as the "Dehn-Affair." Karl Barth's friend and Professor of Practical Theology, Günther Dehn, was to be appointed to the theological faculty at the University of Halle. German-National and Nazi-affiliated students subjected Dehn and the university's administration to extreme harassment because he had declared in 1928 that the prevailing civil religion and Christian theology were to be held apart. He had, in other words, made an argument which Barth had made on numerous occasions since 1915. Barth saw that and knew that indirectly he was attacked too. He wrote an article, published in a Frankfurt newspaper, entitled: "Why not wage war all along the line?" and also circulated a petition among his theological colleagues asking for signatures in solidarity with Dehn and, indirectly, with himself. Only four people signed it! Even though alone and facing "failure," Barth was drawn into the church-struggle. A simple but fateful act, in which Barth experienced the unpreparedness and fear of colleagues to get involved in a new praxis, on the one hand, and his own personal inability, on the other, to make a difference, raised in a poignant way for him the question of where he and his theology were headed.

We know that a shift from radical dialectical theology to radical Christological theology took place. The study of Anselm was a catalyst. As a theory and a praxis, theology needs to be grounded in the sovereign God, not as the One utterly transcendent but as the One who in the lowly, crucified and risen Christ is in our midst. Here the concept of analogy became important. "Conceptually, Barth's turn to analogy meant that 'when the *great* hope is present, *small* hopes must always arise for the immediate future.' Practically it meant that as the emissary of the great hope, the church must fulfill its political task 'as a responsible, forward-looking and forward-moving community . . . regarding developments in state and society.'"[15] For Barth, such forward-looking attitude, namely the hope that feeds the profound longing and the profound longing that keeps hope aflame, can only be in opposition to and in resistance against Western Christianity's deepening embourgeoisement.

The transition is toward a more sustainable way of being and doing what had been Barth's concern before. Here we come face-to-face with the unity of Barth. The freedom and love of God he became acquainted with when he rediscovered the Bible and the Reformation during the First

---

15. Hunsinger, *Radical Politics*, 223; the quotation embodies two citations from Barth's *Church Dogmatics*, IV/1, 121 and 153 resp.

World War helped him discern modern theology, but also capitalism and militarism, as the ideology and praxis of contemporary human claims to totalitarian domination. He worked within and opposed a Christianity which is continually inclined to domesticate God, to establish "fraternal" links between the God of the Bible and God's enemies, the idols, and in so doing keeps itself open for serving numerous different masters simultaneously.

The transition that began in 1928 came to its end weeks after Hitler took power when Barth gave his address, "The First Commandment as Theological Axiom." There he spoke about this Christian and ecclesial service of alien masters. And the way in which the newly conceived development of theological existence today needs to proceed is set out in the opening of the Theological Declaration of Barmen in 1934. It reads (in the recent translation by Douglas Bax of Cape Town): "Jesus Christ, as he is attested to us in Holy Scripture, is the one Word of God which we have to hear, and which we have to trust and obey in life and in death."

5.

Josef Lukl Hromádka

*Theology in Solidarity with the
Wretched of the Earth*

THE QUESTION TO BE explored and, perhaps, to be answered is this: Is there mutuality between the theology of Josef Lukl Hromádka and liberation theology, the theology of those Frantz Fanon called "The Wretched of the Earth" (*Les damnés de la terre*)? If yes, where do we find it and what does it look like? That such a relation between those theologies exists is suggested in a comment by Georges Casalis in a lovely work, written in tribute to Helmut Gollwitzer in 1984, *Begegnungen mit Helmut Gollwitzer*. Describing the convergences and differences between himself and Gollwitzer, he says: "Part of this is the close friendship with Hromádka who in my opinion is the genuine successor of Karl Barth, continuing Barth's original intentions. . . . Hromádka's interpretation of Barth and his friendly matter-of-fact-approach to him was for me during the sixties the point of departure into a new theological phase, in fact the essential entrance into liberation theology."[1] Is what Georges Casalis received from Hromádka that mutuality?

1. I will say something about why I am drawn to Josef Lukl Hromádka and his witness to Jesus of Nazareth.

I met Hromádka in person only once; it was during the General Assembly of the World Alliance of Reformed Churches in Frankfurt, early August 1964. As a student of Karl Barth, I knew about his famous letter to Hromádka in 1938 when Hitler threatened to invade Czechoslovakia; I was curious and wanted to become acquainted with the person and theological existence of that man. Another personal experience joined itself to my curiosity. In 1986, I was invited to join a number of scholars in Washington, DC. in a

---

1. Kabitz and Marquardt, ed., *Begegnungen mit Helmut Gollwitzer*, 45.

symposium on "Religion and Revolution." I decided to talk about the legacy of Jan Hus. I drew extensively on Hromádka because I wanted to illustrate his integration of politics and religion. The praxis that I encountered in him called for and offered new and concrete beginnings, new perspectives and possibilities, not only for the church's actions but also for those of politicians. Concepts such as "theology from below," "God of the lowly," "open church" and the like emerged; it seemed that through the history of the "First Reformation," of the Hussite congregations in the fifteenth century, and the emerging theologies of the "comunidades de base," the base communities in Central and South America, a new form of Christian and theological existence was born. The struggle of the Hussites against emperor and pope, against "the copulation of throne and altar," as Pastor Günter Jacob of the church in the (former) German Democratic Republic defined that centuries-old relationship, was a struggle for a humanity that much resembled the image of human beings that the biblical prophets and Jesus of Nazareth had. The peasants of Bohemia and Moravia, and their counterparts in Nicaragua, understood better than their parsons and bishops that the Gospel was the bearer of a hope, of a yearning for genuine and deep humanity. Its promise of help legitimized the revolutionary actions of the people living at the margins of so-called civilization, in the fields and forests of Bohemia and in Central America's mountains.

And then I came across the following:

> His eschatological anchoring of the reign of Christ—which is to a certain extent part of the Hussite-Bohemian tradition—allowed Hromádka fundamentally to assign positive value to all that is new, to all changes, to all that overcame old mores, in a word: revolution as the expression of the dynamics of Christ's reign. Founded on the revolutionary-dynamic basis that characterizes his ecclesiology, he presents a new perception of the phenomenon of revolution in the historical-social-political domain. All great revolutions seek to bring help to people so that revolution is in its approach and aim a struggle for the human being. Hromádka calls for a new theological estimation of the motives and aims of revolution not least because behind revolution he sees a compassion, a "pathos of humankind" reminiscent of the compassion the incarnate and crucified Christ elicits. [Hromádka] proclaims the compassion of the heart ignited by the flame of the Holy Spirit, a proclamation that itself comes out of his own personal compassion. It is always a concrete, living and moving compassion: it knows itself to be imaged by the road of the human being Jesus Christ: from eternity God in

> Christ is on the road to human beings as they are: the humiliated, tormented, fearful, sinful beings consigned to die but also saved in the resurrection. Jesus Christ puts himself in solidarity right next to these human beings. He is their brother. And that is the Gospel, nothing else.[2]

Because Jesus Christ stands in solidarity next to human beings, because God places Godself into the service of human beings but without ever being at their disposal, humans themselves can now freely and without fear give one another justice, peace, life and freedom in forms of personal and political ways of living. Martin Stöhr, an irreplaceable friend and theological companion, summed up what he had found in Hromádka's work:

> It was the tradition of a church that long before the Reformation had begun with the renewal of the church but also of society, trying to think and act, with biblical intensity, from within the congregational context, and resisted the temptations of a flat two-kingdom doctrine that stultifies the Gospel. . . . A church without privilege, living in the Diaspora, experienced and experiences the challenge of a society that resolutely secularizes itself but at the same time deprives itself acutely of the liberating character of its own secularization by embracing new substitute religions. . . . For that reason the church of J.L. Hromádka was decidedly active in the work of the great tasks given to ecumenical Christianity: helping individuals and nations to implement human rights, making sure that the contribution of theology and church to the search for international justice and peace is more than a condition of mutual deterrence, taking seriously the hopes of humanity to which a world, interpreted by diverse philosophies and ideologies and transformed by corresponding economic and political changes, fails to provide an answer.[3]

For me Hromádka is a man of sovereign freedom joined in wonderful harmony by inner openness, simple assurance of faith, warm philanthropy and, very important for my reflection here, a deep yearning for the wholly other. His Christian hope, that I equate with Max Horkheimer's concept of "longing for the wholly other," sought to set future possibility, that which serves human beings, critically against what the past had put in place, and which the present had become used to and conformed to its interests.[4] Once again Martin Stöhr:

---

2. Ruh, *Tendenzen der Theologie im 20*, 344–46.
3. Hromádka, *Der Geschichte ins Gesicht*, 349–50.
4. Ibid., 346.

> Only those who plant their faith outside the contradiction of a complex reality are safe from contradiction. That is equally true for the truth of Christ turned into practice: it opposes what exists in reality but which, in the interest of human beings and in the name of God, should not remain reality: injustice and war, false relationships and dogmatization that injure the dignity of the image of God and shut off the future. Unlike anyone else, Hromádka. . . . seriously addressed how socialism, in its various forms, contradicts an opiate Christianity and justifiably rails against becoming reconciled with destitution. This did not prevent Hromádka from addressing how the hopes and aims of socialism clashed with its actually existing forms. His disciples in Africa, Latin America and Asia who came to know him, as the itinerant teacher and lecturer in Princeton and Prague, understood this better than the Europeans [I would add North Americans] who were caught up in the Cold War hermeneutics.[5]

Theologian Julio de Santa Ana from Uruguay wrote these sentences after Hromádka's death in 1968:

> Why is this theologian of the generation of the beginning of this century so attractive to the younger generations? It is easy to explain this if we pay heed to the particular situation of Latin America in the last ten years as well as to Hromádka's primary attention to the facts of history in his theological presentations. This openness to history and its dynamics allowed this Czech theologian seriously to assess the radical transformations in history. . . . and helps churches to understand their new situation. . . . To accept the humanity of Jesus Christ means among other things to build a structure of the world around us that enables human beings to live in justice and peace, that is, to live a humane existence. That is why wishing to go back to the past is impossible. Throughout history humankind was always in search of a new community. . . . and that is why we have to wait for the future; all of God's promises to human beings will be fulfilled even though the future as such does not bear the necessary justice in itself. . . . Therefore, church has to become a *Communio Viatorum* on the way to God. . . . We have to start the march that frees up the historical road to God's royal reign.[6]

This moving and yearning emotion, this longing for the wholly other draws me to Hromádka today as it drew me—and still does—years ago

---

5. Ibid., 351.
6. Ibid., 344.

to Karl Barth. Theologians like Friedrich-Wilhelm Marquardt and Dieter Schellong point out how the basic positions of Barth's theology appear in beautiful and wonderfully liberating ways—albeit often nuanced and originating in different contexts—also in Hromádka.

2. The Understanding of Liberation Theology

I must proceed most cautiously here. It is inappropriate, isn't it, for a white male of the "first world" and a university-trained, middle-class academic to define from a position of privilege what liberation theology is? It creates the impression that, once again, someone believes himself to be competent to understand and define what in poverty and exploitation, stained with the blood of victims and tears of children, took its course in communal reflection and listening to scripture and prayer, not as a task of academic labor but as testimony to and in liberating solidarity. Permit me, therefore, *not* to define. I shall try instead to describe what comes to mind when in my small corner in Nova Scotia I hear the term "liberation theology."

I see a church and a theology in bloom. Here is a turning back to renewed witnessing, a forward-striving orientation that, closely linked with radical demands for just participation in the fruits of the earth and in the opportunities life can offer, all set in a radical propagation of the Gospel that is trustworthy. And faced with such demands and propagation I clearly also see the challenge to my liberal-bourgeois church and theology to do likewise: like the people of this theology and church to set out, turn back and convert to the radical Gospel and also confess *in a new form* the God of the wretched of the earth. I hear a call, first, into liberation for solidarity and, second, into the freedom of repentance, of turning back. Both of these aspects seem to me to be inseparable and essential elements of the praxis that we call "liberation theology." Let me elaborate.

It is becoming more and more commonplace that the Bible is read rather differently when one lives in the grip of poverty than when one who, as I do, lives in relative material security, not to speak of utter affluence. My interpretation of scripture is rigorously challenged by people in poverty. I could shrug my shoulders and say: What do they know about biblical interpretation? But it is my experience that I am the one who is asked: What do you know? The Reformation of the fifteenth and sixteenth centuries had placed the Bible into the hands of the people; today the church of the wretched of the earth responds very clearly what the people there have heard: namely *that the Bible addresses all aspects of their lives as people in poverty*. The Bible describes the struggle of people in their social community and helps them present what the more humane and just order looks like in the hope they hold. Here revelation and liberation are fused; the Gospel is good news for tomorrow and not, as Rosenstock-Huessy phrased it beautifully: good news from yesterday. The Bible, in particular the Bible of the Jews, keeps awake the dangerous memory that once the people were slaves and that God revealed Him/Herself as God in the liberation of the people from slavery. Our theology does indeed insist that God is revealed in and through historical events. Liberation theology and its interpretation of the Bible makes that far more specific: God's becoming revealed happens in the struggles of the poor and exploited to throw off their suppression and to create a community in which all can participate as full subjects. In history, God takes His/Her place next to the poor against those who fashion injustice. God's revelation happens in the awakening and the liberation of the poor. God's power becomes manifest when people who are pushed to the margins come together as a new people and is then called to give witness to this view of God through the specific mission: liberate the world from its bondage. I perceive this mission of liberation, for example, in the feminist movements and in how the spirituality of indigenous populations, disfigured by our colonialism, is finding its way into the Christian churches. There are also smaller or larger shifts in the consciousness of people in the so-called first world. Not only in groups of activists who have some experiences of that "third" world but also among theologians something is beginning to be felt of what I describe—borrowing from Ernst Käsemann—as real unlearning and relearning. Something is present that has left behind the "know-it-all" attitude of bourgeois-liberal and conservative-bourgeois theologies, and now invites searching for and entering a still unexplored liberation for solidarity and the freedom for repentance, and into the promising new territory, serving God and our fellow humans there.

Are not all these concepts like exodus, becoming free, humanization, departure into the longed-for otherness, turning back to new witnessing, firmly anchored in Hromádka's understanding of revolution? I think they are and so I ask how his theology leads into the praxis and with it into liberation theology.

3. Hromádka's Theology on the Road to a Theology of Liberation

From 1939 until 1947, Hromádka was professor of Apologetics and Christian Ethics at Princeton University. (He escaped literally a few minutes from the grip of the Nazis after they invaded Prague in March of 1939.)

Until 1941 Millard Richard Shaull was one of his students; in 1942, he went as a Presbyterian missionary to Columbia, and ten years later to Brazil. In 1963, he returned to Princeton and became professor of Ecumenics at his alma mater.

I see in Richard Shaull a bridge between Hromádka's theology and a church that has faithfully listened to the call into freedom of solidarity and into the freedom for repentance and develops a corresponding liberating theology. I think that Shaull heard something in Hromádka's lectures that allowed him to enter into the existence of people in Columbia and Brazil and, upon his return to the United States of America, helped him introduce Hromádka's great concern to today's churches and to enable them to enter in their own fashion on the radical way of the crucified and resurrected one.

I now want to sketch Hromádka's way into the church of "the lowly"— the more biblical term for Fanon's "the wretched of the earth." In Princeton he taught that today's church needs to "leap over the wall" in order to show an epoch that not only radically secularizes itself but also suffocates in its own secularism the way of truth and life in concrete service to humankind. Church and theology in the present period of radical change have to turn back and in doing so make room for hope so that "a refreshing stream of invisible truth will keep the ground of civilization fruitful and creative."[7] Richard Shaull knew of Hromádka's longing for the new *Western* world that had heralded itself in the Russian October Revolution of 1917 and subsequently in the new birth of his own country after World War I. As a missionary of a Euromerican (or should that be: Ameropean?) church, Shaull believed that he now had to make known the Gospel in South America that he had learned in Princeton; like many in Western churches he took for granted that the Gospel as they knew it was the Gospel for the whole world. So he arrived on that Southern continent and was faced by the poverty and concrete oppression of the people there by the economics and politics particularly of the capitalist countries. He nuanced the theology he had learned from his teacher and it became the Gospel on the way to the *poor*. This gave rise to new forms which came to be known as liberation theology. Upon his return to the USA he encountered frightful dimensions of poverty in the richest nation in the world where he then introduced his concrete Columbian-Brazilian theological questions, insights and vistas.

This is well-documented in his essay "The Death and Resurrection of the American Dream." (It was part of a symposium in Pittsburgh in the Fall of 1976 where he and Gustavo Gutierrez spoke about liberation theology.) Shaull describes when and how the American dream turned into a

---

7. Hromádka, *Sprung über die Mauer*, 120.

nightmare for him. It began in South America when he experienced the complicity of the United States in the poverty of the people there. He was convinced that the existence and power of his Western nation offered new possibilities for the economic development and social renewal of Third World countries. But "I realized that the American dream was built on the suffering and exploitation of those peoples, and required the persistent destruction of those movements working for a more just social order."[8] To his dismay, he discovered that as an American he was complicit in that exploitation, an insight that took on even sharper contours after his return home and his experiences of many of his fellow-Americans' poverty.

> My acceptance of the American dream was due, in large part, to my belief that I offered *everyone*—or almost everyone—a chance for a better life. Now I knew that was not the case. I also knew that the fact that I had a chance was somehow related to the fact that others did not. Gradually, I began to see what was happening to so many of my own generation: men and women who trusted in the basic institutions of our society and believed that it was possible to reform them. . . . They took on social and political responsibilities in the expectation that they were doing their part to create a more human world for their children. At some point in late middle age, they realized that their trust had been betrayed. They began to admit to themselves that they had not been offered an opportunity to do good but only to observe and often to perpetuate evil, against their wills. . . . With this, the dream collapsed. As I saw and felt their pain, I could no longer believe that our present structures and institutions offered us the possibility to work for gradual progress toward a more just society. . . . I shall never forget that day my daughter said to me: "Remember one thing: Our generation has known only death from the time we were born. We have no reason to believe we will even be alive twenty years from now, much less hope for a better future. And we can't count on the adults around us to inspire us with a new vision of a world transformed. . . ." The American dream had died, not only for many others *but for myself as well.* And with the death of each piece of which, something more died in me.[9]

The next sentences read as if they had been written by Hromádka:

> As I have experienced more and more deeply the crisis of our life as a nation, I have come to realize that this crisis offers us

---

8. Gutierrez and Shaull, *Liberation and Change*, 99.
9. Ibid., 100.

> an opportunity to begin again. In the midst of the collapse of the old order, I see signs of a new world taking shape; I begin to perceive and work for a *new* future. The loss of those values by which we have lived until now is not primarily something to be grieved about but to be *willed*. You and I can bring death into the center of our lives—individually and collectively—and overcome it. To overcome death is to experience resurrection; to discover that we are, in some sense, new human beings, beginning to live new relationships and to create beachheads of new life in dead institutions.
>
> It means that, as we risk letting go of those things which sustained life for us in the past, we discover not only that we continue to live but to be surprised again and again by possibilities of meaning and fulfillment we did not know before. To the extent that we die *to* the old order, we need to die *with* it.[10]

Shaull's own experience had taught him what to die means; but it had also let him experience resurrection. He speaks of resurrection because the concept of "exodus" does not express sufficiently clearly what it means radically to break with our structures of death. Those structures no longer have power to create a different future. That is why we are free to appropriate those elements of our past with which, together with new elements, better relationships can be established among human beings.

If we cannot pass on to our children a social order in which they will feel more at home, we can at least pass on to them *the legacy of a struggle for a new world*

> order, and expect new life to emerge from the ruins around us . . . If we are to contribute to putting together a new story, we will have to move out of the security of our separate disciplines. We will have to discover once again how to think creatively and symbolically about the human condition as we work together on common problems, share our insights, make use of any tools we find that prove helpful, and develop processes of interaction which push us beyond the categories and perspectives we now have. In this situation, I am convinced that the theologian needs to become more aware of how little he or she has to say and how important the questions are that one is compelled to raise. For the theologian can insist again and again that our intellectual efforts are to be tested by their capacity to clarify our struggle for a more human future, more than by their conceptual integrity and epistemological soundness. The central issue is not how to

---

10. Ibid, 101.

control a world that is falling apart but how to *transform* human nature and the value systems into which we are locked. Hope for the future is not so much a matter of salvaging the present order as it is of discovering how to live for and participate in an order of human life beyond the collapse of present structures.[11]

Shaull speaks of a new theological reflection that takes shape in the new consciousness of Christians. As a response to the God who makes all things new, this theology manifests an openness and, indeed, a longing for new ways of addressing human problems. It is rooted in the struggle of women and men themselves to become different beings and to give their world a different form. That is why this theology is impatient with intellectual efforts that, unmarked by that struggle, remain substantially within the domain of objective conceptuality.

> Today, the new consciousness taking shape around us calls upon us to continue the revolution which began in the sixteenth century. [How can a student of Hromádka's *not* speak here of the fifteenth century, of the "First Reformation"?] The vision that inspires it is that of *every woman and man a Subject, living out new relationships of growth, sharing, and equality throughout the structures and institutions of one interdependent world.* . . . Now, as in the time of the Reformation, a radically different experience and understanding of God's relationship to men and women can radicalize, provide a foundation for and transform the struggle of people to become Subjects. At the heart of this is not a theological affirmation comparable to justification by faith but by a new Christian consciousness, a consciousness taking form as it discovers and responds to Christ, *the one who became incarnate in the struggle of people to be Subjects.* The Creator of heaven and earth, the God of mystery and power, the Lord of history, comes to us incarnate as a humble carpenter of Nazareth, belonging to a people who have no place in the great world of nations. This God empties himself to come into and be present in the world in those who are "nobodies," who have nothing and no place. God becomes weak, exposing himself to death by crucifixion in order to affirm, raise up, and give responsibility and a destiny to the "wretched of the earth," liberating and empowering them to follow an endless road of becoming in a dynamic relationship with him. . . . For those who share this consciousness of which I speak, a stance of faith means involvement in and commitment to the struggle of liberation, the struggle to become subjects

11. Ibid., 102–03.

> over against a system—with its ethos, its structures and institutions—which denied them this possibility.... What [they] are doing is grounded in [their] personal and common struggles, not in [their] reflective processes; the question before [them] is how to get on with [their] struggles; how to generate power as two or three are gathered together, not to inherit power. It is in the midst of this struggle that new understanding emerges. At the cutting edge of it, theological language names and interprets our struggle and thus provides power for it.[12]

Isn't that classical liberation-theology language? Gustavo Gutierrez's response to Shaull's presentation confirms it. He states that the connection between redemption and liberation has always been centered in a political contest. During the Middle Ages society considered itself Christian but the powerful suppressed all social and religious dissent. In the age of the bourgeois revolutions, theologians began to think about the relation between church and world, of Christian community and civil community, even though the idea of political power in opposition to the church's power had not yet taken hold. The ideology of the bourgeois class expressed itself in its progressive groups in the work for what is known today as "liberty." That ideology also influenced European and North American progressive theology. But that theology has had to learn that what for some was understood as modernity, democracy and the free exercise of reason was for others another form of oppression, an aspect precisely of the democracy and deceit of the ruling classes, of the allies and servants of capitalist interests. According to Gutierrez, liberation theology is not some progressive theology, leftist-oriented, from the perspective of political radicalism (*pace* Benedict XVI!), it is a theology in which the poor, that is, the *objects* of history, are the interlocutors of the Bible, of the Gospel.

> In evangelical terms the interlocutor of this theology are the poor. This perspective goes way back to the sixteenth century in Latin America.... The difference between progressive theology and theology of liberation is political before becoming theological.... [w]e are talking of the process of liberation as a conquest of real liberty. For this reason, we have to refer to Europe and North America when we speak of our own historical reality. The popular classes in those countries some time ago, and the crowds of people dispossessed today in the poor countries, are like the opposite side of the coin of a history written by the

---

12. Ibid., 163–66.

dominant sector of the rich countries as well as the oppressor class of the poor countries.[13]

During the gathering in 1966 of the World Christian Student Federation, Shaull said: "We are living in a revolutionary period, where old theological ideas are not satisfactory, therefore, we must start thinking in a different way." Gutierrez cites those words in order to describe what Shaull's theological concern was: the transformation of theology that leads to a theology of transformation. What Shaull calls transformation, Gutierrez calls revolution. And what distinguishes the latter from the former is the understanding of revolution. "It seems to me, there is a need for a clear and concrete explanation of the contemporary revolutionary process. I think that it will be difficult to find a new language and theological rationality as Professor Shaull would like to find, if this language and rationality do not come from a transformation of the history of those exploited peoples, the "condemned of the earth," or if this language and rationality do not come from those who convey the evangelical message."[14] The poor are the bearers of the Gospel; the Gospel comes from the underside of history. Did not Hromádka say that also very clearly, albeit in his context?

4. Why "Church of the Lowly"?

With the concept: "Church of the lowly" I try to articulate the radically *different* experience of God I find in Hromádka's and Shaull's theology from that of the theology and practice of faith characteristic of bourgeois Christianity. Both men show their longing for the wholly other, the longing for the *concrete* reality of the One who speaks in the Bible as well as of the equally concrete reality of what this God promises there to human beings. From Hromádka's political and historical consciousness arose a theological language which, precisely because it rigorously oriented itself by the Bible, talks of God's preferential option for the victims of the world humans have established, and of the way of God to humankind the Gospel lays out or, to put it concretely: of God's way to the humiliated, afflicted, and cowed humans.

But why *church* of the lowly? Isn't solidarity enough? Liberation theology is not a *disposition* of consciousness but a revolutionary societal *praxis* that presupposes a wholly other experience of God and the disposition of conscience that grows from it. Societal praxis calls for a human movement.

13. Ibid., 182.
14. Ibid., 183.

The Bible calls that movement "church." It was clear to Hromádka that a "practicing" church in this sense is not only a matter of being open to others but also a company of pilgrims on the way to God, a *communio viatorum*.

I conclude: I am convinced that Hromádka had in mind a church—in diverse ways a personally incorporated one, that is—that, freed from the interests of the powerful of this world, seeks to find the true freedom of humans. Concretely this meant a church weak in worldly terms. In an interview conducted by a friend of mine in Prague in 1969, Hromádka said that such a church had to find the courage to go against national self-interest in order to keep and protect its freedom. To set oneself apart from the powerful of this world and their interests means to take the step toward the disempowered of this world. And in actual practice that is possible only through direct experience of their reality. For that alone can lead to *genuine* solidarity *with* them. This experience had shaped Josef Lukl Hromádka; it gave his theology and that of his pupil Richard Shaull a totally different orientation. Such experience of the lowly leads to the encounter with liberation theology, an encounter in which that theology is not just another scheme for exploring Christian ideas but a praxis for moving forward to justice, peace, and the integrity of that which God has created. Hromádka's theology pushes us toward where the experience of the reality of the poor lures us into transforming our theology in order to step into the praxis and theology of the transformation of the world that God loves so much. I believe that Hromádka's theology is *in itself* a bridge into liberation theology or at least builds it.

6.

The Political Worship of God

The Example of Beyers Naudé

AT THIS MOMENT, I can feel the ground under my feet moving, for even while I cannot fathom the depth of the honor of being in your midst—in this country, in this university, in the institute that bears the name of a man who honors all of us still with who he was and what he gave—I happily grasp the occasion of your invitation to join you and so many more beyond the walls of this house in a grateful celebration of one, whom to look to is, as I see it, an act of wisdom. But there is a second, different dimension to my feeling of the ground moving: is it not pure folly for a German-born Canadian, a white Euromerican (or is it Ameropean?) male to come here and speak of Beyers Naudé? And if it is not pure folly, then is it not at least a rather cheeky, tall order to ask you who knew this man, you who lived and still live in his context and its multifaceted realities, demands, its anguish, pain, hope and vision, listen to one who met him for three days only and shared his context only from afar?

But here I am and, yes, I do want to speak. After an e-mail prearrangement that my fiancée had made, four persons met at the luggage-conveyor at the Leonardo da Vinci Airport in Rome in June 2004. They were Francine and Nico Koopman, Nancy Lukens my aforementioned fiancée and I. Having gathered our suitcases, we waited outside for a taxi to take us to our conference center, the Casa LaSalle of the Christian Brothers Community, to attend the IX International Dietrich Bonhoeffer Congress. It turned out that our taxi-driver was not licensed to pick up passengers at the airport. We waited for him nonetheless and while doing so, Nico Koopman told us of a recent conference here at Stellenbosch University focussed on Beyers Naudé on the occasion of his eighty-ninth birthday. Plans were developing, Nico told us, for a similar celebration-cum-conference for his ninetieth birthday in 2005. I heard Professor Koopman say to me, "You should come and present a paper." I confess that at that moment I felt like a little dog who has just been given a stick to hold between his teeth and who then, of course, refuses to let go it again. So, that little dog, even more grey than a year ago, is here not ready to let go of his stick but very happy to talk among and with you in the country that has in a variety of forms drawn me for much of my life.

Let my next words now be words of great gratitude. I find it emotionally quite overwhelming to be in South Africa; it is the third time that I am here, again and again drawn to something that, in ways I still try to understand, touches me in my being at the depth of significant aspects: I am a Christian, a person of the church, a theologian, a German who in all those dimensions seeks to come to grips with my native country's, my church's, my own family's twentieth-century history, now a Canadian who is working with the church there that ordained me to the ministry of word and sacrament in seeking ways of reconciliation with the native peoples—we call them First Nations in Canada—whom we Europeans, we late-comers to the shores of the North American continent, treated in ways the United Nations Convention of Genocide of December 1946 defined as "genocide." I am deeply grateful to be allowed to be in your country as a willing learner from you and what you yourself are and have as persons whose beings have dimensions like those I named as being mine. I am deeply grateful to be someone who with you bore love, respect and appreciation for the man who intersected—and still does, of course—many lives, instilling courage, hope, vision, grace, patience and, toward the end of his life joined innumerable thousands here and in many parts of the world in the singing, in freedom, legally without defiant anger and angry defiance, what for me is one of the defining songs of the twentieth century: *Nkosi Sikele' i Africa*. I have a photo taken in the Anglican Cathedral of Cape Town during the opening worship service of the Seventh International Bonhoeffer Congress, of Beyers Naudé with a choir of women and men from Guguletho Township, leading the gathered people in the singing of that song. I saw no one around me from Europe and North America who did not have tears running down their cheeks at that moment. The ground did move under our feet.

A few days later, Mr. Carl Niehaus, then working in a responsible position in the new government of South Africa, had arranged for a visit to Robben Island. When we had completed our stay inside the prison, had stood in the cell of Nelson Mandela and, in a kind of veneration, before the trees he had planted and nurtured in the exercise yard, Beyers Naudé spoke to us. It was not only that again the ground moved under our feet but also—so it felt to me—that the sun stood still to listen. We heard the compelling voice of a human being whose integrity brought healing, whose voice rang true. There is a saying I learned in Canada that goes somewhat like this: Soundso is like a perfect bell; no matter where you strike it, it always gives out the same, perfect and clear tone. That image I want to use for this man: his words ring out, calling, consoling, cajoling. And since most belfries have several bells, it is only proper to say that next to Beyers Naudé's bell, he had other equally true, clear, perfectly tuned bells, voices that together made a gladsome sound in the rainbow-people country.

The night before the Congress concluded, three people joined Oom Bey (that is how the chair of the session, Professor John de Gruchy, called him); the other two were Archbishop Desmond Tutu and Ilse Naudé. The four had a free-flowing conversation about their beloved country. Apparently South African Television had heard about the event and came to record it. Not long before that it would not have been possible for such a remarkable gathering and public exchange. Listening that evening, I learned how true Hlophe Bam's words are: "Whenever people are paying a compliment to a famous man they always say, 'Behind every successful man there is a woman.' I would much rather say, 'Beside every successful man there is a woman.'"[1] Observing those four persons, taking in their animated exchange and paying attention to their theological convictions and the strength of their faith, not only poignantly confirmed the Psalmist's utterance, "How good and pleasant it is when brothers and sisters dwell in unity," (Ps 133:1, RSV, text expanded) but also magnificently demonstrated the depth of the biblical assertion that it is our human maleness and femaleness together and, analogous to the inner-Trinitarian relationship, the mutuality and togetherness of woman and man that is the image of God in which we were created. I saw that image as I looked at Tannie Ilse and Oom Bey.

I think that you see not only that but also how I have been touched by the personalities of Ilse and Beyers Naudé, that an emotional impact on me is there from them to this day. I am telling you this as part of describing to you how I approach my topic.

I need to be somewhat, albeit briefly, autobiographical. I grew up in a family deeply committed to the church; it was part of my parents' strong and good piety to hold regular family devotions with hymns, scripture readings, prayers. I am shaped by that tradition. I was born during the reign of Hitler and National Socialism. Father was an executive member of the industrial conglomeration called IG Farben. His assignments brought him in touch with the use in industry of forced labor and the associated policies, jointly applied by IG Farben and the SS, of *Vernichtung durch Arbeit*, extermination through labor. I have no evidence that Father himself ever ordered such policy-application or participated personally in the selections that determined who was able or not to work. Some years after the end of

---

1. Villa-Vicencio and Niehaus, eds., *Many Cultures, One Nation*, 38.

World War II, we moved to Switzerland; it was an "industrial transfer" like our subsequent move to Canada in 1952, where I first met Jewish persons. My childhood years were indeed *judenfrei*. Gradually I began to ask questions; it was only after my year of study with Karl Barth in Basel from 1961 to 1962 that my questions took on real insight and urgency. Barth had called my attention to Helmut Gollwitzer and Martin Stöhr. Influenced by their theologies and, subsequently by them personally, I learned to deal with my parents' but especially Father's refusal openly to address the history of and around the Holocaust beyond the declaration that they did not know. How to square that refusal to enter into the kind of reflection one would have expected to arise naturally from the personal piety and faith that marked our whole family's life? I was fortunate to have a partner-in-marriage who with her own openness to matters of politics, of justice and peace, and with her love for me sustained my ongoing exploration of the past that marked my country, my church and the theology living in my mother's and father's Christian faith. In the nineteen seventies, Barbara, my late wife, asked me to join her in a demonstration outside a liquor store in the Nova Scotian town of Halifax, where we were then living. The demonstration was about getting South African wines removed from sale. Among those wines was a particular brand of sherry my father kept on buying until Canada finally stopped importing it (Paarl) and all other South African products. Part of our demonstration was a black student from Kenya, attending Dalhousie University. He was dressed in a Santa Claus suit, with a long white beard. From his black face and sparkling eyes came the invitation to everyone entering that store not to buy South African vintages. It was quite the image: a black Santa Claus in our white town telling us what not to do! From that day forward, my work on the Holocaust developed from what I then began to know about apartheid and vice versa. Here, in that interlinkage, faith and politics or, as Karl Barth put it in his Gifford Lectures of 1937: "the political worship of God," became bound firmly together for me. (As an aside, why the English translators J.L.M. Haire and Ian Henderson rendered the title of Barth's nineteenth lecture in that series, in German: "Der politische Gottesdienst" into "The state's service of God," is more than obscure to me except perhaps that they preferred not to be so direct in 1938.)

It was in the course of World War I that Karl Barth found what he called "the strange, new world in the Bible." Among the "strange" or "new" things he discovered, impacted by the wretched supportive embrace and welcome of that war in 1914 by religious and secular persons and institutions alike throughout Europe, was a God who does not tolerate being used as a tool to bless human affairs. One can trace his conversion to that "strange, new" God in his first and, in my view, still breathtaking book *The Epistle to the*

Romans (first edition, 1919). Here Barth develops his opposition to the way Neo-Protestantism had spoken of God in the late eighteenth and nineteenth century, the theology I believe had shaped also the teachers who then taught Beyers Naudé. In its own masterful way, that theology spoke of "god" as an entity that stood for something humans could use to legitimate what they already had in mind and planned to proceed with. In such language, God was just good enough for us humans to accomplish and crown what we initiated on our own. But "on our own" meant what we humans had begun without God. And, so Barth concluded, for that reason the entity used to accomplish and crown our actually godless undertakings—such as a war— was a non-deity, no matter how solemnly we affirmed that this insight about God was not derived from ourselves. Barth counters that we speak of the God who truly is God only when we take seriously that what God is about is exclusively God's concern. That concern resists being used for purposes determined by humans. Therefore, task of theology, its proper task, does not derive its meaning from showing how useful it is for human undertakings, such as war, cultural, economic or male domination, and apartheid, by making them plausible (and saleable) through a religious underpinning. According to Barth, the proper task of theology is to discern God's own concern and then to serve it. Theology does this by always becoming converted in its thinking and by understanding that it is not God who is to serve our plans and ideas but that it is humans who need to become servants of what God is concerned with.

Karl Barth made a clear and, I would say, decisive *theological* response to the political events of January 30, 1933, in Germany, Hitler's accession to power. Comparable in several aspects to the accession to power of the National Party in this country and its imposition of the policies of Apartheid, Hitler's policies were welcomed by Germany's churches and given theological, even biblical underpinning. Barth responded by saying that only a theology that has gone utterly astray would give such support. He published the now famous pamphlet *Theologische Existenz heute* in June of that year in which, close to the beginning, he made the often badly misunderstood statement: today, more than ever, the issue is "to do theology and nothing but theology, as if nothing had happened." And do that in the manner of "the chanting of the hours by the Benedictines in the nearby monastery of Maria Laach, which goes on, undoubtedly without break or interruption, pursuing the even tenor of its way, even in the Third Reich."

How apolitical that sounds![2] But it actually is the foundation for what Barth called "the political *worship* of God." For whenever something like

---

2. In what follows, I base my reflection on the excellent examination of Barth's

Hitler's rise to power happens, even as the result of "democratic" elections like the Apartheid government in this country, theology must not allow itself to be moved and revert to placing God at the disposition of what to humans appears justified and helpful in such an event. *That* needs to be taken seriously in face of such situations, unconfused, as if nothing had happened. Other factors, even the most pressing ones, must not dictate what church and theology must do, for only God declares what their task is. Were they to let themselves be interrupted and distracted by such factors, the God to whom they appeal would be subjected to the critique of being a non-deity. Here Barth astutely links the *theological* substance of the First Commandment: "I am the Lord, your God, who brought you out of slavery in the land of Egypt. You are to have no other gods beside me," with the *ethical* imperative of the Apostles' assertion: "We must obey God more than human beings." And that is why the seemingly harmless statement became a biting affront to those who took Hitler's coming to be a new hour of God, a new *kairos*. Barth's reply to the question on the lips of so many Christians—What does this hour, this *kairos*, signify for Christianity?—was the radical word: Nothing! That hour of National Socialism or, again by extension, of the National Party here, has nothing at all to tell us about what we as Christians must or must not do. Barth's statement is, as well, a spiritual put-down reminiscent of the scorn Elijah heaped on the idols on Mount Carmel and on their hordes of functionaries. And in face of the growing authority of a totalitarian state the assertion that for Christianity nothing had happened at all is a rather bold and highly political stance to take. Such an assertion is, by its very nature, highly critical of churches and theologies whose *theological* statements are dictated by a particular *political* judgment and are subsequently used to legitimatize that judgment or to identify it with God's concern. Barth's critique in that 1933 pamphlet was equally directed to the Christian churches' affirmation of it. That is why he did not counter those affirmations with different *political* judgment, similar in kind but not in substance to that given by the churches to Hitler or, again by extension, to the Apartheid regime. Instead he emphasized that his own judgment of Hitler, which he did not deny having, had nothing to do with his theological task which, being the task of *theology*, was determined and bound solely by scripture and the confessional statements of the Evangelical Church. It follows that Barth could offer a credible critique of National Socialism only if he resisted crowning his own, however different, political judgment with theological dignity. Barth's analysis of the German Christians' claim that

pamphlet by Eberhard Busch, "'Doing theology as if nothing had happened': The freedom of theology and the question of its involvement in politics," in *Studies in Religion/Sciences religieuses*, 459–71.

their support of Hitler had theological justification is that their political enthusiasm for Hitler was rooted in a deep theological error, namely that their political judgment had been formed independently of God's Word and then wedded to a theological interpretation giving rise to a marriage in which the *political* judgment dictated to theology what to say. The hearing of God's claim rules out in principle the simultaneous hearing of another claim: "You are to have no other gods beside me," says the commandment; "we must hear and obey God's claim more than the claims of humans."

It is in this sense that Barth went on the attack in 1933, although his attack was not aimed directly at the political system but rather at the combination of the task given to the church with a Yes to that system. Indirectly it was very much a matter of taking a political stance. The Gestapo headquarters in Berlin understood it precisely as such; a memorandum of May 1934 noted that Barth's position presented a real danger in that his theology created enclaves that allowed people to isolate themselves for religious reasons against and from the demands of the new state. Thus, the Nazi authorities banned him in 1935 from Germany and his position there and forced him back to his native Switzerland.

If that is what taking an indirect political stance means, then one understands that "indirect" does indeed not require others to guess what is implied; instead what had been spoken followed from listening to God's Word in the testimony of the Bible. Barth's sermons of 1933 were "political preaching" in that he spoke out for Jews, not because he felt like doing so but because he had to on the basis of the biblical text itself. And thus, they became the strongest imaginable word(s) of solidarity with the already then badly mistrusted Jews. In a later writing, "The Christian Community and the Civil Community," 1946, he wrote that wherever Christians cooperate with others in the political sphere they ought not to *call* themselves Christians but ought to *act* like Christians, anonymously, so to speak, and translate their reasons into arguments everyone can understand. And, I would add, as such they render political worship of God. Isn't that what Bonhoeffer had in mind when he spoke of "arcane" Christianity?

This form of theological reflection became for me the lens through or with which I began to look at the testimony, the words and actions, indeed the personal "fate" of Christiaan Frederick Beyers Naudé after my close theological companions and friends Martin Stöhr and Dorothee Soelle drew my attention to this, as they called him, authentic voice in South Africa. I can still see Dorothee Soelle, standing on the base of a monument in the town of Barmen in 1984, cheering a large, several-days-long commemoration of the important "Barmen Confession" of 1934, and hear her mentioning the name of a man, still banned since 1977, for his opposition to the Apartheid rulers of South Africa, Beyers Naudé. We had left our Barmen conference halls to go out to protest the imminent visit to West Germany and Helmut Kohl of Prime Minister P.W. Botha. Martin Stöhr, speaking with me a year or so later about the then new "Kairos Document" of which Naudé was a signatory, said that the Kairos Document was developmental aid—in matters of Christian witness—from the South for us in the North. It demonstrated that and how the New Testament—and through it, the Christian Church—took the gospel of the First Commandment from and with the Hebrew Bible, the so-called Old Testament, when it declared (Acts 8:29) that we must obey God more than humans which was the text of Beyers Naudé's sermon bidding farewell in 1963 to his congregation in Aasvoëlkop. I would like to characterize that sermon and his subsequent Christian witness in the words a recent interpreter of Karl Barth used for Barth's witness: "Preferably unpleasantly noisy than pleasantly quiet."[3] Two significant dimensions of faith were reaffirmed and demonstrated in Naudé's witness, as I have come to see it. He named the profoundly undemocratic attitude that "politics is a matter of politicians only; politics is a dirty business." Against that he set the necessity that one should learn that the Christian faith and democracy have one thing in common, namely that both accept that *all* people are not only responsible for leading their own lives but are also capable of it, too. A *direct* repudiation of Apartheid (as it had been, of course, of Nazism). The second dimension is this. Naudé challenged the belief that one should not expect the Bible to have answers to political, economic and social problems and, therefore, should not even look for them there, that salvation, liberation or justice dealt with the relationships between God and humans and their innermost life or perhaps even only the hereafter. What the Italian chemist Primo Levi once noted from the underground resistance in Turin against the Nazis, I see mirrored in Beyers Naudé's testimony. Reminiscing on those earlier days, Levi recalls how they met in the Talmud-Torah school and taught each other how to find justice and injustice and the power that overcomes injustice in the Bible. In his resistance against Apartheid, Naudé saw how clearly the Bible gives incentives to action, clarity of vision to distinguish between justice and injustice and strength to work for that justice, the human right that is of God.

There is an insightful story told of Martin Niemöller that pictures for me the nuanced theological shift from an inward, private relationship to God and the preoccupation with investment credits for the hereafter, to what I call the broader, contextual substance of political worship of God. After Niemöller was liberated from a concentration camp he declared that

---

3. See Naudé and Soelle, *Hope for Faith*.

he no longer wanted to preach "how do I find a merciful God?" That was, of course, Martin Luther's question on his way into the monastery. But in Protestantism it had often become the egotistical question regarding only the personal salvation of a person, of her or his personal relationship to the Saviour. Instead, Niemöller resolved to preach for the rest of his life, "how do I get a merciful neighbor?" In it resides the more direct, "whose neighbor am I?" than the more detached one, "who is my neighbor?" *That* question allows for discussion, for assessing, for more "information seeking" which lets one postpone the decision for or against action, for inclusion or exclusion.

More importantly, in our context today, is the next question that forces itself upon Christians when they let themselves be grasped by the demands imposed by the question: "but whose neighbor am I?" In that remarkable conversation, broadcast by the Dutch ecumenical broadcasting company, IKON Television, on June 20, 1985, between Beyers Naudé and Dorothee Soelle, interviewed by Professor Lammert Leetouwer,[4] Beyers Naudé phrased that question himself, with, I suspect, deep anguish.

> I constantly ask myself, how is it possible that a community, claiming to be devoutly Christian, building its whole life—or claiming to build its life, and also its political structure—on the recognition of God's sovereignty as it is stated in our constitution; how is it possible that we could, for instance, remove forcibly three and a half million people from their land, from where they live, from where they had settled down, from where they are happy as a community, force them into arid, remote areas where the possibility of livelihood, of income, of existence is in fact so small that for all practical purposes it is a slow process of death which they are facing? . . . And you know, I must feel the agony of this because I know that the people who are in control and in power doing this, these are my people. I cannot deny that I am an Afrikaaner. I don't want to deny it. How can I? I am nothing else but an Afrikaaner, and yet in that sense I don't see myself to be there—then the agony of that separation. What are the basic roots, what are the deepest roots of such an injustice, of such inhumanity? How do we continue to justify it, and that in the face of the fact that the whole world outside is turning like South Africa? This is wrong, this is inhuman, and this is evil. I am still struggling because I find certain answers but yet I sense here in myself this is not yet the full answer. There is some

---

4. Ibid.

> deeper perspective of human existence, of human justification of such acts which I have not yet been able to discover.[5]

Oh, how those words resonate with me, a child of Nazi Germany, struggling with that past that is not over, a member of a nation that gave birth to people who enriched profoundly the culture of the Western world (and not only of it), a person in and of the Christian church! How the probing of this honest man of your country—honest to himself, to his fellow-citizens, to his communities of faith and, perhaps most of all, honest to God—paying the price of such honesty, how his probing teaches, illumines and, indeed, liberates me: from a self-focussed, introspective guilt, from the easier, but finally imprisoning assertions of not having known what really went on, liberates me for the joy of repentance, of mourning, of new and true solidarity and, as a result, or at the very heart of these, of the gift of new and glad worship of God!

At the basis of what I call "the political worship of God," which, of course, is ours only as a gift of the Holy Spirit, is what I learned from several of my significant theological teachers, is that in situations of crisis, the last thing that is demanded of us Christians is neutrality. Let me interject. Sometimes I have the sense that the old adage applied to the theological reflections of Karl Barth, especially in his early years, that it was a "theology of crisis," is misplaced when it is taken to mean that he *responded* to a crisis in theology. But it might be accurate if it means to signal that he *created* a crisis *in* theology by abandoning neutrality, by taking sides—to be specific: the side of victims. Naudé identifies this point for me when—again in the TV interview referred to—he said: "There is no neutrality possible, or no true neutrality, in a situation of crisis and I think one of the major problems of the church is that it was in a certain sense educated to see itself as a neutral body. [I interject: liberal theology at its height!] We have . . . . misunderstood the concept of reconciliation so that the church, or many parts of the church leadership, believe that you can only truly be a reconciling agent if you remain neutral, and that's not possible."[6]

The abandonment of neutrality as something not only of the *bene esse* of the church, but, instead, and completely of its *esse*, and the concomitant commitment in word and act to solidarity with the excluded, is a decisive hallmark of the political worship of God. What Karl Barth eventually termed "the political worship of God" in his Gifford Lectures of 1937 grew from his activities as an organizer of labor-unions in his Safenwil parish, and his opposition to the defaming of Jews by the Nazi regime.

5. Ibid., 9–10
6. Ibid., 27.

Concurrently with Dietrich Bonhoeffer, he stood up for Jews by insisting in his sermons of very early 1933 that the church now had to preach that Jesus was a Jew. Solidarity with and advocacy for those whom a state targets for "exclusion" is political per se precisely because the God of Abraham and Sarah, of Rebecca and Isaac, Rachel and Israel, the God of the Son of David, Jesus of Nazareth, is the God who takes sides—that of the excluded through whom, in the form of the call to justice, God calls the excluders back into community. And if I understand the Bible, especially the Bible that Jesus knew and preached, at all correctly, that is the most authentic form of the call that *this* God issues. It is the shape of what Germans call *der Anspruch Gottes*, the claim of God, that holds in it the very *Zuspruch Gottes*, the promise of God's grace and mercy.

In my view, that is exactly what Beyers Naudé began to grasp and to live out as his witness after the Sharpeville massacre and solidified through Cottesloe, his farewell sermon at the Aasvoëlkop congregation, into the Christian Institute and right into his banning.

At the end of the interview in June 1985—now over twenty years ago—Beyers Naudé asked Dorothee Soelle (may both rest in peace) "Do you, in yourself, have the strength to endure whatever may come to you by way of disappointment, by way of rejection, by way of non-recognition, by way of waiting, perhaps your whole life, without being able to participate in the outcry of the truth that you are standing for? Do you believe that you will be able to sustain yourself through those years up to the very end?"[7]

In place of Dorothee Soelle's answer, I will provide one myself. I referred to it already. By the always astonishing, surprising and amazing grace of God, Beyers Naudé led us international participants in the Seventh International Dietrich Bonhoeffer Congress in Cape Town in 1996 with his own black and white, coloured and Indian co-patriots in the singing of what I often consider the perhaps most glorious hymn of the twentieth century: *Nkosi Sikele' i Africa*. God had granted this servant the experience of hope fulfilled. But immediately Naudé went back to work: to help shape this—in Archbishop Tutu's words—"rainbow" nation. And I see *that* aspect of Christiaan Frederick Beyers Naudé's work as the direct continuation, albeit in a new form, of his earlier political worship of God.

To this teacher, mentor, companion and saint, to this fellow Christian whom you, his people, gave to us, I, gratefully, humbly, but also deeply honored, pay my unending respect and with you, gratefully, give praise to God. If I am allowed to do this, let me join in the words of his mother tongue: "Baie dankie, Oom Bey!"

---

7. Ibid., 37.

7.

To Helmut Gollwitzer on His Eightieth Birthday, December 29, 1988

". . . those who are close to you, you test; like a father you keep awake their remembering."

IN 1986, THE FILM entitled *Dark Lullabies* premiered in Canada. The script was written by Irene Lilienheim-Angelico; she herself appears in the film. Her parents, Jews, had been shipped by the Nazis to Dachau. Both survived the Shoah; not long after the Allies had liberated Germany in 1945 their daughter Irene was born. Their subsequent emigration to Canada gave the Lilienheims, in particular their daughter, the necessary distance from the generation of those who had planned and then implemented the "final solution of the Jewish problem." That space made room for questions; she knew much about children of those who had been targeted by the final solution, but nothing about children whose parents and relatives were its perpetrators. She had learned what it means to be a child of the persecuted and—as in her case—of survivors. But what would it mean to be a child of those who had sent human beings to their death, a child of people who had "handed over" their sense of morality to Hitler and then, after the end of the war, returned to family life and raising children?

Questions like those pursued Irene Lilienheim-Angelico. Her film was born in long, often disturbing conversations with Jews in Canada and Israel, but then she realized that she wanted to encounter children of perpetrators and find out how they faced their past. And one hears her asking: How do you relate to what is in you of your parents? What have you learned from them? How do you relate to what they were, what they wanted and what they did? And she hears answers like these: What I know now has completely destroyed the wonderful times I had with Opa! I have to get free from my father, for otherwise I won't have the strength to do what I believe in!

She searches for understanding—to understand a world she cannot understand even though it is all around her, a world within whose history she lives but the connection with which the Shoah had destroyed. In the process, she meets the young German filmmaker, Harald Lüders from Frankfurt. In the film, he says something to Irene one evening as they were talking in his flat that has deeply touched me. "I envy you, Irene. You can have a positive relationship to your past, to the history of your ancestors. It surely is a relation filled with mourning, but a mourning that allows you, if not even commands you, to stand with your ancestors. Your entering-into-your-past gives you an intimate relation with your people. For me it is the utter opposite."

I interpret Lüders distinction as follows: There is no profound or compelling reason for Lilienheim-Angelico to distance herself from her ancestors, including her parents. Instead, she can identify with what they were, what they wanted, believed, and did. She has a "usable" past; it can create identity. Lüders, on the other hand, has difficulty engaging his past, not to speak of coping with it, for he either has to silence and minimize it or confront it openly, which means to acknowledge guilt. The enormous difficulty of the generation of children of Holocaust-functionaries lies in having to look for their roots, to find the connection to their past in their future. They have been handed a past that they cannot *understand,* one they have to *reject* as well as what their parents believed in, wanted and did, but which nonetheless they have to *take upon themselves* and *work through.*

It is not enough to reject the ideology and practice of the past. It has to be addressed openly and attended to. Here you, Helmut Gollwitzer, have become a good companion to me and many others in this endeavor. You do *not* leave us alone in our questions of guilt and repentance in connection with our German past, for you know that the death of the perpetrators does not signify closure for their children in their engaging of the legacy with which they have been burdened. Between me, now a Canadian citizen, and the discussion in the two German Republics concerning the common German past, there is an ocean—in a literal and figurative sense. The great majority of my Canadian colleagues, especially in the church, counsel me again and again finally to put behind me what happened in the name of my people between 1933 and 1945. Jews and people of Canada's First Nations understand that a repressed past imprisons us human beings theologically and psychologically in a place without exit. But very few Canadians understand this. In my own experience this was particularly the case with my father's silence on the question of Germany's guilt and repentance. I have *no* access through him to that past and, for that reason, also none to a *different* future. As I see it now, with him I am disabled. In what I must be, I am "father-less."

But that is true only in the literal sense. In the figurative sense, you Helmut, are "Vater" to me. In our personal relationship, as in your theological existence, I find myself "tested; you keep awake my remembering," following the beautiful verse in the *Wisdom of Solomon* (11:10). Right from the beginning of your work, you have insisted that only a concrete, unqualified and unconditional acknowledgment of guilt can be met with forgiveness, creating the possibility for a way into freedom and a *realistic* future. In such a future, I do not need to conceal my/our past but can openly face it in concrete hope for liberation from it.

During a sabbatical in 1982, I spent four months in the magnificent library of Yale Divinity School voraciously reading the writings of "Golli"—as we affectionately call you. Beginning with your powerful Day of Repentance sermon of November 16, 1938 (on the Sunday following the November 9 pogrom often called Kristallnacht) up to *Befreiung zur Solidarität* (Liberation for Solidarity), from your provocative collection, *Forderungen der Freiheit* (The demands of Freedom) to your conversations with Rolf Rendtdorff on the subject of Jews, Christian and Israel, on to *Vietnam, Israel und die Christenheit* (Vietnam, Israel and Christianity) and *Die reichen Christen und der arme Lazarus* (The Rich Christians and Poor Lazarus), *Krummes Holz—aufrechter Gang. Die Frage nach dem Sinn des Lebens* (Twisted Wood—Upright Stride: On the Meaning of Life), your work, while attentive also to the World Council of Churches 1983 Vancouver Assembly, *Justice, Peace and the Integrity of Creation*, is a consistent, loving and hope-giving invitation into repentance. It is "repentance" in the sense of "turning back": to life, to the neighbor, whether a Cold War enemy Soviet soldier, a member of the 1970s "extremist" Baader-Meinhof-Group, or a worker of a kibbutz. As liberation that the God of Abraham and Sarah gives us and who lives among us human beings in Jesus of Nazareth, it is a liberation for solidarity with the victims of the politics, economics and religion of the powerful in the world. Helmut Gollwitzer, you keep my/our remembering awake theologically by your constant emphasis that God's forgiveness and the future grounded in it is not unmediated, given directly to us the powerful, privileged people. It becomes ours only through the solidarity of those the world victimizes, imaging the solidarity of him whom the powerful of the world had crucified: the solidarity of the Christ with his executioners.

Yet I experience your "Fatherliness" almost more directly in our personal relationship, even though your theological work moves my remembering into the critical center of my own work. I declare with gratitude and joy that you "test" me too, precisely because we are "close" to each other. I wrote you once about my sense that I had no way out from the past that

Harald Lüders had so eloquently described. In your reply you characterized my lines as the

> retrospective of a German of your generation (born in 1935), from a bourgeois background like nearly all of us, and a narrative of being set free from the limited perspectives of that generation. In so doing we look with forgiveness and understanding at our parents who grew up with those limits and lived with the limits. Among this parent generation only few perceived that the gospel to which they gave allegiance demanded a more radical opposition to the dominant powers of the time than they thought. The gospel tells us that we ought not to create a new sense of superiority but instead to be thankful for the liberation from old bonds, the liberation which correspondingly creates new responsibilities for us so that the arrogant sense of being superior to our fathers is amply dampened as well as excluded. The fact that in our lives the actual reality of life often falls far short of our understanding is due to external limits as much as to us ourselves, to our cowardice, our misplaced considerations, the peace we keep on making with the world. And so there is little cause for pride and presumptuousness; yet at the same time, we are not allowed to refrain from critically subjecting the fathers and the boundaries that we have transgressed.

Here you ask me to test my understanding of the Fifth Commandment: "Honor your father and mother" just as you did in your book . . . *aus der Sklaverei befreit* (. . . Freed from Slavery). It is just such testing that I see to be the psychologically necessary opening to that critical solidarity with those who write my generation off, perhaps all to quickly and easily, with the phrase "Father is dead, long live father!" With your testing, "Father" Gollwitzer, you want me and my generation not to follow such counsel; instead you admonish us to remember, not to forget, not to look away.

It would seem then that is it *indeed* possible to turn back without silencing the past, without banning parents and their generation from critical new understanding. I believe that you "Father Gollwitzer" offer us a road on which to travel into the future does not have to break with the past but to include it in our identity through the grace of forgiveness and repentance. And that surely means to honor father and mother.[1]

Thank you, Father Golli.

Martin

1. *Junge Kirche*, 683.

8.

Something About Bonhoeffer

IN AN UNDERGRADUATE COURSE in philosophy of religion in 1957, our professor at McGill University introduced us to the work of Søren Kierkegaard. The iconoclasm of Kierkegaard fascinated me. I asked Professor MacKinnon for additional reading material; he suggested that I purchase David F. Swenson's *Something About Kierkegaard*. I promptly went to my favorite bookstore and ordered the book. A week or so passed and I went to pick up my order. It was a rather different book that had arrived at the store. It took a few moments until the manager confessed that she had taken the title to mean just something about Søren Kierkegaard. Eventually I got the recommended book.

This essay has components from both my professor's specificity about the substance of Swenson's book—still a classic on Kierkegaard—and the bookstore manager's vague sense that anything about this Dane would do. I want to address specifically why Dietrich Bonhoeffer has such an impact in theological discussion, particularly in the confluence of theology and public policy. But I shall do so from my perspective that goes now here and then there. I forego a systematic approach in order to commend the man whose one hundredth birthday we celebrated earlier this year.

Eberhard Bethge was a student of Dietrich Bonhoeffer and subsequently by marriage to Bonhoeffer's niece Renate Schleicher, a close relative. Bethge wrote the authoritative biography of his teacher, friend, confidant and "uncle-in-law." On the title of this biography are three characteristics of Bonhoeffer: "Theologian, Christian, Man for His Time." It becomes quite apparent a few pages into this 1,048-page book that those three terms are not separable in Bonhoeffer but, instead, they constantly flowed into and mutually shaped one another. In the course of my more than forty years of engagement of Dietrich Bonhoeffer's work, I have come to learn ever more deeply that it is the confluence of those characteristics, which theology and church have all too often kept apart, that draws me to this man and stimulates my own reflection.

When I borrow Bethge's three terms to structure this essay, I seek to pinpoint the "something" about Bonhoeffer that has constructively guided me in seeking to do theology appropriately, in endeavoring to be a disciple of Jesus, and in both to be present in and committed to the time I live in.

A few, brief words about how I depict that time from my perspective. I am a child of Hitler's Germany, a defeated and, for over forty years, a divided nation. Since my late teens I have lived in Canada, in its diverse ethos of First Nations and immigrants' peoples, inter-religious, increasingly more secular, shaped by a spectacular geography that has given rise to numerous and beautiful traditions. A land where, indeed, cultures and civilizations labor to bring about something new by simply living together while, at the same time, clinging to the perceived promise of this land: that of freedom and justice.

So, how does Dietrich Bonhoeffer, a person of what we sometimes affectionately, at others derogatorily call the "old world," provide direction to one who, coming from that same world, has his place in what may possibly yet really become "the new world" and is responsive to that context? For example: how does addressing theologically the burden of the German nation's guilt for the genocide of Europe's Jews in the Shoah impinge on Canada's apartheid history with the First Nations here? Or how can the Christian Church's traditional imperialist exclusiveness be abandoned in Canada's multiple diversity without losing the substance of Christianity's mystery? Or as Douglas Hall might put it: What is post-Constantinian theology and church to look like in this country?

Dietrich Bonhoeffer was born in the city of Breslau, now Wroclaw in Poland. He was one of eight children. The family was of the German upper-middle class, of aristocratic background, embodying a creative mixture of conservative and politically radical values. The Bonhoeffers were not a church-going family, but Christianity was present in the household through music, literature, and the rich contact with the university. Theologian and historian Adolf von Harnack lived in the immediate neighborhood in Berlin, where the Bonhoeffers had moved in 1912 when Karl Bonhoeffer was appointed to the prestigious chair of psychiatry and neurology. Harnack would gather the various neighbors' children and read stories to them. Later Bonhoeffer became his student and teaching assistant. Still in high school in Berlin-Grunewald—an educationally demanding, advanced institution—the fifteen-year-old announced that he would study theology. The course of World War I, during which his older brother Walter was killed at the front, impacted that decision. After his university studies, which he completed with a doctorate in theology at age 21(!) and the publication of his first book *Sanctorum Communio*, he served on the staff of a German congregation in Barcelona (1928–29.) He returned to Berlin to qualify for the doctorate that would allow him to teach at university. After successfully achieving that goal, he was a post-doctoral fellow at Union Theological Seminary in New York (1930–31.) Then back once again to Berlin to teach in the faculty of theology at the university. There Bonhoeffer experienced firsthand the ascendancy of the Nazis, who in January 1933, assumed power. Right from the start Bonhoeffer was opposed to their policies, which in August 1936 cost him his teaching position.

In those years, he also served as chaplain to the students at Berlin's Technical University and, in addition, took over the confirmation-class in a working-class congregation in the city. He became very active during those years in the churches' ecumenical work, attending numerous conferences both inside and outside Germany.

From October 1933 until April 1935, he served two German-speaking congregations in Sydenham and in the East End of London. He needed space, on the one hand, for a time away from the fiasco of the German churches' widespread embrace of Hitler's National Socialism. On the other, he wanted to make use of his international ecumenical relationships and contacts to help refugees from Germany and to advance the work of opposition to the new German regime.

He was called back to Germany to establish and direct an illegal seminary, at Finkenwalde, for the small number of those seeking to serve that part of the church which refused to accommodate itself to the way the so-called "Faith Movement of German Christians" directed the life and witness of Christianity in Germany. Eventually, the Gestapo stepped in and closed the seminary in September 1937. By that time, it was apparent that war was imminent. Hitler annexed Austria and, as we now know, with the acquiescence of France and Great Britain, marched into Czechoslovakia; all this in the guise of reuniting the German-speaking peoples. Bonhoeffer continued to educate people for service on the so-called "Confessing Church" while also working in that church's administrative section. In that work he came to know, both through direct personal relationships and emerging contacts, many of those who later were involved in the efforts to achieve a regime-change in Germany. Through the efforts of some of those persons, after World War II had broken out, he was assigned to the German counter-intelligence where he acted in fact as a double-agent. He made contacts in Switzerland and Sweden with people who, learning of the plans to remove Hitler from power, were to contact the Allies' governments to establish conditions for peace-negotiations after the fall of Hitler.

In January 1943, Dietrich Bonhoeffer and Maria von Wedemeyer became engaged; less than three months later, he was arrested and eventually charged with "subversion." After the failed assassination attempt on Hitler on July 20. 1944, his involvement in the conspiracy was discovered. On the personal order of the then-already bunkered dictator in Berlin, Bonhoeffer was summarily tried, convicted and hanged on April 9. 1945, at Flossenbürg concentration camp.

Bonhoeffer published six books and numerous articles, reviews, sermons and other materials before he was prohibited from publishing by the Nazis in March 1941.The previous September, his right to speak in public was revoked. All that time he worked on a book that had taken on prime importance for him: on ethics. But he did not complete it. It was published posthumously, entitled simply *Ethics*. The correspondence he was able to keep up while in the Tegel prison in Berlin (April 5, 1943 to August 10, 1944), most of which was smuggled in and out by a sympathetic guard, was published as *Letters and Papers from Prison*. It comprises much of Bonhoeffer's reflection on the renewal of the witness to Christ today.

1. Bonhoeffer the *theologian* speaks to me persuasively primarily in two areas: the imperative of ascertaining always that we speak indeed of *God* when we *speak* of God, and the necessity of knowing the reality of those to whom we speak when we speak of God.

Bonhoeffer encountered in his lifetime the slide into idolatry and the subsequent falsification of the living God, that is, the transgression against the First Commandment. There was the co-optation of "God" in World War I when chaplains and bishops blessed the armed forces' weapons and "God" was said to be "with us" on soldiers' belt buckles. This was followed later in his experience of how white churches in the United States defended their racism, denying the inclusiveness of God's creation. The most aggressive idolatry he lived in was the elevation of Hitler and his "Nordic" ideology to the level of divinity. For him those were specific and explicit manifestations of what Karl Barth, from whom Bonhoeffer had come to learn a lot, depicted the idolatry of modernity: when today we speak of God, we really solemnly speak of ourselves in elevated tones and loud volume. Bonhoeffer saw quickly that an idol-god is always at the center of the attempts and their policies of setting one group of humans over another group or groups. The God of Holy Scripture, the Living God, seeks the freedoms of humans, their co-existence in relations of justice, inclusiveness and peace. He asserted that idolatry robs us of our sight, our vision of God's revelation in its concrete manifestations. In his view, it was not disobedience that we are so little religious but, rather, that we love to be religious, that we are so much at ease when the authorities mouth the Christian world-view. Our disobedience is that the more pious we are we let ourselves be told less and less that God is dangerous, that God is not mocked.

The clarity with which Bonhoeffer saw that idolatry necessarily leads to separation between people and between churches is impressive as is his renewed focusing on scripture and creed. So that the testimony found there may be seen, an approach and interpretation is required that is not "religious" in the sense of the assertion referred to. It must suffice here to say that when he explored the concept so closely associated with his name, that is the non-religious interpretation of Christian concepts, what he was after was an approach free of the assumption that we humans either innately or through the influence of our culture have a capacity for God that lets us access God apart from God's own manifestation to us. Bonhoeffer's rebuttal was that a god whom we can prove to exist does not exist, nor is it a god. It is more an elevated, noble portrayal of ourselves. The other significant theological term for me is "arcane discipline." When he draws on that concept of ancient Christianity, he does not have in mind an exercise to maintain something arcane in the sense of obsolete or beyond the comprehension of most people. It is quite the opposite. The Christians' arcane discipline is their vigilance in protecting what is sacred from being profaned. I cite two examples of profanation, one from his and another from our context. Hitler claimed, and many of his Christian followers accepted his claim, that he was an instrument of, and that his aims were inspired by, Providence. Today, a President of the United States of America and leader of a nation even more powerful than Hitler was in his time, asserts that his is a divine mission and that, in response to his prayers, he receives the deity's guidance for his military and political imperialism. There was no doubt for Dietrich Bonhoeffer: such claims are an unadulterated profanity and followers of Jesus Christ must resist it.

2. Bonhoeffer the *Christian* speaks to me persuasively primarily in his insistence on taking the Sermon on the Mount seriously, on distinguishing costly grace from cheap grace and on honestly grasping the realities of following Jesus.

Bonhoeffer's sense of being a Christian is of one who has heard Jesus's call: come follow me! and then accepts the consequences of having decided to follow him. What he saw instead everywhere was that becoming "Christian" required at most a little discomfort such as having to take religious instruction and paying for the maintenance of the church's institutional dimensions. Being Christian in that sense is being fed "cheap" grace: something that fails us in hard times in that it cannot prepare us for the tough decisions to be made especially when they are decisions of resistance and opposition. Such "Christianity" does not lead to a life lived according to the Sermon on the Mount. His most influential and most read book, *Discipleship*, (the lectures delivered at the illegal seminary at Finkenwalde) explores what Christian existence in discipleship to Jesus would be when it attends to two things. It is alert to idolatry and, secondly, it desires authentic Christian life by not so much asking, What would Jesus do now? but, What is my responsibility here as someone committed to Jesus? This, of course, raises the question he addressed in his prison correspondence, "Who is Jesus Christ for us today?" What impresses me here in particular is how he works at that question less in terms of the classical doctrine of the two natures of Christ and their interrelationship. He does address that in lectures delivered in Berlin in 1932. In *Discipleship*, he reflects on who Jesus is for us in terms of what the late Dorothee Soelle once called the greatest spiritual gift of Judaism: the concept of "the neighbor."

The scripture's understanding of the neighbor is rooted in the utterly clear recognition that it is God who "defines" the neighbor. When human categories become the defining factor, often, all too often, they embody exclusion. "Loving" the neighbor requires God's revelation, Karl Barth had argued in a public debate with his (and Bonhoeffer's) teacher Harnack. It seems that Bonhoeffer did not meet Martin Buber, his great Jewish contemporary, but he would surely have known Buber's fine rendering of Judaism's greatest commandment: "*Liebe denn IHN deinen Gott mit all deinem Herzen, mit all deiner Seele, mit all deiner Macht. Halte lieb deinen Genossen, dir gleich.* Love HIM your God, with all your heart, all your soul, all your might. Love your neighbor who is like you."[1] This "the neighbor who is like you" was for Bonhoeffer the radicality of God's prohibition of every form of human exclusion.

The Beatitudes in the Sermon on the Mount are an illustration of the neighbors whom God places before us and of how God blesses them *and* those who are neighbors to them. Human "neighborliness" or "hospitality" here become a reflection and enactment of God's "neighborliness" or "hospitality" to us. But it is also a matter of "costly" grace for it involves being reviled, persecuted and having all kinds of evil uttered against one falsely accused on account of Jesus (Mt. 5:11).

3. Bonhoeffer the *Man for His Times* speaks to me persuasively primarily in the clarity he achieved as he struggled with the questions of responsibility and guilt.

---

1. Buber, *Die Schrift*, 220 and 149.

When it comes to making ethical decisions, Bonhoeffer argued that the real question to ask, as we have already seen, is not What would Jesus do? or What would Jesus have me do? but, What in my freedom is my responsibility as a follower of Jesus in this situation? That question directly relates to the two inseparable questions: Who is Jesus Christ for us today? and Who is my neighbor in the present context?

In the Sermon on the Mount, Jesus commands his followers to be perfect as their Heavenly Father is perfect (Mt. 5:48). The immediate response, sincere in its way, is that nobody is or can be perfect, except God. But that belief gets around obedience to Jesus's commandment. Bonhoeffer reflected on that verse noting that the Greek word for perfect is *téleios*, meaning: "being determined, focused on a single goal; not simultaneously aiming for two goals; it means not being *dipsuchos* [with two souls]."[2] This is reminiscent of Kierkegaard's assertion that the purity of heart is to will one thing. In this sense, "perfection" is not an unattainable matter. It rather becomes a matter of free responsibility. As I understand Bonhoeffer here, he is saying that as God is free and single-mindedly chooses one goal: the covenant between God and God's creatures, acting with undivided covenantal love, grace, mercy, forgiveness and judgment toward the creatures, so are we, the creatures, free to choose and focus on the single goal of loving God and the *neighbor*. And that is actually our perfection. To act in free responsibility and in responsible freedom is God's and our perfection.

This is exactly the place where the question of our guilt is so much more weighty than in the view that no one is perfect. It arose for Bonhoeffer most sharply when he decided to become a co-conspirator, that is, to enter into the resistance against Hitler on the side of those who planned to assassinate the dictator.

Bonhoeffer was not a "theologian of the resistance" but, instead, a "theologian in the resistance." He struggled to become clear about the significance of planning to take a human being's life through an act of violence for one who knows that violence and murder are both willful transgressions of the divine commandment: murder not! Bonhoeffer stood by his Christian fellow-conspirators with theological-pastoral-spiritual counsel in their mutually taken decision that the killing of innocent peoples by the Nazis had to stop. Where the church failed them, as it failed the victims of the Nazis' murders, was in insisting that obedience to God's commandments took priority for the salvation of the soul over bringing to a halt the ongoing killing thousands of human beings daily.

An important point has to be interjected here. The conspirators prepared for the assassination of their *own country's dictator*. When Bonhoeffer

---

2. Bonhoeffer, *Discipleship*, 278.

remarked to Willem Visser' t Hooft in the fall of 1941 that he prayed for the defeat of Germany, of his *own* country, he was not opening the door to the generalization of his prayer or of the conspiracy he was involved in. When the president spoken of a moment ago now uses Bonhoeffer and his theological reflections, in his speech to the German Bundestag on May 23, 2002, to buttress with religious rhetoric his war against another country and the removal of the dictator there, Bonhoeffer is abused and dishonored, and the God of whom Bonhoeffer spoke and in whom he believed is profaned.

To the end of his life Bonhoeffer lived in and by the hope in God's greater truth and reality; in that sense, he was indeed a pioneer of hope, as Sabine Dramm calls him. He lived simultaneously with hope and with guilt. After having weighed rationally all other options to achieve the removal of Hitler from power and having concluded that no alternative was available effectively to bring the killing to an end, the free decision was taken to kill Hitler. That decision included taking guilt upon oneself. But in trust on God's mercy, one can with one's guilt throw oneself on God's judgment. The dilemma was crystal clear: not to act would bring guilt upon them just as acting would. Hence the planned action meant that one would *consciously* take guilt upon oneself and that one has to live before God with it. Here is where Bonhoeffer, in my view, advances the reflection on guilt. We shall be guilty, yes, but we must do what we have decided to do; we shall be guilty of taking a life, yes, but we can live before God with our guilt. In that conviction, Bonhoeffer not only strengthened hope but also freedom and responsibility.

In what is known as Bonhoeffer's "spiritual testament," the reflections written for his fellow conspirators entitled "After Ten Years," he wrote something that is a good way to conclude this essay. Entitled "Some Statements of Faith on God's Action in History," he said:

> I believe that God can and will let good come out of everything, even the greatest evil. For that to happen, God needs human beings who let everything work out for the best. I believe that in every moment of distress God will give us as much strength to resist as we need. But it is not given to us in advance, lest we rely on ourselves and not on God alone. In such faith all fear of the future should be overcome. I believe that even our mistakes and shortcomings are not in vain and that it is no more difficult for God to deal with them than with our supposedly good deeds. I believe that God is no timeless fate but waits for and responds to sincere prayer and responsible action.[3]

---

3. Bonhoeffer, *Letters and Papers from Prison*, 46.

9.

Discipleship between Conflicting Commandments

Dietrich Bonhoeffer in the Conspiracy against Hitler

"Whenever Christ calls, his call leads us to death," wrote Dietrich Bonhoeffer in his *Discipleship*.[1] The original German is: "*Jeder Ruf Christi führt in den Tod.*" The first English translation rendered it as: "When Christ calls a man, he bids him come and die."

This sharp aphorism is the climax of a section where Bonhoeffer links *faith* and *obedience* by saying: "only the believers obey" and "only the obedient believe." I see what I call "discipleship between conflicting commandments" in his understanding of obedience. What happens when, in obeying God's commandments, one finds that acting on one of them one has to deny another? Or: Is following Jesus Christ's call not disobeyed when in acting faithfully in relation to one commandment one has to trespass against another?

Let us look at some passages from *Discipleship*. In the section "Simple Obedience," Bonhoeffer names forces that seek to get between the word of Jesus and obedience and says:

> Jesus [breaks] through all of this and mandate[s] obedience. It [is] God's own word. Simple obedience [is] required. If Jesus Christ were to speak this way to one of us today through the Holy Scripture, then we would probably argue thus: Jesus is making a specific commandment; that's true. But when Jesus commands, then I should know that he never demands legalistic obedience . . . what he [really] intends is that it is not important if [I] do [what he commanded] literally, outwardly . . . . Our obedience to Jesus' word would then consist in our

1. Bonhoeffer, *Discipleship*, 87.

rejecting simple obedience as legalistic obedience, in order to be obedient "in faith." . . . [S]imple obedience is supposed to be wrong, or even to constitute disobedience . . . . Jesus' concrete call and simple obedience have their own irrevocable meaning. Jesus calls us into a concrete situation in which we can believe in him. That is why he calls in such a concrete way and wants to be so understood, because he knows that people will become free for faith only in concrete obedience. Wherever simple obedience is fundamentally eliminated, there again the costly grace of Jesus' call has become the cheap grace of self-justification. But this . . . constructs a false law, which deafens people to the concrete call of Christ. This false law is the law of the world, matched by an opposing law of grace. The world here is not that world which has been won over by Christ and is daily to be won over anew in his community. Rather, it is the world which has become a rigid, inescapable law of principles. But in that case grace is also no longer the gift of the living God, rescuing us from the world for obedience to Christ. Rather, it becomes a general divine law, a general principle, whose only use is its application to special cases.[2]

Those whose theological perspective is formed by the work of Martin Luther may well find a Lutheran theologian's insistence on obedience surprising; after all, we are saved by faith and not by works, even the works of obedience. But Bonhoeffer's point is that following Christ is a matter of doing what Jesus says concretely, such as what he said to the rich young ruler: "Go, sell your possessions, and give the money to the poor, and you will have treasure in heaven; then come, follow me" (Mt. 19:21). In an earlier work, *Creation and Fall*, Bonhoeffer had made the same point about simple obedience to a concrete commandment of God. Having been commanded not to eat of the fruit of a specific tree, it occurred to the couple to question whether God had really meant it quite so specifically; in so asking, the two sought to gain a deeper understanding of God's meaning. In their desire to have deep communion with God and full understanding of what God says, they turned simple obedience into a matter of their own judgment.[3]

It is not works as such that is the issue but the reality of Christ's grace in calling us. I cite Bonhoeffer again from *Discipleship*.

Fundamentally eliminating simple obedience introduces a principle of scripture foreign to the Gospel. According to it, in order to understand scripture, one must first have a key to interpreting

2. Ibid., 77–81.
3. Bonhoeffer, *Creation and Fall*, 115.

it. But that key would not be the living Christ himself in judgment and grace.... Rather the key to scripture would be a general doctrine of grace, and we ourselves would decide its use.[4]

The freedom to judge, to dare to use one's reason, to be autonomous—the very gifts of the Enlightenment to humankind—here clash directly with the form of obedience, the *simple* obedience Bonhoeffer sets forth as a key component of discipleship.

The two commandments I speak of as "conflicting" are these: *You shall not commit murder* and *You shall love the Lord, your God, with all your heart, with all your soul, with all your strength, and your neighbor as yourself.* Martin Buber and Franz Rosenzweig translated these two commandments as follows: *Morde nicht.* Murder not! and *Liebe denn IHN deinen Gott mit all deinem Herzen, mit all deiner Seele, mit all deiner Macht. Halte lieb deinen Genossen, dir gleich.* Love HIM your God, with all your heart, all your soul, all your might. Love your neighbor, who is like you.[5] Let me develop this "conflicting" in relation to Bonhoeffer's participation in the conspiracy against Hitler.

After their intense, secretive and highly dangerous deliberations, the conspirators were convinced that to remove Hitler from power could be accomplished only by assassination, that is, by murder. And even though the commandment *Murder not!* demands simple obedience, they went ahead, planning to murder him.

Interjection: My having been born in Nazi Germany influences how I interpret Bonhoeffer. When the Third Reich collapsed, I was ten years old; until well into my twenties, I did what all too many Germans did: I focused on the suffering of my people and, specifically, of my family and relatives during the War and during the occupation of Germany afterwards by the Allies. What my country, my people—some of them as close as my father—had inflicted on "the others" was secondary to what had been "inflicted" on us. It was not until after my ordination and post-graduate studies that I began to ask about and research the horrific history of Nazi Germany and its legacy to my people, my church, my family and—most urgently—to Christian theology. I would like to name with gratitude some persons who became "significant others" to me: companions, critics, supporters and healers on the long and hard but utterly unavoidable journey: Karl Barth, Helmut Gollwitzer, Friedrich-Wilhelm Marquardt, Paul Lehmann, Emil Fackenheim, Albert Friedlander—may they rest in peace!—Irving "Yitz" Greenberg, Richard Rubenstein, Susannah Heschel, Martin Stöhr, Franklin

---

4. Bonhoeffer, *Discipleship*, 82.
5. Buber, *Die Schrift*, 97, 220 and 149.

Littell (of blessed memory), Andreas Pangritz, Eberhard Busch. Then there are Charles Villa-Vicencio of the South African Truth and Reconciliation Commission, Barbara Rumscheidt, my late partner in marriage who bore much of her husband's burden of the anguish and often sick despair that marks the road into facing Germany's past, and Nancy Lukens-Rumscheidt, my partner in marriage now who, with her own work on the resistance against Hitler, supplements my labor splendidly as I proceed.

It was Karl Barth who urged me to read Bonhoeffer and explore his life and work in the actuality of Hitler's terrorism. I began by reading *Discipleship* and was gripped by his depiction of what following Jesus means. I read that book after I was ordained and wonder whether I would have sought ordination had I read it before. Then I read Helmut Gollwitzer's *Und führen wohin du nicht willst* (*Unwilling Journey*), the account of his years in a Soviet prisoner of war camp. That book opened my eyes wide to my country's and my people's terror in the Hitler years and helped me form the hermeneutic for Bonhoeffer's life and theology, for his own discipleship.

Simple obedience: simple obedience to Jesus's call to follow him, to God's Word, God's commandment, simple obedience and no prior examination or substantiation of whether the Word really means what the words say! For Bonhoeffer, this came face-to-face with *Murder not!* with its demand for unquestioning obedience in the context of the dreadful actuality of Germany's murderous terror that made the blood and the ashes of the victims cry out to heaven, to God and others on earth. But it also came face to face with *Love your neighbor, who is like you!* In the discussion between Jesus and some Pharisees narrated in Mt. 22:34–40, Jesus roundly declares that the commandments to love God and the neighbor are, in fact, the greatest of all commandments. Might this not be taken to mean that we are to decide when those "great commandments" should or should not supersede obedience to other commandments? I do not interpret Bonhoeffer that way.

His entry into the plot to kill Hitler and, thereby, to end Nazi rule and the murder of Jews, Slavs, homosexuals, Sinti and Roma, the feebleminded, Communists and ever so many others, put him in a position of having to decide between *disobedience* here or there, between "conflicting commandments." So, what does he do? What were his options, if there were in fact any at all? Bonhoeffer's biographer Eberhard Bethge addresses the question thus:

> For the church, peace and non-violence seem to be the simplest things to imagine. Woe to the Christians, woe to the church who let the peace and non-violence commandment lapse into

obscurity and let non-violence be what others ought to embrace rather than make it their own solid commitment. Yet, at the same time, peace and non-violence are something highly complicated. Woe to the church when it pulls back and does not offer resistance when violence is perpetrated against those who cannot defend themselves. The danger on one side is that, having involved oneself with the peace of Christ, one slips into dreams of the absolute which then turns all too often into their very opposite [of peace and non-violence]. The danger on the other side is that one becomes a cynic about reality the like of which one finds also in the bosom of the church.[6]

Those words trouble me deeply: "having involved oneself with the peace of Christ, one slips into dreams of the absolute" and "one becomes a cynic of reality." The danger of the former is that, as an absolute, the implementation of Christ's "peace" requires "absolute" measures, such as crusades or jihads, or else is seen as something not of this world, unachievable and not to be tried for our earthly conditions. The danger of the latter is that, in the face of violence, one withdraws into an inward, individualistic realm and cynically asserts that that's just how the world is and nothing can be done about it.

Bonhoeffer understood this perfectly and rejected such an either-or. He introduced the distinction between "ultimate" and "penultimate" things.

In 1932, aware of the danger of Hitler's National-Socialist Worker's Party and determined to oppose it, he gave an address at a conference of the World Alliance for Promoting International Friendship Through the Churches at Černohorské Kůpele in Czechoslovakia. He said that peace and non-violence are not a reality of the Gospel itself, not an aspect of the reign of God; they are a commandment of God, an aspect of the integrity of creation. Peace among the nations is God's command; it is not an absolutely ideal condition, but an order aimed at something else, not something valuable in and of itself. It is something penultimate. Nevertheless, the establishment of that order, the work for peace among nations, labor in the service of non-violence, is urgent and commanded by God. And this commanded peace and non-violence has two boundaries: truth and justice. The community of peace can exist only when it does not build itself on injustice. Here peace and non-violence have their limit and that limit calls us into readiness for struggle. Here Bonhoeffer introduces a significant differentiation: war under no circumstances, yes, but we must struggle against lies and injustice, struggle for truth and justice. Therefore, the order of external peace and

---

6. Bethge, *Bekennen*, 87.

non-violence is not of the ultimate and has to be breached when the rape and mockery of truth and justice threaten the word of the peace of Christ, which is of the ultimate. Struggle as such is basically possible as an action in and of discipleship. But, he goes on:

> Today . . . there is a widespread and extremely dangerous error that says that in the *justification of struggle* there is already the justification for war, that this contains the *fundamental Yes to war*. The right to wage war can be derived from the right to struggle no more than the right to inflict torture can be derived from the necessity of legal process in human society . . . Our contemporary war does not fall under the concept of battle because it means the certain self-destruction of both warring sides . . . . Today's war destroys soul and body. Because there is no way for us to understand war as God's order of preservation and therefore as God's commandment, and because war needs to be idealized and idolatrized in order to live, today's war . . . must be *condemned* by the church.[7]

This implies that breaking external, "penultimate" peace does not destroy the peace and the peace-community that is based on the struggle for truth and justice and, for Christians, on God's forgiveness and grace alone. Rather, "ultimate" peace can exist in the struggle for truth and justice.

In 1938, the danger Bonhoeffer had foreseen in 1932, had become stark reality. I mention just three factors to highlight this point. Through his minister for religious affairs, Hitler had ordered that all clergy swear a special oath of allegiance to the Führer. After initially refusing, most clergy of the Confessing Church did what other Nazi-aligned clergy had no scruple doing: swear the oath. Then, in September, the letter Karl Barth had written from Switzerland to the Czech theologian Josef Lukl Hromádka had become public. In it, Barth declared, among other things, that every Czech soldier resisting Hitler's advance into Czechoslovakia does so for the sake of Christ. But the Confessing Church in Germany declared that it had nothing to do with that Swiss democrat and with such unpatriotic theology. Finally, on the eve of November 10, the Kristallnacht pogrom, the deportation and killing of Jews took place. By then Bonhoeffer had been apprised of plans for a plot against Hitler; members of his immediate family were part of those plans.

It was clear to them that critique of the National-Socialist regime had become pointless. The regime's war-mongering, its euthanasia-murders and organized deportation of Jews from the territories of the Reich and, subsequently, the information concerning the genocide of Jews and of

---

7. Bonhoeffer, *Ecumenical, Academic, and Pastoral Work*, 365–66.

certain segments of Eastern European peoples, had made it irrefutably obvious that the Nazi system was not an occasional system of injustice and lies but the quintessence of falsehood and injustice. It was no longer worthy of being called a "state."

Bonhoeffer had not "slipped into dreams of the absolute" nor become "a cynic of reality." The struggle for truth and justice had to be taken up within and against that regime. Here, without naming it, is how he identifies it in the significant essay "After Ten Years," written at the turn of 1942/43. "That evil should appear in the form of light, good deeds, historical necessity, social justice, is absolutely bewildering for one coming from the world of ethical concepts that we have received. For the Christian who lives by the Bible, it is the very confirmation of the abysmal wickedness of evil."[8] Bonhoeffer then develops how "our tradition's world of ethical concepts" fails in face of such "abysmal wickedness of evil." It is not that he tosses traditional ethics on the junk-heap of the past; no, it had failed in the "masquerade of evil," the masquerade that turns everything upside down. It had failed because it was exercised in isolation and lacked the ability to see through the disguises and dissimulations of evil. "The person is wise who sees reality as it is, who sees into the depth of things," he wrote at that time.[9] In the absence of this wisdom lies rooted the danger of becoming "a cynic of reality." It manifests itself in the lack of courage to face reality. And in another section of that essay, "Who Stands Fast?" Bonhoeffer states that insisting on the virtue of "the clear conscience" provides the way for escaping reality, especially escaping the reality of complicity in evil.

"The word of the Bible that the fear of God is the beginning of wisdom (Ps. 111:10) declares that the internal liberation of human beings to live the responsible life before God is the only genuine way to overcome"[10] these dangers. It appears to me that in Bonhoeffer's view, it is ultimately faith, a clear relationship to the living God, that sets free an unclouded view of reality and assigns tradition's ethics and its virtues their appropriate functions. I see this confirmed in what he writes in "Are We Still of Any Use?"

> We have been silent witnesses of evil deeds. We have become cunning and learned the arts of obfuscation and equivocal speech. Experience has rendered us suspicious of human beings, and often we have failed to speak to them a true and open word.

---

8. Bonhoeffer, *Letters and Papers from Prison*, 38.
9. Bonhoeffer, *Ethics*, 81.
10. Bonhoeffer, *Letters and Papers from Prison*, 44.

Unbearable conflicts have worn us down or even made us cynical.... Are we still of any use?[11]

In the fullness of the concrete situation and in the possibilities it offers, the wise person discerns the impassable limits that are imposed on every action by the abiding laws of human communal life. In this discernment, the wise person acts well and the good person acts wisely. There is clearly no historically significant action that does not trespass ever again against the established limits set by those laws. But it makes a decisive difference whether such trespasses against the established limit are viewed as their abolishment in principle and hence presented as a law of its own kind, or whether one is conscious that such trespassing is perhaps an unavoidable guilt that has its justification only in that law and limit being reinstated and honored as quickly as possible.[12]

In no way did Bonhoeffer propose that the notorious character of injustice and violence of the Hitler regime "justified" or "legitimated" his and his fellow-conspirators' resistance and its ultimate aim, or that they needed no justification at all. What he saw was the necessity of being liberated for free, responsible action, including action against laws and mores and, I stress, against commandments of God, when faced with horrible crimes against humanity, against the rape and violation of human rights. The killing, killing, killing had to be ended.[13]

The origin of responsible action for Bonhoeffer does not lie in a theology; after all, theology can both block and smooth the way to such action. The Christian's responsible or political action derives from, or comes out of, a situation where faith is called into responsibility. Something like the sensibility of faith for the present situation, for concrete reality frees the Christian person for the action of resistance. Such action is not the implementation of a previously designed theological-ethical concept; for if it were, it would still be an act of unfree anxiousness; it cannot deliver what is longed for, namely the experience of freedom. There is still the groping for the safe railing of advance or subsequent guaranteed justification for what one does. Justification is and remains God's alone! Believing that a situation exists that calls for responsibility, faith grasps with the responsible action the garment

---

11. Ibid., 52.

12. Ibid., 45–46.

13. The threefold repetition of "killing" is drawn from an interview with Eberhard Bethge in the documentary *Bonhoeffer* by Martin Doblmeier. Bethge is describing the horror of the mass killings in the death camps and the countries occupied by Germany. The documentary was produced by Journey Films, Alexandria, Virginia, 2003.

of freedom for oneself and for others; it does not thereby create justification for itself, not even a theological one. What faith does is open itself with abandon to accountability for actions taken responsibly in the existing situation. Accountability, responsibility is authentic and, therefore, free when it is radically open to acknowledging, accepting and confessing guilt.

It is here where ethics pinpoints the reason for necessary *political* action in openness to and willingness for the *responsible* action proper to or inherent in Christian *faith*. Wherever faith looks only to the yearnings of the passive human being for meaning or consolation, for being loved and held, it turns grace into a cheap commodity. In those classic formulations of *discipleship*, grace then costs nothing, becomes something for the isolated, monadic individual that so much of present Western culture celebrates. Radical openness, on the other hand, and willingness for responsibility materializes itself, becomes concrete entity, in the liberation for accepting guilt or culpability and for overcoming scruples before one acts. What bears and sustains such openness and willingness is the knowledge that the world, including the political world (does anyone live in a world other than politically?) is accepted, judged and renewed by God. That openness and willingness live in the faith which learns from Christ that the norms of Christ's commandments are firm, that they call and bear us AND that, even when we break the commandments in sensitivity for our fellow human beings and their security, thereby taking guilt upon ourselves, *we are not abandoned by Christ*.

That we are not abandoned by Christ, the one whom we seek to follow in discipleship, is the rock upon which Bonhoeffer's political engagement *against* Hitler and *for* Hitler's victims rests. His openness to and readiness for freely choosing and accepting responsibility derives from that "blessed assurance."[14] "Free responsibility" is founded in a God who calls for the free venture of faith into responsible action and who promises forgiveness and consolation to those who, on account of such action, become sinners. Here forgiveness relates to the unavoidable personal guilt that those, who in taking a stand and acting upon it, accept the risk of free responsibility and in so doing burden their conscience.

In Bonhoeffer's prison correspondence we find these lines, written immediately after the failed attempt on July 20, 1944 to overthrow the Nazi regime by assassinating Hitler.

---

14. He must have heard that expression in Abyssinian Baptist Church in Harlem while in New York, 1930–1931.

> Not always doing and daring what's random, but seeking
>   the right thing,
> Hover not over the possible, but boldly reach for the real.
> Not in escaping to thought, in action alone is found freedom.
> Dare to quit anxious faltering and enter the storm of events,
> carried alone by your faith and by God's good commandments,
> then true freedom will come and embrace your spirit, rejoicing.[15]

Bonhoeffer was a pioneer of hope. What one can learn from him is to live by hope and, perhaps more importantly, to live with guilt. His understanding of Christian faith enables an ethical freedom which in turn enables action. It was clearly his intent that his conscience and that of his fellow-conspirators would be free for the action they had decided upon: the murder of Hitler, and for the acceptance of the inevitable guilt taken upon themselves by that action. The freeing characteristic of his approach to guilt is that it allows one to live with the dilemma that non-action in response to the murder of whole peoples meant guilt[16] and that action to stop it by murdering the perpetrator meant guilt, that this latter action knowingly renders one guilty, and that it was a guilt that had to be accepted knowingly. The freeing characteristic of this way of thinking is that it lets us live before God with such guilt. Being an insider to the assassination plans and participating in the conspiracy, Bonhoeffer knowingly burdened himself with guilt, yes. He consciously and freely incurred guilt in what he knew he had to do but he clearly knew also that he could live before God with that guilt. We speak here of "liberation for guilt" as an interpreter of Bonhoeffer recently put it.[17]

Of course, the issue is not that we are set free to choose between one guilt and another, as if guilt were a matter of preferences. The "freedom" spoken of here is that in the choices we make—and in the context of Bonhoeffer's situation addressed in this presentation, it is the choice between conflicting commandments and the subsequent conflict of obedience—we can live before God with the guilt we incur by having chosen the way we did. We heard earlier Bonhoeffer's assertion that "people become free for faith only in concrete obedience." And that means that faith in God's covenantal promise of forgiveness, faith in the "grace of our Lord Jesus Christ," sets us free to obey the commandments and then, making our choices for concrete,

---

15. Bonhoeffer, *Letters and Papers from Prison*, 513.

16. The former executive director of the Canadian ecumenical agency, Project Ploughshares, Dr. Ernie Regehr, coined the term "non-violent culpability" to characterize such non-action for reasons of principles of non-violence in face of oppressive assaults on vulnerable people.

17. Dramm, *V-Mann Gottes und der Abwehr?*, 243.

responsible action, we can live gratefully before God with the guilt we incur because of God's faithfulness to God's promises.

To conclude, we recall the remarkable credo by Bonhoeffer, written just a few weeks before the Nazis arrested him in April 1943:

> I believe that God can and will let good come out of everything, even the greatest evil. For this to happen, God needs human beings who let everything work out for the best. I believe that in every moment of distress God will give us as much strength to resist as we need. But it is not given to us in advance, lest we rely on ourselves and not on God alone. In such faith, all fear of the future should be overcome. I believe that even our mistakes and shortcomings are not in vain and that it is no more difficult for God to deal with them than with our supposedly good deeds. I believe that God is no timeless fate but waits for and responds to sincere prayer and responsible actions.[18]

---

18. Bonhoeffer, *Letters and Papers from Prison*, 46.

10.

A Calling in a Higher Sense

Dorothee Soelle's Theopoetics

"What her prayer shows above all is that Dorothee Soelle is a translator of the Bible's poetry," writes Luise Schottroff in her essay: "Come, Read with My Eyes: Dorothee Soelle's Biblical Hermeneutics of Liberation."[1] Dorothee Soelle speaks of Luise Schottroff as "my best friend."[2] Prayer as poetry and, conversely, poetry as prayer: this is Schottroff's imaginative key to the hermeneutic of Dorothee Soelle's theological work.

This essay seeks to examine why Soelle turned to poetry and the literary genre in order to communicate theology, how she connects the two entities, what functional characteristics distinguish them and, finally, what she desires her theological poetry to make known to her hearers and readers. There is little direct citation here of the poetry that by now fills several volumes; instead, the intent is to show why the poetic medium is so much more appropriate today for "god-talk," and all that is related to it, than "theology" as it is commonly understood, if it is understood at all.

When Dorothee Soelle speaks of herself as a "theologian," which she rarely does, one detects in her voice a note of hesitation, of reluctance. The word itself is of ambiguous coinage. Dorothee Soelle once visited Martin Buber in Israel; during a conversation, he asked her: "Theology—how do you do that?"[3] By the time Soelle studied theology at university, that critical question was beginning to form itself on the lips of many of her generation, particularly in post-World War II Germany. Buber wondered about the nimbleness with which the adept, authorized and blessed of society dealt with the *logos*, with what humans declare they can know with certainty of the Transcendent. Buber's question was not anchored in the craving for method and almost nothing but method that marked (and marks) the theo-

---

1. Pinnock, *Theology of Dorothee Soelle*, 45–53.
2. Soelle, *Against the Wind*, 158.
3. Soelle, *Thinking About God*, 2.

logy of the academy. His question arose in the face of the accommodation of a great majority of Germany's theologians with the régime of Hitler, and the burden of guilt and shame it bequeathed to the people of that country. The horrors visited upon Jews, upon the population of countries occupied by the German armed forces, especially the Slavic people, and the terror exercised by the secret police on nearly every segment of the population radically challenged nearly all certainties. What was becoming clear was that the reign of the National Socialists was part of the "long history of calamity and guilt . . . that is on the record of my people."[4] This is how a German World War II soldier put it. In 1944, he wrote and published eight poems written under the impact of the German army's offensive against the Soviet Union and his participation in it. That soldier, Johannes Bobrowski, became a notable literary figure in what was the German Democratic Republic. His work became known to Dorothee Soelle just as she was beginning to explore how she could "do" theology. What she found in Bobrowski helped her significantly in identifying the profound aspect of poetry for the theological, and the necessary but perhaps impossible task of rebuilding theology.

However, what Dorothee Soelle described provocatively in the opening sentences of her address to a plenary session of the Sixth General Assembly of the World Council of Churches in Vancouver in 1983, was not the sole reason for her asking Buber's critical question on her own. "Dear sisters and brothers, I speak to you as a woman from one of the richest countries of the earth, a country with a bloody history that reeks of gas, a history some of us Germans have not been able to forget." To this she added, in her typical fashion of always linking past with present: "I come from a country that today holds the greatest concentration of atomic weapons in the world, ready for use."[5] Alongside of a history she cannot forget were three additional factors that pushed her theological inquiry. The first was her increasing alienation from the existing theology of the academy, the second the emergence of a new understanding of "spirituality," and the third her entry into the women's movement.

Dorothee Soelle describes these factors in the chapter on her "best friend" Luise Schottroff. She speaks of an erosion of her respect for university theology. "Not only was that theology removed from praxis, it even prided itself on *not* having a praxis, that is to say, it gave its blessing to a false one." It was in the context of just that praxis question that Soelle then spoke of the need for a "new piety" or what in French is called "*spiritualité*." Contrary to the diffuse English meaning of "spirituality," the meaning in French

---

4. Schäfer, *Almanach*, 67.
5. Soelle, *Against the Wind*, 93.

is more precise: "becoming more radical and more pious." "More pious" is defined by Luise Schottroff as the "'conversion' to the power of tradition, to the necessity of rereading Scripture, to hope even in times when the empirical basis of hope seems ever so thin—in other words, conversion to worship and prayer." The "more radical" grew particularly out of the perhaps slowly growing recognition of sexism as *the* place where false theology and its academy and institutionalized church structures, together with the false, hierarchical ordering of life, are to be resisted and broken open.[6]

In this essay, I work with three epistemological conclusions. The first is that Auschwitz and all that it embraces signals the collapse of the so-called Western World's value systems and epistemic structures. Secondly, as I see it, the indispensable, symbiotic relation between theology and literature or, more broadly, between the ethical and the aesthetical, has been so centrally affected by the reality of the Holocaust that it may well be irreparable. And finally, theology, in its now widely known form as an undertaking of the academy and the institutionalized church, has since the Western World's Enlightenment, distanced itself, to its very detriment, from the aesthetical. In so doing, it has undermined its own power in and for the ethical.

Institutionalized theology in the Christian West relegated literature, poetry, music as well as the visual arts to the role of a decorative servant. Under the rigorous control of the two chief structures wherein they became housed and maintained, these expressions were to provide a subsidiary or complimentary interpretation to theology, the "queen" of the human spirit's expressions. As it has done for the other domains of life, both physical and spiritual, the Enlightenment loosened the bonds of theology over the work of the creative human spirit. As a consequence, that work could and did develop into something of quasi-religious, indeed, theological significance. For example, historian and theologian Adolf von Harnack (1851–1930) interpreted the art of Johann Wolfgang von Goethe and how the religious renewal movement of Anthroposophy had elevated that poet's famous *Faust* to the level of sublime liturgy.[7]

This is not the place to discuss the turn to the "cultural" that so marked the Protestant liberal theology of the latter part of the nineteenth and the earlier part of the twentieth centuries. In my view, in its positive approach to the broader domains of the artistic, it failed the deep dimensions of the human spirit's search for and encounter with the transcendent "Thou."[8] How-

---

6. Ibid., 158–60.

7. See Rumscheidt, *Revelation and Theology* on Harnack's views and use of Goethe's poetry and the place of Goethe's *Faust* at the high temple of Anthroposophy at Dornach, Switzerland.

8. Rumscheidt, *The Making of Modern Theology*, 41.

ever, it is noteworthy that in many ways and for many people, literature and poetry in particular, but also music and the visual arts, reflectively subsumed the content of theology and "secularized" it. The poets Johann Christian Friedrich Hölderlin (1770–1843) and Rainer Maria Rilke (1875–1926) come to mind here; the former became the focus of the philosophy of "Being" of twentieth-century philosopher Martin Heidegger (1889–1976.) Hölderlin had asserted that what abides is fathomed by poets. Such a view is not the mystification of people who have become disenchanted with established religion. Rather, it critically exposes the false orientation, if not even the very failure of theology. Why else would poetry set out to become the "secular" bearer of what is at the heart of the theological endeavor?

The "religion" that predominated in the Western World for more than sixteen centuries is Christianity in its numerous and varied denominations. The charge that can, or needs to, be laid against nearly all of them is that they have held (or still do hold) the human being in bondage. What I mean is that religion was (is) presented in the language of dominance. Being declared the domain of the initiated, the adept and the experts, theology has for many Christians turned into a mysterious and esoteric discourse, inaccessible to the great majority of the population. The regular preaching of the churches of the Protestant reformations, the celebration of the Eucharistic liturgy in Roman Catholicism, Anglicanism and, to a certain extent, in Orthodoxy manifest clerical control both of the assembled congregation and of the sacred itself. Even reformative or renewal attempts to halt such nimble domestication often fall short of freeing human beings from the petty orderliness of hierarchy, allowing various forms of domination to maintain themselves, however chastened, and even to strengthen themselves.

What is traditionally referred to as "the Word of God" is something "literary." It is spoken and written communication. When turned into language of domination, the "Word" is blocked from what even in that language it is claimed to be, namely the liberation of human beings. Instead, their being in tutelage is cemented, the freedom to become and remain of age is a matter of what Dorothee Soelle and Luise Schottroff call a "false praxis." (The critique of religion Dietrich Bonhoeffer presents in his exploration of "a religionless Christianity" has precisely the same features Soelle and Schottroff envisage. He names them: inwardness, partiality and other-worldliness.) Many Christians who embraced the Enlightenment and its cry *sapere aude!*, (dare to use your mind!), substituted "the good, beautiful and true" for "religion," if they did not, like Hölderlin, see literature, poetry, music, painting, etc., as religion itself. However this development is to be evaluated, the Western World's "Enlightenment" bequeathed its children the firm conviction that the aesthetic is, unlike religion in its prevalent mode of existence, a means of liberation, of coming of age, in a word: of humanization.

Dorothee Soelle's circle of friends has always included poets, writers, painters and representatives of other forms of what Germans speak of as *die schönen Künste* (a well-nigh untranslatable term). One of them was the Nobel Laureate Heinrich Böll (1917–1985) to whom she dedicated a chapter in her memoir and on whose death she wrote a Psalm-like poem.[9] As if in intercession or invocation, Soelle calls on the unnamed "Who" (always with a capital W) "Who protects, shields, reminds, comforts, promises, strengthens, intercedes?" knowing that the call is not into a void but to the Unnamable One who has many names. Soon after she came to know Heinrich Böll in 1967, he and fellow writer Johannes Poethen had a conversation on religion and literature; it was broadcast on German radio. I cite the following excerpts from that conversation since it may be a source of an answer to why poetry became, willingly or not, a bearer of theological substance. It may also indicate what "purpose" Dorothee Soelle pursues in her theological poetics.

> Literature and art are means of humanization . . . they respect human beings in their lostness. That is why they can never be optimistic, whereas religion, religion-substitutes like Marxism and doctrinaire political teachings have to be so; they therefore render art and literature inhumane. Human beings are qualified by mourning, by love and transitoriness. Creating itself: painting a picture, composing music, writing a poem, or prose, is an erotic process creating relationship. Initially, the erotic relationship is between the artist and the artifact . . . . The eros that comes into being can, of course create also a relationship to human beings, possibly to God or the devil . . . . Here looms the danger of a new myth emerging, the myth of the author or the artist. This is a mistake, in my view. I believe . . . that authors and artists, all creative people must enter into a relationship of equality with the non-privileged so that they do not create for an educated elite who turn the art created into a pseudo-religious esotericism.

The cult of the genius, of "great men," (Adolf von Harnack is an example of this "cult")[10] that characterized the West's nineteenth century and its pseudo-religion, needed to be resisted with the imperatives of *equality*. To resist in such manner, Böll continues, is

---

9. Soelle, *Against the Wind*, 143.
10. Rumscheidt, *Revelation and Theology*, 232–68.

most likely the task of twentieth century artists; they need to create the myth of equality. No more elitist notions! [Did Böll also think of the elitism of anti-Semitism here?] Religion, the churches and denominations, having envisaged nothing but authority, are in a state of being completely remaindered. They existed by authoritarian means only, falsely believing that religion was inheritable, to be passed on by doctrine, transferable. [As a result of the collapse of religion caused by this false belief,] art is put into a position that it really cannot defend: it becomes religion, the only expression of the Word, while the Word of God, corrupted by its representatives, is barely audible, barely understandable. So many intermediary steps were interposed, so many stages of domestication. It might just be that it is precisely the decidedly non-Christian, that is, anti-Christian, even blasphemous literature . . . that will lead forward to humanization and create the human being who can be addressed with the Word of God who became, as we are taught, a human being.

Later in the conversation, Böll and Poethen expand on the "myth of equality" that a genuinely "democratic" literature needs to create. It needs

> to create the myth of the human being, of the everyday life of humans, and create anew the mythical elements of everyday human life, the poetry of that everyday life. We basically still think in terms of the categories of "educated" and "uneducated." I believe that a democratic literature must first demolish this myth of "educated" and "uneducated": it must be jarringly popular and popularizeable. . . . Here, there emerges the myth of the human being who is subject to transitoriness, capable of love and hate, living an everyday life. And that life, too, is a myth.[11]

When Böll surmises that theology, as a scholarly discipline, never became something important, he expresses what Dorothee Soelle also affirms. What has been important for people has always been what was secondary in and for theology, "in other words, the unimportant," as he puts it.[12] But it was the unimportant with which control was exercised over people: rules, regulations, church-law, catechetical injunctions, etc. People have left behind the institutionalized church and academic theology in order to discover and live the great insights of theology that rarely found their way to the wider populace; to lift the veil off those insights and to live

---

11. Schäfer, *Almanach* 4, 95–102.
12. Ibid., 102.

their praxis is what, in Böll's and Soelle's view, "democratic" poetry can do for the basis of humankind.

Without expressly stating it, the radio conversation of Böll and Poethen names the process that became utterly exposed in the Holocaust: the inability of religion to provide through its institutionalized and scientific media a praxis of resistance, that is, an ethics *for* human beings. Those media were elitist, readily amenable to the elitism of the planners and practitioners of the "final solution." This elitism could and did root itself in religion, church and academy, all of which, being in false orientation, failed the human being. While Böll and Poethen directly name the elitism of religion established in the church institution and its structures, they also identify it, albeit in its varying forms, in the aesthetic domain. Here they incidentally provide a persuasive answer to the question why it was in the very nation of Bach, Beethoven, Goethe and Hölderlin that the Shoah came into being. This creation of German will, organization, technology and coercion brutally manifests the apex of a process one-and-a-half-centuries long: the utter impotence of art and religion to concretize themselves in a praxis of resistance, perhaps even to imagine one at all.

Dorothee Soelle's book *The Silent Cry: Mysticism and Resistance* portrays such a praxis in conjunction with a democratic, non-institutionally based theology.[13] She maintains that in shunning every attempt to impose definitions, the language of poetry is able to render meaning audible and resonant exactly because of its narrative freedom and the range of linguistic means available to it. In particular, she names those used in mysticism: frequent repetition, comparison, exaggeration, hyperbole, antithesis and paradox.[14] When the relationship between theology and literature is severed, the result is that both suffer. In that separation, theology seeks refuge in "science," which, Soelle argues, is finally something of no ultimate concern to much of humankind. What theology then produces as a secondary product for the general population: ordinances, pronouncements, "how to" manuals, etc., declaring them to be for the good of the people, turns out to be detrimental to the real, the profound insights of theology. They are viewed with suspicion instead; the broadly aesthetic, even in its weakness, comes to be seen as more credible and, for that very reason, more decisive and significant.

When a strong relationship exists between them, there is mutual benefit. But the dogma of modernity is a hurdle to be overcome: the separation of the aesthetic, of politics, church, religion, into distinct domains. The Holocaust radically exposed the weakness of that dogma, for existing

---

13. Soelle, *The Silent Cry*.
14. Ibid., 64.

side by side in a spiritual apartheid, a religion separate from politics ends up venerating power and its idols; a politics separate from religion decays in despising humanity, and a politics and religion separate from the aesthetical turn into mere utilitarian instruments of the principalities and powers of this world.

In 1970, Dorothee Soelle published the "Theses concerning the criteria of theological interest in literature." There she says that the theological interest in literature is directed primarily on "what ultimately concerns us" and that is hidden in the pure profaneness of the artistic form. It is the task of theology to uncover this hidden dimension. In the language of art, theology finds a "non-religious interpretation of theological concepts" (Bonhoeffer.) These concepts are those that address human beings in their totality and relate them to their eternal, that is, their authentic life. In its discovery process, theology cannot restrict itself to myth or to the Bible, however significant both are for the self-formulation of human beings. What is theologically important is not just to revert to myth or the sources of faith but to reach out for authentic life, to anticipate it in praxis. The understanding of what is of ultimate concern to us is in reference to the conditions of finitude; hence, theology is particularly, albeit not exclusively, interested in what brings transitoriness into our consciousness. Art that so covers up transitoriness as no longer to hold before us the victims of a culture is hardly of interest to theology. For both theology and art, banality is a mortal danger. That which is theologically relevant opens us up, lifts us out of the assurances of what we know, confronts us with our own clichés, unmasks us and changes our relation to the world and, hence, ourselves.[15]

> This kind of poetry is no luxury item; it is bread. It turns our planet, ever so beloved in spite of everything, more and more into home. . . . [Poetry] creates a boundary dissolving freedom. . . . I really do not believe in the modern program of *poésie pure*: Wherever it happens successfully that the unmixed purity of the beautiful becomes sound and language, poetry is no longer "pure" and "for itself. . ." When I learned Greek, the concept *kalonkagathon* became very dear to my heart. In my seventeen-year-old unintelligence, I wondered how the Greeks could take two words that for us have nothing to do with each other, and turn them into one word: beauty-good. Where on earth would one find aesthetics and ethics in the same dish? . . . In order really to do theology we need a different language. Poetry and liberation are topics central to my life.[16]

15. Schäfer *Almanach* 4, 206–7.
16. Soelle, *Against the Wind*, 151.

Poetry as prayer, prayer as poetry, poetry and liberation-praxis: when coupled with the other does each not lead to the subversion of both? In his *Frankfurter Vorlesungen*, Heinrich Böll made it clear that whenever literature enters into any context whatsoever, it becomes itself the object of diverse interests which, themselves vulnerable and possibly even wounded, may well in turn wound literature.[17] But perhaps even more crucial is the question whether the aim of being about the praxis of liberation does not in itself turn a poem into something propagandistic and thus ceases to be poetry and becomes just that: propaganda. Some critics, such as Theodor Adorno and Hans Magnus Enzenberger, believe that the theological or political intent of a poem, let us say, has to be contained solely in the artistic *quality* of the poem. The relation of an artistic creation to the theological, social or political must not lead from, but more deeply into, the work of art. That to which a poem seeks to relate itself must, so to speak, enter through the cracks, behind the author's back on its own, without the author, as it were. Others known for their "political" agenda, such as Bertold Brecht or Walter Benjamin, insist that in addition to the linguistic-artistic quality (the form,) a poem with theological intent (the content) needs a specific technique: how is the envisaged readership to be addressed so that the desired result is achieved? How is the linguistic-communicative aspect so to be shaped that the public to be addressed understands the artistic creation? Dorothee Soelle herself makes it plain, in her essay on Brecht, that she identifies with the hermeneutic of poetry espoused by him and Benjamin. To her, Adorno and Enzenberger strive more for a form of poetry that she called *poésie pure* and for which she has little interest. I think that she identifies in the "dislike" what made "poetry" something that, according to Adorno, could no longer be properly written after Auschwitz. Her response is precisely that Auschwitz demands a response, one which intentionally sets out to bring about a conscientization and transformation that will prevent another Holocaust. And here theology, that is, what it is about and seeks to make known and understandable, has a contribution to make, namely, what has already been referred to as the "liberation" from tutelage to the powers and ideologies of the age and for a solidarity with the neighbor whom we are commanded to "love," even when that neighbor is not to our liking or meets with our approval, as she puts it in her essay on Bertold Brecht.

In this context, it is helpful to turn to yet someone else from her circle of friends: theologian, preacher, teacher and poet Kurt Marti (1921–2017). Together with Wolfgang Fietkau and Armin Juhre, he and Soelle edited and published the instructive and rewarding series *Almanach für Literatur und*

---

17. Böll, *Frankfurter Vorlesungen*, 7–9.

Theologie, beginning in 1967. An essay Kurt Marti wrote for the Festschrift for Swiss preacher and theologian Eduard Thurneysen in 1968 is included in the 1969 *Almanach*. The essay is entitled "Wie entsteht eine Predigt? Wie entsteht ein Gedicht? Ein Vergleich mit dem Versuch einer Nutzanwendung" (How does a sermon come into being? How does a poem come into being? A comparison and attempt of practical application.)[18]

Like Soelle, Marti prays through his poetry while also seeking to present the profound depths and heights of theological knowledge, which is what he also does in his preaching. Are his sermons then artistic creations and his poetry a homiletical endeavor? His proposal to compare poem and sermon and then seek for a possible practical application is highly illuminating for an interpretation of Dorothee Soelle and what I call her poetry as a vocation in a higher sense.

Marti declares that neither a sermon nor a poem comes into being on its own but are "made," and "making" them is work. But work on a poem and on a sermon are comparable; in both cases the medium of language is used. Yet each work has different presuppositions and aims.

> Preachers preach commissioned by their churches. Lyricists are not commissioned by any institution to write poems. . . . The task of preachers is to proclaim the Word of God as it is attested to in the biblical witness. Lyricists, on the other hand, set out from their unarticulated experiences, emotions, ideas, fantasies, observations, and the like. The *aim* of their work is the articulated text. An already articulated text, that of the Bible, is the *point of departure* of preachers. With their commission, preachers also receive the general theme of their sermons. They are to make known "the great acts of God." (Acts 2:11) No theme is given to the lyricists; they must find it themselves or let themselves be found by it. Preachers, beginning their work of writing the sermon, know that they *must* deliver the sermon, irrespective of whether they succeeded fully, or only half or not at all, in their work. Setting out to work on a poem, lyricists do not know whether what they have begun will ever become a poem. As soon as a poem is published, lyricists submit it to the free, often merciless, often just and often also bribable competition of the literary market and critique. This compels them from the very outset to be rigorously self-critical. . . . From their first sermon on, preachers have an audience while lyricists have to gather a readership first. . . . The fact is that initially no readership awaits the lyricists and even later, the circle of those awaiting

---

18. Schäfer, *Almanach*, 94–109.

their work remains small. Unlike preachers, lyricists work alone without being called or commissioned. Driven by pleasure or dismay, ambition or despair or whatever else, they write into an anonymous sphere. Both lyricists and preachers have their own uncertainties: lyricists as to whether their work will find a hearing at all and is meaningful, preachers as to whether their work is adequate to their assigned commission and the demands of the congregation.[19]

Theology speaks of "the Word of God," which is to say that God is not an unarticulated existence. God is not timeless or abstract but, as articulated communication, is historical, concrete, here and now, this and not that. The Bible gives testimony to this articulated Word, to the here and now of God. The preacher's task is so to present this testimony in the sermon that all present become expectant, quasi impatiently and excitedly asking: And now? What of us? Is there a future for us in the Word? And what kind of future here and now? The work of preparing and delivering the sermon includes exegesis and interpretation, to which theological study at university pays much attention. But, in addition, in order to let the hearers come to ask those highly existential questions, sermon preparation requires meditation: to reflect prayerfully on the text, to weigh it, to think oneself into it, to carry it around within oneself in the midst of the encounters, experiences and problems of everyday. In this phase, the text quasi besets the preachers, their habits and prejudgments. Conversely, the preachers beset the text with their questions, experiences, doubts. One may also say that the text courts the preachers and the preachers the text and often this mutual courting resembles a struggle.[20]

Marti continues his comparison, still dealing with theology and poetry as separate entities. For him the poet (lyricist) too is "receptive." Poets do not listen to "him," that is, God, but to "it," the world as they experience it. Not the world *as such* but the world as each poet experiences it; it is, therefore, not an objective entity but one wherein it is not possible to distinguish between subject and object. Poets

> listen to their world (which is "the" world for them) by meditating on their subjective experience of the world. The object of their meditation, their receptivity is therefore not "he," God, but "it," the world. This distinction is not a simple one of method; it embodies a fundamental position that wants to keep "he" and "it," God and world, revelation of God and experience of the

---

19. Ibid., 94–5.
20. Ibid., 97.

world clearly separate. In poetry, [poets] do not mediate divine revelation but experience of the world. If in their poems there is talk of God then it is an element of their subjective experience of the world or an invocation of a power which to call God appears appropriate to the poets.... What they call God could be God.[21]

Kurt Marti names a profound danger for every poem that makes being understood one of its primary aims. Striving to be understood invites accommodating oneself to the conventional language of society, thereby becoming overtly or covertly subverted by the interests of those who dominate in society. Both Marti and Soelle draw on the prophetic element of theology here to stay clear of this danger. This is manifested well in her work, already referred to, *The Silent Cry: Mysticism and Resistance*. She shows repeatedly there that and how a theology that has no practical agenda is relevant only for those who have nothing to resist to except what threatens them in their places of elitism.

Marti's conclusion of his comparison is, in my view, illuminating and provocative. He asks: When is a poem, a sermon "complete?" A poem is complete when, in its author's judgment, it has become a linguistic entity, autonomous and no longer to be improved upon, self-contained, that is, rhythmically and metaphorically compact. How different the sermon! It seeks to draw listeners into a dialogue. What to an outside observer may seem to be a dialogue between congregation and preacher is really an attempt to enable the deeply existential dialogue between congregation and God within God's own dialogue with the congregation. A sermon can, for that very reason, never be complete as a poem may be said to be. Only *God's* Word, when it meets and transforms a human being, completes the sermon, which is a human word, and allows an "Amen" to conclude the sermon and, in that sense complete it.[22]

Marti's "practical application" shows how theology and poetry, poetry and theology, relate without mutually subverting each other or ceasing to be what each is. He manifests his suspicion of what we earlier called the "nimble dealing by the adept of what we may know of God." Like Dorothee Soelle and Luise Schottroff and their critique of theology "administered" by the institutions of church and academy, Marti believes that the idea of a Word of God under the "management" of the church encouraged the misunderstanding that this Word is "objective" in the sense that it now needs only to be recited and no longer needs to be witnessed to. To witness means to communicate or articulate God's Word *with* the subjectivity that is given

---

21. Ibid., 100.
22. Ibid., 103–4.

to everyone. And in the witnesses' articulation they do not primarily, but clearly secondarily communicate also themselves.

Preachers are to proclaim the Word of God, not their subjectivity. But that Word is refracted in the human subjectivity of Jesus of Nazareth and those who seek to follow him, attaining to its radiance only in such refraction. The same is true for the testimony of the biblical witnesses. What poets know, namely, that experience and articulation are "genuine" only when the subjective is knowingly introduced, is important for preachers. They speak as witnesses and not as scientists who make operational use of the terminology of objectivity. As witnesses, preachers need to insert themselves, their subjectivity into their testimony no less decidedly than poets do in their poems.[23] This means that preachers will make use of subjectivity clauses such as: "In my view" or, "as I understand it." The concept of subjectivity clauses was coined by Dorothee Soelle in an essay on the poetry of Johannes Bobrowski; there Soelle showed how Bobrowski marked "Christian" statements with such clauses.

> The more preachers express their views and understandings as their *subjective* views, their *subjective* understandings, and in so doing open their statements to discussion, the more credible they become ... when they must speak prophetically, when they do actually declare a word to be indisputably *God's* Word: thus says the Lord now and not in another way, this and nothing else is what *God* wants from us now. ... Only a sermon that is vulnerably open ... can open others for that dialogue in the course of which God's Word ... both activates and assures the consciousness, the conduct and finally also the subconscious of humans so that hearers of the Word become doers thereof (James 1:22) who as active witnesses to God's shalom (peace, salvation, justice, well-being) help change society.[24]

By setting the poem's language apart from or opposed to the conventional, ideological and interest-bearing language of society, a poet hopes that society may change its language as a result. Poetry seen this way has linguistic traces of a more humane world. In that sense poetry also opens dialogue. This does not automatically cause it to become "engaged" poetry closer in line with what Brecht and Benjamin proposed.

> [Poetry] is more than what is commonly understood by engagement. Its category is that of possibility. Reality too is understood [by poetry] to a large extent as possibility. ... The category of

23. Ibid., 104–5.
24. Ibid., 106–7.

possibility is what points in a poem beyond the past and the present... to the future. By meditating on and playing with possibilities, which takes place more or less in every poem, poetry quietly contradicts what is now and envisages an individual and social situation where humans can develop their possibilities more freely, better, where, instead of being pushed into neuroses, they are freed to themselves and so also become free for all that is not the ego.... [Poets] should become more aware that they too are drawn into dialogue with their readers and hearers about the future of this changeable world."[25]

What distinguishes poets and Christians but also brings them into conjunction is that for the former the future is a multi-formed and still undetermined possibility, while for the latter the future took form and was decided in the subjectivity of the Word of God made flesh.

Dorothee Soelle eloquently expresses that conjunction. She gives very concrete contours to Marti's "category of possibility" in that she relates "possibility," "future" to what above was called "authentic life" as it took expression in the life of Jesus of Nazareth. But instead of repeating the both definitionally precise but inexhaustive *theological* terms, such as redemption, reconciliation, sanctification and others, she paints word pictures such as the one that gives title to her presentation on the poetry of Johannes Bobrowski: "For a Time Without Fear."[26] Soelle is determined, for reasons already signaled, "to speak of God in worldly language," as Dietrich Bonhoeffer's biographer, Eberhard Bethge, put it. (Bethge and Soelle were good friends; he stood by her in all of her "troubles" with the church, and his insight into the work of Bonhoeffer made a strong impact on her theological articulation.)[27]

Bobrowski (1917–1965) grew up in Eastern Germany and, after World War II, lived in what was until recently the German Democratic Republic. He openly declared that he was Christian but not a "Christian writer." Society in the East *and* West, then *and* now, looks on "faith" as something of the ecclesiastical establishment; it is seen as having to say more about the maintenance of law and order than to the encouragement of conscience. Having served in the German army that had wreaked havoc on the people and territory of the Soviet Union, having seen the destruction of European Jewry and realizing that this was part of the long history of disaster and guilt that rested on his people, he saw in the creation and encouragement

---

25. Ibid., 108–9.
26. Schäfer, *Almanach*, 143–65.
27. Soelle, *Against the Wind*, 92.

of conscience and of a different future, a chance for poetry and not only for Christians. He referred to his war and Holocaust experiences as his "war injury."[28] Not until 1949 was he released from the Soviet prisoner of war camps. Before the outbreak of the Hitler war, Bobrowski was associated with the Confessing Church movement in Germany.

Dorothee Soelle characterizes Bobrowski's poetic language as something that is close to what in the Bible is known as "calling," as "a voice calling in the wilderness. . . ."[29] Such "calling" is not communication or information *about* something; rather it is a matter of invocation and adjuration, even conjuring. Above all else, "calling" in that sense promises a future.

Whenever Bobrowski speaks of, or names God, he does so in the term that Kurt Marti adopted from Dorothee Soelle: subjectivity clauses. The poet speaks of God in the indicative case, since God cannot be spoken of in the manner we speak of "objects." What Bonhoeffer meant to say in his dictum "there is no God that is there" (*einen Gott, den es gibt, gibt es nicht*) namely a god that can be spoken of in the mind-set of objectivity does not exist, is expressed here in clauses of subjectivity. That language is "non-religious" or "secular"; it has abandoned the sense that one can speak of God, of the dimension and aspects of the transcendent, in "objective" terms, as does the scholarly theology of academy and institutionalized church rejected by Soelle and others. The "objectivity" that is alleged to be necessary for genuine scholarly pursuit and, subsequently, for "correct" communication of the Christian "truth," claiming to have no praxis—as that would only subvert the objective pursuit of truth—is actually blessing a false praxis, as Soelle maintains. She asserts that theological reflection has to cross the threshold of conscience where praxis is critically analyzed. Here language itself changes from description, mythic naming and even injunction; it becomes language of the yet unseen. "Vision of a more humane world, utopia of the life that is promised . . . home. Not the home that nature provides beforehand, not that of blood and soil, but the one yet to be won." Here Soelle quotes the same text that she uses nearly three decades later in her work on mysticism and resistance. "The root of history is the human being working, creating, reshaping and surpassing what is now. When humans have laid hold of themselves and rooted what is theirs, without relinquishment and alienation, in real democracy, something comes to be in the world, that shines into the childhood of all and in which no one had yet been: *Heimat*, home."[30]

---

28. Schäfer, *Almanach* 2, 145.
29. Ibid., 147.
30. Ibid., 158. See also Soelle, *The Silent Cry*, 11.

This is a prominent feature in Bobrowski's poetry and in it Soelle recognizes historical consciousness. Not that of the observer; "the observer sees nothing," she quotes Bobrowski. It is the consciousness of one who, gripped in the long history of disaster and guilt and its traditions (such as elitism), has crossed the threshold of conscience and now "calls up," "invokes" the yet unseen, the promised world of authentic life. It is a time without fear. In Bobrowski, the language of Christian faith and tradition has the function of representing the messianic expectation of the human being, the "more brightly colored years."[31]

Soelle describes the complex meaning of "calling" or "invoking" in Bobrowski; in my view, it fits her poetry precisely.

> Human beings attain to their reality through calling and speaking, asking and responding.... One ... dimension of this word [calling] is the religious . . . the Jewish-Christian tradition, which is not further secularized because it is . . . already secular enough. In some places "calling" has the limited and clear sense of "praising God" . . . of "calling hosanna. . . ." This absolute use of the word—without dative or accusative—is known from the language of the Psalms. This calling is synonymous with praying, the one addressed is not specifically named. The specific term "praying," monopolized by church language, does not occur in Bobrowski's poetry, but "calling" as a broader gesture contains within itself the dimension of praising and pleading.... Calling is a form of being alive, it belongs to that kind of life that cannot come to its reality in aloneness.... Everyone who calls ... is not content with the "object"; calling is a kind of transcendence over the time of fear; being able to call is something that is not at our disposition any time, any place.[32]

"Calling" means composing, writing poetry. The word—Soelle calls it a Jewish word[33]—perceives the person in her relationship to another; it perceives God in that same way. "If one understands Bobrowski's poetry as 'calling,' then it serves as an example for a Christian poetry that is possible today, one that does not talk 'about' God but calls God, to or upon God, for a time without fear."[34]

> For me, praying and writing poetry, prayer and poem, are not alternatives. The message I wish to pass on is meant to encourage

---

31. Schäfer, *Almanach*, 161.
32. Ibid., 163–64.
33. Ibid., 165.
34. Ibid.

people to learn to speak themselves. For example, the idea that every human being can pray is for me an enormous affirmation of human creativity. Christianity presupposes that all human beings are poets, namely, that they can pray. That is the same as seeing with the eyes of God. When people try to say with the utmost capacity for truthfulness what really concerns them, they offer prayer and are poets at the same time. To discover this anew, to bring it into reality or make it known, is one of the goals I pursue in my poems.[35]

Recently two women in Germany, Bettina Hertel and Birte Petersen, published what may well be called a "Soelle reader." They entitled their 240-page anthology of texts by Dorothee Soelle, *To Feel the Rhythm of Life: Commonplace Inspired*. Each of the twelve chapters derives its title from a line of one of Soelle's poems, followed by two words conjoined by the little word "and," words that name "what really concerns" human beings. I cite these twelve titles because they are a form of "calling," of "adjuring."

1. "We are all called to hallow time." The Now and Eternity.
2. "And it is not plain yet what we shall be." To Be Human and Destiny.
3. "Give me the gift of tears, give me the gift of language." Fear and Consolation.
4. "You are to let love bloom." Yearning and Giving the Self.
5. "God's pain embraces my pain." Suffering and Vulnerability.
6. "What are you doing? the angel asks me." Justice and Responsibility.
7. "Someday the trees shall be the teachers." Creation and Solidarity.
8. "Peace is a millet-seed, teeny-weeny." Gentleness and Non-violence.
9. "The bright morning star rises in my soul." Joy and Happiness.
10. "Not we give life meaning, life gives us meaning." Seeking and Being Found.
11. "I shall sing and wrest a chunk of land from death with every note." Dying and being raised up.
12. "We go to the city of our hope." Wishes and Visions.

In their Afterword, Bettina Hertel and Birte Petersen write that

> what we wish for our lives need not be little and timid but can be just as big as the wishes and promises of the one to whom

---

35. Soelle, *Against the Wind*, 153.

> we belong.... It is not that greater and greater demands be put on life; what concerns [Dorothee Soelle] is that wishes become reality through one's own action and in responsibility toward fellow humans and fellow creatures.... Her texts took us into a spirituality that joins profound personal questioning to an alert attention to the world. It is a spirituality that never gives smooth answers to life's questions. On the contrary, there is great tension in those twelve themes. Happiness cannot be thought without pain, death without life, future without memory. It is precisely in the strongest and deepest experiences of love, mystical union and happiness that Dorothee Soelle also reflects on the dark side.... Dorothee Soelle has an artful and, at the same time, willful way of articulating her thoughts. She interrupts herself with objections, contradicts tradition and speaks in paradoxes. In a poem on "resurrection" she writes "Oh don't ask about resurrection a tale of ages long ago" only to conclude it by calling out "Oh do ask me about resurrection Oh don't stop asking me!" ... The rhythm of life that Dorothee Soelle feels is multi-layered. It is a joy to let ourselves be drawn into that rhythm.[36]

In that rhythm, according to Soelle, human beings and God, human beings and human beings, human beings and all of creation experience their mutuality and interdependence. It is through "calling," "invoking" and "adjuring" or even "conjuring" that this mutuality is expressed and, in fact, made real. And then it is possible to see images of resurrection, to learn hope, to love and to resist.

In English, the distinction is made between "calling" and "vocation" even though both may mean the very same thing. *Vocare* means "to call" and to be called is to be invited into a "vocation." In German, there is a parallel differentiation between *Beruf* and *Berufung*. The former is an utterly secular term, referring to one's job whereas the latter has the clear dimension of having been called, most closely related to the religious aspect of having been addressed by the divine. It is this aspect that is heard in the phrase: "a vocation in a higher sense." I imply unambiguously that Dorothee Soelle's vocation—"job" or *Beruf*—as a theologian and poet is a "calling," a *Berufung*, to witness to the future that is the substance of our hope, the future that is not entirely at the disposal of us human beings. And the witness that we give, and which is found abundantly in Soelle's poetry, appropriately takes the form of "calling" (in German: *rufen*) or "invoking" (in German: *anrufen*). The "higher sense" refers to the inescapable and central aspect of being *berufen*: being called by the One whom humans cannot

---

36. Soelle, *Den Rhythmus des Lebens spüren*.

name objectively but only through subjectivity clauses, on the one hand, and decisive acts of solidarity with the neighbor. "Vocation" in this sense rests in the call into freedom for the neighbor, liberation for a praxis of living already in the promised future that is in the hands of God and is shared by God with us humans to be fulfilled, to live out in anticipation the *Heimat* of which Ernst Bloch speaks and thereby create it in the world already. What Luise Schottroff characterized as the hermeneutic of Soelle's writing, namely poetry as prayer and prayer as poetry, depicts the vocation in a higher sense in that prayer itself is a "calling," an *anrufen* or invoking of the One whose spirit leads those who pray into a more radical and more pious *spiritualité*, as Schottroff and Soelle see it. Dorothee Soelle calls on, enters into conversation with, God; her "calling" invokes the conversation God has with human beings in which they are called into the vocation of the future promised to humanity. And, hence, her conversation with God, addressed as it is also to her readers, becomes a form of God's conversation with and calling to them. To be called to do that is to have a vocation "in a higher sense."

In Dorothee Soelle's hands the poem becomes, both in substance and form, shelter or refuge, even rescue in the face of hopelessness and utter inconsolation. That is why the accolade applies to her: hers is "a vocation in a higher sense."

11.

The Gift of Hospitality

President Beresford, Madame Chair of the Board Sagar, Chair of the St. Mary's University Naulls, honored representatives of the churches, colleagues of Sister Universities and of Atlantic School of Theology, alumnae, alumni of the School's founding parties and of AST, friends, my fellow graduates and our families, ladies and gentlemen: It is an honor to share with you in this forty-second convocation of Atlantic School of Theology. Would someone happen to have a fiddle and give us a rousing crescendo as an emphatic jubilation! (Natalie McMaster, the Nova Scotian folksinger and fiddle-player, was the other recipient of the school's degree of Doctor of Divinity *honoris causa*.)

Deep gratitude moves me as I receive this honor, but a sense of ambiguity as well. Just over fifty years ago, my teacher Karl Barth was awarded a prestigious prize in Copenhagen for his work; at the ceremony, he reminded people that it was the city where the rabble-rouser theologian Søren Kierkegaard roamed the streets. "What if I should meet his ghost and hear him saying: 'What is the world coming to when serving God in church and world with theological labour is being rewarded with honorary doctorates?'" Is there such a ghost here in Halifax? You, Dr. MacMaster, need not worry!

Sixty-eight years ago, Dietrich Bonhoeffer was hanged by the Nazis for participating in the plot to assassinate Hitler. Bonhoeffer viewed his participation as an integral component of his being a follower of Jesus. He distinguished between cheap and costly grace and asserted that because it is Jesus of Nazareth whom we seek to follow, discipleship is grace, and because it is Jesus the Jew, it is costly grace. Bonhoeffer was sure that had Jesus lived in Nazi Germany he would have been murdered in the course of the "Final Solution of the Jewish Question." In his participation, Bonhoeffer offered resistance against those who planned and worked the machinery of destruction; it cost him his life. But he indicted not only the Nazis but also exposed the complicity and co-responsibility of Europe's political and religious institutions in and for the Holocaust. As a good pastor, however,

Bonhoeffer let us see that facing the burden of complicity as followers of Jesus is not unaccompanied by grace.

For close to four decades now, I have been looking for the ways of costly grace and how we may walk them after the Holocaust. I have found great help in the work of Hank Knight, the 2002 Nicholson Lecturer and Ed Aitken Workshop leader at AST. The lectures are published in his book *Celebrating Holy Week in a Post Holocaust World*, where, as in his other writings, he develops a profound understanding of "hospitality." His exegesis of hospitality informs me in what I want to say today about discipleship as costly grace.

The Shoah was a volcano-like eruption of utterly evil inhospitality. In Nazi Germany, where I was born and raised, Jews were radically unwelcome to share place and life and breath. In Canada, the country that had welcomed my family in 1952, someone expressed such inhospitality to desperate Jewish refugees in the dreadful phrase: "None is too many." Countering inhospitality with hospitality is, quite simply, "making room for the other in our lives and our worlds of relation and significance," as Hank Knight puts it. I regard that statement to be a magnificent way to interpret what the Apostle Paul calls "a still more excellent way." He names three dimensions of that more excellent way; women mystics of the Middle Ages spoke of them as "the three sisters," as Dorothee Soelle told us in the 1999 Pollok Lectures in our School: Faith, Hope, and Love.

Sister Faith. In Jerusalem, close to Yad Vashem, Israel's Holocaust memorial, there is the Avenue of the Righteous. It is lined with trees planted to celebrate righteous gentiles, people who practiced hospitality to persecuted Jews, rescuing them from the death machine. Rescuers demonstrated that they valued the stranger as someone bearing the image of God shared by all humanity. The Torah has a name for the "other": *neighbor*. What Dorothee Soelle calls the inestimably significant gift of Judaism to religion: the concept and meaning of "neighbor," comes directly from what the Bible calls the covenant. It is covenantal faith that asserts "We are not alone" precisely because it believes in the One who is not alone: God who creates all creatures to be her neighbors and welcomes them into his hospitality. Again and again I am surprised by the insight of Cyril and Methodius, those ancient Greek Orthodox missionaries to the Slavic world who translated the Greek *Kyrie eleison* as *hospodi pomiluy*. *Hospodi*—here in the vocative case—means the One whose hospitality is grace. *Hospodi*, in its liturgical usage, cannot be translated into English as "Lord" but only as: She/He who is open in hospitality to the neighbor. But that word also has a human parallel: if you ever get to the Czech Republic and need a place to eat or sleep, look for the word *hospoda*.

Sister Hope. Because acts of hospitality happened in the midst and of the Shoah's inhospitality, we can know that hospitality to the other was possible—even to the quintessential "other" of Christendom: the Jews—and we can hope with confidence that it can happen again and again and watch for it around us. Our hope for the promised and, indeed, already present rule and realm of God is connected in its very essence to hospitality. When Jesus sent the disciples "to the lost sheep of the house of Israel" to proclaim the good news that God's realm had drawn near, he told them to look for hospitality. When they were welcomed with hospitality, they were to bless the home that had taken them in, that is, they were to identify the significance of that hospitality: God's realm has broken forth here. Hospitality nourishes hope in and for God's rule and realm, just as hope comes alive in the presence of hospitality.

Sister Love. In the Gestalt of hospitality, we meet the promise of God's creation breaking forth in respectful encounter with the other. In sending the disciples in search of hospitality as the sign of God's realm breaking forth, Jesus also sent them to heal. We know that hospitality heals, that is, its practice serves life and restores life to a greater, albeit still wounded wholeness. When and wherever it is truly practiced, the intention of creation is fulfilled. Fractured ties between others and within communities are re-established; isolated, marginalized individuals and communities are reconnected with resources needed for meaning and support. Hospitality restores respect when the regard of one person recognizes the infinite value and work of another. Closed worlds are opened up as boundaries of community and care are extended to include others who stand at or beyond their thresholds. Broken relationships are mended, as are shattered communities, when wounded souls meet, acknowledging fragile ties that bind them together, even in their pain. In the words of Henry Knight: "In our broken world, hospitality heals when it is practiced by vulnerable hosts and extended to wounded guests." Whenever hospitality happens, the cup of life overflows. I believe this is what is meant when we take the word *agapé* on our lips and seek to live it.

If I have one wish for you who today formally receive our school's recognition of fitness for service, but not only for you, it is this: may you, called by God into service through following the Jew Jesus of Nazareth, in every moment of your life be so blessed with God's grace that, with courage, commitment and joy, you practice this indeed costly hospitality, this costly grace and that you are enabled also to receive such hospitality. And, please, know that you are not alone in that service and also that those among us here who are a few yards or a life-time ahead on that same road are at your side. Know that in our service we need you at every step for our frequently flagging courage and, above all, know that we hold you in hospitality.

II: Quaestiones Disputatae

12.

To Intervene or Not to Intervene

Is That the Question?

IN THIS TEXT, I seek to assist the churches in the theological quandary that the doctrine of The Responsibility to Protect vulnerable people puts them in. In addition, I seek to provide a theological approach to the dilemma that confronts especially, but not only, those who espouse an ethic of nonviolence in their search for how they can respond to the plight of those threatened with aggravated harm who are crying for protection. The obligation to come to the neighbors' assistance in such times as it is formulated, for example, in the biblical commandment to "love one's neighbor," creates quandaries for those who also seek to keep the commandment declared in nearly all of humanity's sacred texts not to take another's life. The theology of this essay holds that it is the neighbor in need who matters primarily and not the quandary of intervention or non-intervention.[1]

The exploration of this problematic proceeds as follows: after briefly clarifying what the issue to be addressed is and what it is not, and acknowledging that the human search for a nonviolent world embraces indeed diverse and, at times, opposing positions all of which need to be honored rather than judged, the doctrine of The Responsibility to Protect (henceforth R2P) is discussed. The World Council of Churches' invitation to its member churches to develop theological responses in accordance with their understanding of the Christian faith and tradition is highlighted. As a member of the United Church of Canada, the author approaches this invitation from the perspective of the Reformation tradition and especially from the theologies of Karl Barth and Dietrich Bonhoeffer. The reality of the destruction of vulnerable peoples by the régime of Germany's National Socialists,

---

1. Lest there is confusion as to whom the paper addresses itself, it is important to emphasize, that the church specifically, as the community of those who follow Jesus, is envisaged here and not the state or the community of nations. I assume that when churches address governments of individual states or of communities of nations, they will do so on the basis of theological conviction and argument.

in particular the neighbors of Jewish descent, stimulates the reflection concerning intervention with or without the use of armed forces.

In this essay, intervention and non-intervention in relation to the responsibility to protect, if depicted as ethical virtues or obligations, are identified not as moral choices between good and evil, right and wrong, but as courses of action that both render their actors guilty. There is, as will be argued, culpable violence and culpable nonviolence; neither can claim the high moral ground when it comes to how vulnerable people are to be protected.

The theological-ethical orientation presented here maintains that the *people crying for protection* have ethical priority over the ethical *principles* of those who may or may not intervene. Or, as the essay develops this point, the commandment to love the neighbor overrides the morally equivalent commandment not to murder. This is explored theologically at some length. The final part focuses on Bonhoeffer's reflections during the course of the "final solution of the Jewish question" and in the planning of the coup d'état and the murder of Hitler on how freely chosen action to intervene with violent force or not opens the door to accept culpability freely and to give oneself over utterly to the judgment of God's mercy in the knowledge that we can live before God with our guilt.

In relation specifically to the doctrine of R2P, in this essay I seek to assist churches in responding theologically to the doctrine's stipulation that under clearly defined circumstances nations may be called upon to deploy military forces in order to aid people in aggravated harm's way. The ethical issue for the churches is whether they should or should not call on their national governments to deploy their armed forces in military interventions. For churches related to other churches in ecumenical relationships, this means working through with one another what following Christ implies in the situations R2P speaks about. This is where the matter of guilt before God *and* neighbor has to be addressed with urgency.[2] The help I want to offer here is to move the R2P dilemma away from the moral decision-making process based in the rigidity of firmly held principles of right and wrong, good and evil, to the more flexible space of discerning what the responsibility of religious persons and communities is *before* God and *to* the

---

2. In a recent private conversation among theologians and peace-workers, a comment overheard by one of the group at a conference on R2P brought into clear focus what forms nonviolent culpability may take. The comment was to the affect that followers of Christ committed to nonviolence may have to put up with the albeit inconvenient fact that sometimes innocent people may have to suffer for the convictions held by persons committed to nonviolence. Views such as that clarify what the issue is that I seek to address.

endangered neighbor before whom they stand.[3] I argue that the exercise of regulated violence as it is proposed by R2P can be given theological and moral support by the churches in calling on a nation's government to send the troops to protect people.

Yes, "War is to be avoided, the use of force is to be minimized, and conflict is to be resolved as much as possible in the interests of justice and without resort to violence."[4] This statement by Dr. Ernie Regehr, the co-founder, former executive director and now senior researcher of the Canadian ecumenical coalition Project Ploughshares, is accepted without reservation in my reflection. In addition to that clear formulation of what is demanded of churches and Christians in their discipleship, the obligation to *prevent* conflicts from erupting and, should every effort to prevent them have failed, to *rebuild the conflict-torn communities*, are equally affirmed here. It may be useful, therefore, to state at the outset that neither *war* nor *the theory of just war* are at issue here; what is at issue are the cries for protection of vulnerable peoples in aggravated harm's way and how those cries are to be answered by Christian communities and individuals. Is the answer to be given in terms of the use of force and as a matter of Christian conscience or in terms of pacifist non-violence or a contextual decision to delay intervention until it is more clearly a last resort?

One further preliminary note: What is proposed here fully acknowledges and respects that there are in the church different and, indeed, opposed positions based in the same embrace of Jesus, the Prince of Peace, and in the same determination to follow him. These positions are not rejected but honored as fully valid and faithful. An "either-or" approach is not at work here.

Meeting in Porto Alegre, Brazil, in 2006, the World Council of Churches adopted a report entitled "Vulnerable populations at risk: Statement on

---

3. This point was driven home at a recent conference of Holocaust scholars by Father Patrick Desbois, the author of *The Holocaust by Bullets*. In his address, he said that we cannot build a world of peace and demand that Abel's blood be silent, that our problem is not the existence of God but how we can stand before God with all the murdered, to stand with them and say to God: here we are! We dare not obliterate the murdered in order for us to believe in God today. The ground under our feet keeps moving with Abel's blood. Here the cries of Abel's blood—a metaphor for the victims of those lacking the protection of their own states and crying for help from the outside—clearly have priority over the however well-reasoned principles of those to whom the cries are addressed.

4. These words encapsulate the basic convictions of the coalition. See Hutchinson, *Defence Beyond Borders*, 1.

the Responsibility to Protect." The Assembly approved the report's resolutions by consensus.[5] Its understanding of what R2P means is this:

> The concept shift[s] the debate from the viewpoint of the interveners to that of people in need of assistance.... This innovative concept focuses on the needs and rights of the civilian population.... Hence, the shift from intervention to protection places citizens at the centre of the debate.... The churches are in support of the emerging international norm of the responsibility to protect.... The responsibility to protect and serve the welfare of its people is central to a state's sovereignty. When there is failure to carry out that responsibility, whether by neglect, lack of capacity, or direct assaults on the population, the international community has the duty to assist peoples and states, and in extreme situations, to intervene in the internal affairs of the state in the interests and safety of the people.[6]

This passage spells out what is the substance of the assertion that it is an ethical duty to respond to the cries of the vulnerable.

It is in the "how" or the form of the kind of "intervention" described here that the diversity in the churches' support of the R2P norm becomes apparent. Behind a subsequent statement on the WCC report lies what was earlier called "different, indeed, opposing positions" within the communities of Christ's followers about the use of force or, more accurately, the application of violence. That statement says:

> In calling on the international community to come to the aid of vulnerable people in extraordinary suffering and peril, the fellowship of the churches is not prepared to say that it is never appropriate or never necessary to resort to the use of force for the protection of the vulnerable. This refusal in principle to preclude the use of force is not based on the naïve belief that force can be relied on to solve intractable problems. Rather, it is based on the certain knowledge that the objective must be the welfare of the people, especially those in situations of extreme vulnerability and who are utterly abandoned to the whims and prerogatives of their tormentors. It is a tragic reality that civilians, especially women and children, are the primary victims in situations of extreme insecurity and war.

---

5. www.oikumene.org/gr/resources/documents/wcc-commissions/international-affairs/responsibility-to-protect/vulnerable-populations-at-risk.

6. Ibid.

Even in its careful phrasing, declaring that "the fellowship of the churches is not prepared to say that *it is never appropriate or never necessary to resort to the use of force* [violence] *for the protection of the vulnerable*"⁷ is a challenge, to put it gently, to principles of pacifism or non-violence held by many of the "fellowship" of Christians as matters of faith if not as matters of *status confessionis*. But the Assembly of 2006 clearly recognized and affirmed—felicitously, in my view—that "some within the churches refuse the use of force in all circumstances. Their form of responsibility is to persist in preventative engagement and, whatever the cost—as a last resort—to risk non-violent intervention during the use of force."⁸ And, in acknowledging this form of Christian witness, the Assembly added three clear profoundly theological/ethical convictions:

> The churches do not ... believe in the exercise of lethal force to bring in a new order of peace and safety. By limiting the resort to force quite specifically to immediate protection objectives, the churches insist that the kind of long-term solutions that are required ... cannot be delivered by force.
>
> The use of force for humanitarian purposes can never be an attempt to find military solutions to social and political problems, to militarily engineer new social and political realities. Rather, it is intended to mitigate immediate threats and to alleviate immediate suffering while long-term solutions are sought by other means.
>
> The force that is to be deployed and used for humanitarian purposes must also be distinguished from military war-fighting methods and objectives. The military operation is not a war to defeat a state but an operation to protect populations in peril from being harassed, persecuted or killed.⁹

---

7 141 Italics and insertion added. Here the Assembly appears to acknowledge one of the problematic aspects of ethical and/or theological systems. Since it is conceivable that such systems so strictly codified to allow no flexibility will fail in some situations, ethics and theology should demand a combination of guiding principles or rules and allowable exceptions. And so, the statement leaves open the door to flexibility in relation to the R2P component of "reaction" or, specifically, intervening with military force. And instead of capitulating to the inflexibilities of the either-or between absolutist and contextualist approaches to the problem of the use of force, the Assembly invites the distinction between fundamental convictions and conclusions reached on concrete questions of actions required in support of people in need, and by showing how some of those conclusions could be supported by communities with differing or, indeed, opposing positions. I am grateful to Professor Roger Hutchinson for this insight.

8. Ibid.
9. Ibid.

In these statements, the WCC acknowledges that the difficulty contained in the doctrine and practice of R2P derives from the fact that it calls for a decision between two unpleasant and wicked issues rather than between a clear-cut good and evil; in his article "Culpable Nonviolence. The Moral Ambiguity of Pacifism," Ernie Regehr calls it "a devil's choice . . . because it is not a simple choice between nonintervention that abandons people in perilous circumstances and military intervention that liberates them. The choice for military intervention, even for explicitly humanitarian purposes, runs the risk and the likelihood that peril will be expanded rather than alleviated."[10] The issue is which kind of force is to be used: the force of nonviolence, such as, for example, that used by Mahatma Gandhi, or the force of violence, such as, for example by NATO forces in the Balkans? How does one make an ethical decision or present a theological case when the schemata of "good vs. evil" are not the point but the murky "which of the sinful options to go with," if one wants to be involved at all?

The position this reflection takes is that, from a theological perspective, to intervene or not to intervene with military force [violence] is not the question. When striving for a model of the churches' conversation that say says "No" in principle to resort to violence but addresses what our responsibility is in a world where violence is being used, the question becomes rather: How does faith in God, following God's commandments, shape our understanding and, hence, our actions of responsibility before God and to the neighbor? What concrete and contextual shape does discipleship of Jesus call for when the cries of vulnerable people are heard and to be acted upon? How do we stand *with* them before God?

It may help to cite an actual case here. Reporting on an international assessment team's fact-finding tour to the southern Sudan, Ernie Regehr writes:

> When the Sudanese IDPs [internally displaced persons] asked why the churches were not calling for immediate military intervention to stop the bombing and expulsion, one articulate young man, discovering that I was a Mennonite, pressed the point even harder. Mennonites, he argued, have a reputation for compassion and peacemaking, and if they really were for putting people first, wouldn't they be leading the call for just such relief? Military intervention to protect those who are utterly without protection would surely be a supreme act of compassion, he challenged. I explained that our refusal to call for military protection was not evidence of callous indifference, but

---

10. Regehr, *Voices Across Boundaries*, 42.

was part of a principled commitment to nonviolence. He wasn't impressed. How, he asked (as I knew he would as soon as I had uttered my stock answer), is the principle of nonviolence honoured by the international community's refusal to lift a single finger against ceaseless, egregious violence directed at unarmed and unprotected people in southern Sudan? The failure of the international community to bring protection to the vulnerable of Sudan makes them, in their own eyes and experience, victims of inaction—and for them, whether that inaction is the product of indifference or of a principled commitment against military intervention amounts to the same thing.[11]

What responses are open to Christians in face of such cries for help and "neighborliness"?

The theological argument presented here refuses to approach that question in terms of the false dichotomy of nonviolence versus justice. Seeking God's justice and doing it is as integral to those whose faith in and obedience to God rejects military intervention on behalf of vulnerable populations as it is to those whose faith in and obedience to God supports it. As well, the argument presented here does not approach the Bible, to which Christian faith appeals, as the referee for our stories, positions and decisions; it maintains instead that, in our diverse concrete situations and contexts, we regard and use Scripture as our deep source of our stories, positions and decisions. "Using" the Bible means "appealing" to its language and spirit as the authority for thinking and acting appropriately to and responsibly in following Jesus of Nazareth. The "controversy" of God with the people of Israel, to which the sixth chapter of the prophecy of Micah addresses itself, has a classic statement, to which churches today readily appeal: "It has been told to you, my people, what is good; and what does the Holy One require of you other than to do justice, to love in kindness, and to go humbly with your God?"[12]

An excursus is required at this point to provide the biblical basis of the theological insistence that the neighbor has priority even over strongly affirmed principles. Throughout, the First (a.k.a. "Old") Testament wrestles with the question of how justice is to be done, how love in kindness is to be exercised, and how people walk humbly with God. Furthermore, it commands its readers and hearers "Do not kill!" or, as I prefer to translate the Hebrew version: "Murder Not!" In the Second (a.k.a. "New") Testament, Jesus provides a further formulation of how the people of God are to

---

11. Ibid., 39.
12. Micah 6:4.

walk in the way of justice, kindness, and humility. Asked what the first and greatest of God's commandments in the scriptures is, he replied: "Hear, O Israel, Adonai our God, Adonai is one; love Adonai, your God, with all your heart, all your soul, all your might. And love your neighbor who is like you" (Mark 12: 28-31).[13]

Jesus's reply, bringing together Deuteronomy 6:4 and Leviticus 19:18, points to love as the "soul" of the Bible. What has to be recognized is that the Bible's sense of "love" embraces *both* the love of God for humans and the love of humans for God. Which means that in *our* loving God in the manner of the greatest commandment, that is, in our doing justice, loving kindness, and walking in humility with God, God's *own* will on how to be God to and for us is being fulfilled. Correspondingly, in God's loving us creatures (and all other creatures!), in blessing, inspiring, healing, forgiving, guiding us, our desire to be what God wills for us to be is answered. Thus, God is God and humans are humans only in the mutuality of the love the Bible envisions here: in God's love for us and for our neighbor (who precisely because of God's love is like us) and in our love for God and for our neighbor. More, an essential condition for this love to be the love the Bible speaks of is that it is given freely and for its own sake. Thus, to love in freedom is to give oneself to the neighbors, to be before them by being for them before they call upon us and certainly when they do so. And to be for the neighbors, as the Bible demonstrates in ever different variation, is to be there responsibly, that is, in their concrete context, in the situation they are in fact experiencing and out of which comes their cry for our appropriate presence to them. In that understating of love, priority unquestionably belongs to God's call on us to *be* the people of his/her love and equally to the neighbors' call on us to *be* neighbor to them. In God's covenant-faithfulness to humans, there is, as scripture testifies, a predilection for the marginalized, the weak and helpless, the abandoned, oppressed, and exploited; recent theology speaks of it as "the preferential option of God for the poor." Theirs is a "commanding voice," as Rabbi Emil Fackenheim puts is. For our discussion, the cries of vulnerable peoples for protection are a commanding voice to both God and to us humans.

Ernie Regehr's account of his conversation with the young man in the southern Sudan makes the case for claiming that the cries of vulnerable peoples have priority over commitment to a principle. It is not too much to say that his experience of the conversation with that young man in the context of the internally displaced persons' camp and its reality was an encounter

---

13. See the translation of the Jewish Scriptures by Buber and Rosenzweig, *Die Schrift*, 220 and 149.

with the commanding voice and its priority over an article of faith. But it was also more than that. It was a moment where his faith in God called him into responsibility and into the freedom that faith creates for responsibility. If Mennonites really were putting people first, then calling for military intervention would surely be a supreme act of compassion, was the challenge to be answered. And how is the principle of nonviolence honored if there is no intervening action commensurate to the ceaseless, egregious violence directed at unarmed and unprotected people?

In the posthumously published collection of Dietrich Bonhoeffer's prison writings and letters there is an extended memorandum he composed just before his arrest in early 1943 by the Nazis. Entitled "After Ten Years," it contains a variety of reflections he composed for those with whom he was involved in the plot to assassinate Hitler. We draw on two of them in the development of the theological argument made here. In "The view from below" and "Who stands firm?" he writes:

> It remains an experience of incomparable value that we have for once learned to see the great events of world history from below, from the perspective of the outcasts, the suspects, the maltreated, the powerless, the oppressed and reviled, in short from the perspective of the suffering. If only during this time bitterness and envy have not corroded the heart; that we come to see matters great and small, happiness and misfortune, strength and weakness with new eyes; that our sense for greatness, humanness, justice, and mercy may have grown clearer, freer, more incorruptible; that we learn, indeed, that personal suffering is a more useful key, a more fruitful principle than personal happiness for exploring the world in contemplation and action.
>
> Who stands firm? Only those whose ultimate standard is not their reason, their principles, conscience, freedom, or virtue; only those who are prepared to sacrifice all of these when, in faith and in relationship to God alone, they are called to obedient and responsible action. Such persons are the responsible ones, whose lives are to be nothing but a response to God's questions and call.[14]

What Bonhoeffer calls "the view from below" and the biblical conception of "the neighbor,"—the late German theologian Dorothee Soelle called the concept of the neighbor the greatest gift, on the inter-religious scale, of the Jewish people to humankind[15]—interpret and shape each other deci-

---

14. Bonhoeffer, *Letters and Papers from Prison*, 52 and 40. (Transl. altered.)
15. Soelle, *The Mystery of Death*, 33.

sively. The former clears the way for seeing the priority of the vulnerable for God's *chesed*, God's passionate covenant-justice love, and as a consequence, what *being* neighbor to the vulnerable demands. The latter clears the way for the "new eyes" to see that our credibility as "neighbors" to vulnerable populations is based in accepting the priority of their cries for protection over our reason, principles, conscience, etc. If we accept the remarkable interpretation of love as it manifests itself in the covenant of God with God's creatures, namely that in our "doing neighborliness" how God wills to be God to and for us becomes fulfilled, something remarkable happens: the commanding voice of those who suffer becomes God's voice crying out to us, appealing to us to act now so that God can indeed be God to the vulnerable *as well as*, if not indeed primarily, to those who bring help to them. Our credibility of neighborliness derives from the appropriateness we bring in our actions towards the suffering neighbor.

If we interpret Regehr's reflection on his experience in southern Sudan in terms of what Bonhoeffer says in "Who stands firm?" we may say that Ernie's faith in God was called at that moment into responsibility. Secondly, the sensibility of his faith for that situation, for the actual, concrete reality that the Sudanese people had to live in, freed him for a decision about what to do and accepting responsibility for that decision and its consequences. And the free and responsible action of one who follows Jesus, according to Bonhoeffer, is not to apply an already existing, pre-designed ethical or theological principle or doctrine. For if it were an action of that kind, it would be "unfree" in the sense of satisfying the motive of having a good conscience, of feeling justified by having kept one's "good conscience," of doing what allows one to live with one's unsullied conscience. The explanation that "our refusal to call for military protection was not evidence of callous indifference, but was part of a principled commitment to non-violence" failed to impress that young Sudanese and, more importantly, also failed as a justification for the refusal to call for such protection on the basis of principle of acting nonviolently. And if we look for "the view from below" in Regehr's description, we find it in what he writes about watching the burial in "the ever-expanding field designated as the graveyard." His "view from below" takes the form of a mathematical calculation related to the estimated two million people claimed by war in Sudan since 1983. "That comes to about 100,000 per year, and that's 2,000 per week and 300 a day.... After September 11, 2001, the *New York Times* ran personal accounts of the victims, at least momentarily rescuing all those who had died from anonymity, putting a face on the statistic, giving public acknowledgment to loss. For the victims of Sudan to be similarly acknowledged it would take three hundred photos and brief biographies each and every day for the next twenty years. And that would do it only if the killing stopped today—*which it won't.*"[16]

The expression attributed to Saint Augustine of Hippo: "Love God and do what you will" signals something of the character of free, responsible action: in loving God and the neighbor as the Bible specifies it, love sets one free to decide oneself what is seen to be appropriate and necessary action in a given, concrete situation without advance assuredness that one is justified (or "righteous") before God in what one wills to do. Augustine, like Bonhoeffer, captures the component of "freedom" in the relationship between God and humans and between humans that is described in the word "love." It is precisely in God's freedom that God loves all creatures; were it not for the freedom of God, the love with which God binds Himself/Herself to the creatures, that love would be something other than love. And so, to love God and to do what one wills means to decide in freedom what is seen to be appropriate and necessary in and for the love one shows to God and neighbor.

This is the point Bonhoeffer wrestled with when he composed the essay "After Ten Years" at Christmas time in 1942. The circle of conspirators had concluded that resort to violence was inevitable if Hitler was to be removed successfully from power. But "to kill or not to kill" had become the deeply troubling question. To some of them the divine commandment was clear and absolute: "*Murder not!*" to others resorting to the violence of murder would stress conscience beyond endurance, to yet others the principled commitment to what is honorable, for example not reneging on an oath, was sacred. Bonhoeffer rejects none of those positions but submits them to the perspective "from below," from how those who suffer see things. Two excerpts of what he wrote at that time suffice to grasp where he is going.

> The man of *conscience* has no one but himself when resisting the superior might of predicaments that demand a decision. But the dimensions of the conflict wherein he must make his choices are such that, counseled and supported by nothing but his very own conscience, he is torn apart. The innumerable respectable and seductive disguises by which evil approaches him make his conscience fearful and unsure until he finally settles for a salved conscience instead of a good conscience, that is, until he deceives his own conscience in order not to despair. That a bad conscience may be stronger and more wholesome than a

---

16. Regehr, *Voices Across Boundaries*, 40. Emphasis added.

deceived one is something that a man whose sole support is his conscience can never comprehend.[17]

Not long before composing "After Ten Years," he penned the following sentences in his study on ethics, a work that remained unfinished. Asking who can endure (i.e., who stands firm?) he says:

> Only the person who combines simplicity with wisdom can endure. . . . A person is simple who in the confusion, the distortion, and the inversion of all concepts keeps in sight only the single truth of God. . . . Because of knowing and having God, this person clings to the commandments, the judgment, and the mercy of God that proceed anew each day from the mouth of God. Not fettered by principles but bound by love for God, this person is liberated from the problems and conflicts of ethical decision, and is no longer beset by them. This person belongs to God and to God's will alone. . . . The person is wise who sees reality as it is, who sees into the depth of things. Only that person is wise who sees reality in God. . . . Wise people know the limited receptivity of reality for principles, because they know that reality is not built on principles, but rests on the living creating God. So they also know that reality can be helped neither by the purest principles nor with the best will, but only by the living God. Principles are only tools in the hands of God; they will soon be thrown away when they are no longer useful.[18]

These astute insights of Bonhoeffer allow us to recognize two important things. One is that what drives much of the debate about R2P, as it touches especially Christians, is precisely the question of conscience, of how we are to stand before God and the neighbor with a good or bad or salved conscience. The other is that as long as conscience is the key component in the discussion, the reality of God's mercy, grace and forgiveness is obscured if not even denied, for what allows us to stand before God is not our conscience but God's love alone.

The "commandments, the judgments, and the mercy of God" to which the simple and wise person clings, are but another way of speaking of God's love, of the God who loves in freedom. And thus, when it comes to making ethical-theological decisions and to act in accordance with them in a concrete situation, to see reality in God, is to throw oneself on the judgment and mercy of God. To put this in a different way: What the simple, wise person, the person of faith does here is to open herself, himself unconditionally to

---

17. Bonhoeffer, *Letters and Papers from Prison*, 39.
18. Bonhoeffer, *Ethics*, 81–82.

accountability for the actions taken freely and responsibly in that situation. And that accountability, that responsibility is truly authentic and, therefore truly free, when it is radically open to accepting and confessing guilt.

This is the surprising and amazing turn in Bonhoeffer's reflection; for one, it helps us break free from the "either-or" of pacifism and just war, violence and nonviolence, and accept the claim by both sides to seek to be faithful in following Jesus of Nazareth; and secondly, it provides a way of living with the quandaries that arise when commandments of God are in conflict for those who strive to live by them.

In relation to the responsibility to protect, the issue, if seen in this perspective, is clearly not which choice is justified before God and which is not, whether the decision for one course of action leaves us non-culpable while the decision for another renders us culpable. It is not even a matter of which culpability we choose. The issue is that radical openness to God and willingness for responsibility for the neighbor materializes itself in liberation for accepting culpability.

> What bears and sustains such openness and willingness is the knowledge that the world, including the political world . . . is accepted, judged and renewed by God [in Her/His mercy]. That openness and willingness live in the faith which learns from Christ that the norms of Christ's commandments are firm, that they call and bear us *and* that, even when we break the commandments in sensitivity for our fellow human beings and their security, thereby taking guilt upon ourselves, *we are not abandoned by Christ*. . . . "Free responsibility" is founded in a God who calls for the free venture of faith into responsible action and who promises forgiveness and consolation to those who on account of such action become sinners. Here forgiveness relates to the personal guilt that is unavoidable for those who take a stand and act upon it, accepting the risk of free responsibility and thus burdening their conscience.[19]

"Liberation for accepting guilt" is an elaboration of what is found in both the term and the description of Ernie Regehr's "culpable nonviolence." The freeing dimension of that term and its approach to culpability is what allows different and even radically opposite approaches to the horrors of genocide, etc., to live with the guilt that arises from, as the young Sudanese man put it, the international community's refusal to lift a single finger against ceaseless, egregious violence directed at unarmed and unprotected people, and also with the guilt that arises from taking

---

19. Rumscheidt, *Analecta Bruxellensia*, 19.

military action, that people will be killed during it and that peril might be expanded rather than alleviated.

What a recent interpreter of Bonhoeffer called "liberation to accept guilt"[20] is a direct consequence of seeing reality in God, it characterizes those who, because they know and have God, cling to God's commandments, judgments and mercy alone, those who belong to God and to God's will alone.

Transposed into the context of the Responsibility to Protect and its inclusion of the option to resort to military intervention in order to protect vulnerable peoples as an appropriate and necessary action, belonging to God and to God's will alone enables us consciously and freely to burden ourselves with culpability in the actions we deem responsible. It lets our accountability to God and to neighbors rest on the covenantal promise of forgiveness made by God and, consequently, lets us know that we can live with our guilt, our culpability before God. In Bonhoeffer's own words:

> I believe that God can and will let good come out of everything, even the greatest evil. . . . I believe that even our mistakes and shortcomings are not in vain and that it is no more difficult for God to deal with them than with our supposedly good deeds. I believe that God is no timeless fate but waits for and responds to sincere prayer and responsible action.[21]

---

20. Dramm, *Dietrich Bonhoeffer and the Resistance*, 241. (The German original has: "Befreiung zur Schuld" which I translate preferably as "liberation for guilt.")

21. Bonhoeffer, *Letters and Papers from Prison*, 46.

13.

Dying as an Act of Defiance

I

My biographical context is that of a German, born in Hitler's "Third Reich," taught in elementary school by teachers who were members of the Nazi Party and raised in a family that attended worship services conducted by a clergyman whose theology was oriented by the direction of the so-called "German-Christians" and their embrace of aspects of Nazi ideology. But what most deeply impacts my context is my father's complicity in the Holocaust through his work in Germany's IG Farben conglomerate, its extensive reliance of forced labor and the close cooperation with the SS that climaxed at the IG Farben project Auschwitz-Monowitz where the inmates' work was "a horrifying parody of work, useless and senseless—labor as punishment leading to agonizing death."[1] The generation of my father burdened my generation with shame about how my native land, my church, and my people failed humanity, defied ethics and poisoned theology. What occupies me—in the sense of both "engaging" and "having taken hold of" me—is not so much that burden, although it "keeps me going," nor is it *Vergangenheitsbewältigung*: coming to terms with my German past in order to be done with it. I seek to obey "the commanding voice of Auschwitz," as Emil Fackenheim taught us, which, among other things, means doing justice to those who are to be heard in that voice: those who were killed by the Nazis, those who survived, and those who chose to bring about their own death. And the first word I have heard in that voice is *Zachor!* That has both epistemological and hermeneutical implications.

Within that context, I sum up the death camps' intentionality in terms of a categorical imperative: Dying is the inmates' highest duty,[2] and in attempting to "face mortality," I cannot but give their death in the Shoah absolute hermeneutical priority. The evidence about inmates deciding to defy

1. Levi, *Survival in Auschwitz*, 178.
2. Rumscheidt, *Studies in Religion/Sciences religieuses*, 487–96.

the Nazis ultimate purposes for the death camps comes to us from survivors and observers in the camps; that is to say, from what they remember. Memory is subjectivity-dependent: its logic is inseparable from the actuality of the inmates' experiential reality. In this essay, therefore, I seek to connect the state of consciousness of death camp inmates, their experience of the camps intentionality, and the decision of some to defy the ignominy of that intentionality through acts of freely bringing about their own death and thereby affirming their authenticity as human beings.

Primo Levi's book *Survival in Auschwitz* begins with a poem that tells the reader to consider if the inmate in that hell is a woman, a man; it ends with this admonition in the form of a post-Shoah coda to the *Shema* of Deuteronomy 6:

> Meditate that this came about:
> I commend these words to you.
> Carve them in your hearts
> At home, in the street,
> Going to bed, rising;
> Repeat them to your children,
> Or may your house fall apart,
> May illness impede you,
> May your children turn their faces from you.[3]

II

WHAT PERCEPTIONS OF DEATH, of dying, prompt statements such as these: "A strange thing has happened to us: all our ideas and feelings have changed. Death, quick death that comes in an instant, is to us a deliverer, a liberator who breaks our chains.... The Jews... embrace death as their liberator.... I die at peace, but not pacified, conquered and beaten but not enslaved, bitter but not disappointed, a believer but not a supplicant, a lover of God but not His blind Amen-sayer."[4] These words are put into the mouth of a resistance-fighter in the Warsaw Ghetto by Zvi Kolitz in his fictional narrative of that fighter's last hours before he pours gasoline over himself and ends his life. Whatever differences there are between dying in ghettos and dying in extermination camps, the Germans' intentions were the same for both: Jews were to die—in myriad ways—in the process of dehumanization and humiliation

---

3. Levi, *Survival in Auschwitz*, 11.
4. Kolitz, *Yosl Rakover Talks to God*, 4, 13, 23.

and with their dignity shattered. But what is that note which sounds in the resister's words and in these: "The ghetto was starving, and the starving lay like rags in the streets. People were prepared to die any death, but not the death of starvation. This is probably because in a time when systematic persecution gradually destroys every other human need, the will to eat is the last one that endures, even in the presence of *longing for death*."[5] It is surely not a note of resignation and submission, of conceding one's being a slave and an object of the oppressors' lust for domination; it is a note of defiance, of breaking one's chains, of liberation and of agency, however small the act. Primo Levi also sounds this note:

> Then for the first time we became aware that our language lacks words to express his offence, the demolition of a man. In a moment, with almost prophetic intuition, the reality was revealed to us: we had reached the bottom. It is not possible to sink lower than this; no human condition is more miserable than this, nor could it conceivably be so. Nothing belongs to us any more; they have taken away our clothes, our shoes, even our hair; if we speak, they will not listen to us, and if they listen, they will not understand. They will even take away our name: and if we want to keep it, we will have to find [in] ourselves the strength to do so, to manage somehow so that behind the name something of us, of us as we were, still remains. . . . Imagine now a man who is deprived of [everything]. . . . He will be a man whose life or death can be lightly decided with no sense of human affinity, in the most fortunate of cases, on the basis of a pure judgment of utility . . . precisely because the Lager was a great machine to reduce us to beasts, we must not become beasts. . . . We are slaves, deprived of every right, exposed to every insult, condemned to certain death, but we still possess one power, and we must defend it with all our strength for it is the last—the power to refuse our consent. . . . We must walk erect, without dragging our feet, not in homage to Prussian discipline but to remain alive, not to begin to die.[6]

The refusal to consent to dying as beasts so that something remains "of us as we were" is an act of defiance wherein death is not only embraced as liberation but also as self-affirmation in and through the freely chosen manner of how one will die. Under the circumstances of both ghetto and death camp, the choice of how one will end one's own life is an act of dying with dignity; that we must all die is now instrumental in defying and

5. Kolitz, *Yosl Rakover Talks to God*, 7. (Italics added.)
6. Levi, *Survival in Auschwitz*, 26–27, 41.

defeating the Nazis' aim destroying the dignity of being human. Even though it meant death, dying by one's own will is the refusal to participate in the victory Hitler desired.

The distinction between "active" and "passive" death is absolutely important. The Nazis were determined that all to be eliminated should die a "passive" death, that is, their manner of dying was to be entirely decided by the executioners. They were to be shot, gassed, starved to death, beaten, and—in relation to my father's work—worked to death. To this end, a thoroughly thought-out and rationalized program of commercialized death was worked out between IG Farben and the SS that rested on the sophisticated system of planned dehumanization of the inmates by working them to death. The "Buna works," as IG Auschwitz-Monowitz is known, after first exploiting and oppressing the workers, "liberated"— using Kolitz's word—them into freedom only when death was the only remaining freedom they could hope for. But to be liberated by extermination is exactly what is at the heart of "passive" death. "Active" death, on the other hand, is where the "victim" is the subject in the act of dying. We know that inmates threw themselves into the high-tension wires where they were instantly electrocuted; others deliberately bolted away from their marching columns or work places in order to be killed by their guards' gunfire, and yet others starved themselves to death so as to accelerate their dying. But in such "active" deaths there lies the possibility of asserting one's dignity and identity, one's agency and authenticity of one's humanness. In this act, the subject escapes from being forced to live only to be exterminated when and however it pleases the perpetrator. When base purposes impose themselves so that one stays alive, then to die an "active" death by one's own hand is an act with noble purpose.

The Belgian Benedictine monk George Passelecq, who was a fellow prisoner of Dietrich Bonhoeffer, the German theologian and a co-conspirator in the planned assassination of Hitler, describes the reality of the prison they shared: "death, wretchedness, hunger, hatred, torture, inhumanity, things that even Dante couldn't imagine."[7] Several of the co-conspirators chose to end their lives by their own hands; Bonhoeffer considered but refused that option for it would have led to reprisals by Hitler's henchmen against his family. But still he writes the following about taking one's life: "One cannot deny that with this act a person plays out and enforces [his or her] . . . humanity against blind, inhuman fate. . . . [It] is the ultimate and extreme self-justification of the human being as a human. . . . The origin [of this act] is . . . the freedom of the person, even in despair, to carry out the highest form of self-justification. . . . Therefore making an end to life remains

---

7. Poelchau, *Die Ordnung der Bedrängten*, 74.

the final human possibility for giving one's life meaning and making it right again, even though this happens at the moment of its annihilation."[8]

The reflection on mortality in an age of atrocity cannot avoid addressing the commandment: "Do not kill!"[9] But the very fact that the imperative "Dying is the inmates' highest duty!" had become such a horrible reality in the Holocaust, inevitably elicits rethinking the nature and meaning of that commandment. As the symbol of the devaluation of nearly all values, of the crossing of thresholds of ethics, Auschwitz compels us to interpret the values and commandments by which we seek to live in a manner that will not do injustice to those whose lives were subject to the death camps' imperatives. What meaning do those values and commandments have in the presence of those who in the ghettos and camps freely chose to kill themselves?[10]

Here I turn to Jean Améry and his illuminating reflections about "laying hands on oneself." His book *Hand an sich legen. Diskurs über den Freitod* was published in 1976 and published in English in 1999, *On Suicide: A Discourse on Voluntary Death*. The first part of that title, as I see it, is an unfortunate distortion of the German. The German word rendered there as "suicide" would be "Selbstmord" or self-murder but that is not the word Améry used. "Suicide" is part of a series of terms that clearly express the violence of killing someone else: patricide, fratricide, regicide, deicide, homicide, etc., i.e., murder. But Améry's book argues exactly against the notion that violence is an aspect of voluntary death, of what in this essay is spoken of as "freely choosing to end one's life." The use of "suicide" to describe dying by one's own hands permits the interpretation which this essay seeks to reject because it does terrible injustice to the inmates who refused to consent to the intentionality of the Nazi's death camps which were in fact murder industries. After his last public reading—at Marburg in 1976—Améry expressly told someone who had asked for an autograph, that the book was not a "user manual."[11] Instead, it is an appeal to society to

---

8. Bonhoeffer, *Ethics*, 197–98, 202.

9. According to the translation of the Tanakh by Buber and Rosenzweig, a rendition closer to the Hebrew phrase is: Murder Not!

10. A parallel discussion is going on now in relation to what is called "death with dignity" or "doctor-assisted suicide."

11. Heidelberger-Leonard, *Jean Améry*, 327. Like Primo Levi, Améry was a worker at the IG Farben's Auschwitz-Monowitz installations. He had been captured in Belgium in 1943 and severely tortured at Fortress Breendonck, shipped from there to Auschwitz in early 1944 (about the same time as Levi). When the Soviet army advanced towards Germany, he was part of the death-march to Dora-Mittelbau and landed finally in Bergen-Belsen, where he was liberated. Like Levi, Améry took his own life (in Salzburg on October 17, 1978).

acknowledge the freedom for voluntary death as an inalienable human right and, consequently, not to excommunicate persons who in this freedom have chosen to "lay hands on themselves."

Améry quotes Nietzsche: "Death is only a death that is not free under despised conditions, a death at the wrong time. . . . Out of love for life one ought to want death differently, free, conscious, without surprise,"[12] an apt juxtaposition of "passive" and "active" death. The former is death under despised conditions, an unfree death imposed by the conditions of the death camps, a death at the wrong time. The latter is freely and consciously chosen out of the "something of us, us as we were," a death at the right time, without surprise. In dying the "active" death, the conditions of the camps are repudiated and dying the "passive" death defied. "I die, therefore I *was*, at least in a foolish way in the moment before the leap, what I could not be because reality would not allow it to me,"[13] reality being that of the camp's relentless logic of dehumanization. In "active" death the logic of the fool prevails: I will be who I was by ceasing to be at all. "*I die, therefore I am*"[14] or: true self-realization, self-justification and utter affirmation of one's freedom and dignity through self-annihilation.[15] The wisdom of this "fool's logic" is precisely that in the self-annihilation the inmates "constitute themselves in voluntary death."[16]

The conception of "freedom" is shaped by two prepositions as if by inevitability: *from* and *for*. Every freedom from implies freedom for.

> Freedom is not an unchangeable space to be conquered once and for all: it is a process of new and ever new liberations. . . . And if freedom is not an existential, acts of liberation, one after the other, are. They belong to the fundamental project of every individual and last throughout one's life. . . . As a product of the basic human condition, every act of liberation changes both the past and the future. A new project is conceived. This not only alters whatever has been valid up to now, but also the past related to it.[17]

If we turn for a moment to ontology and repeat the observation just made, we might say that "being a subject" is not a condition that is ours from birth; it is an act or movement; "being is in becoming" through ever new acts of becoming. In the context of the inmate's decision to die a voluntary

---

12. Améry, *On Suicide*, 26.
13. Améry, *On Suicide*, 27.
14. Ibid.
15. Ibid., xx.
16. Ibid., 97.
17. Ibid., 125-26.

death, the act of liberation through an "active" death is, even as the choice for not-being, an act of becoming, an act of "being a subject." Choosing to be free *from* the Nazis' intention to destroy one's being a subject with dignity and rights is the choice *for* the freedom that alone allows one to become a "subject." But in the death camps, the decision of freedom was the decision for being in becoming non-being, an embrace of the possibility of regaining one's subject-ness in the freedom for non-being.

Elie Wiesel renders such ontology into powerfully expressive narration:

> My father's voice tore me from my daydreams: "What a shame, a shame that you did not go with your mother. . . . I saw many children your age go with their mothers. . . ." His voice was terribly sad. I understood that he did not wish to see what they would do to me. He did not wish to see his only son go up in flames. . . . Still, I told him that I could not believe that human beings were being burned in our times; the world would never tolerate such crimes. . . . "The world? The world is not interested in us. Today, everything is possible, even the crematoria. . . ." His voice broke. "Father," I said. "If that is true, then I don't want to wait. I'll run into the electrified barbed wire. That would be easier than a slow death in the flames." He didn't answer.[18]

Wiesel did not choose to run into the fence but what he said to his father testifies to "the urge to be free *from* something-*to* nothing."[19] Améry too did not choose to end his life in Auschwitz, or Mittelbau-Dora, or Bergen-Belsen, to mention only three of the places of his incarceration. But he phrases the essence of what I call "active" death under the conditions of the camps: It "removes us, delivers us from a state of being that has become a burden and from the *ex-sistere* that has become nothing but fear. . . . [This death] which promises freedom *from* something, but without also being freedom *to* something, as logic requires, is, more than just affirmation of dignity and humanity. . . . It is liberty in the most extreme and final form we can attain."[20]

The Nazis' imperative: Dying is the inmates' highest duty! was to be implemented according to plan through the "passive" death of stripping the inmates of their humanity, dignity and value, working them to death and, finally—unless this was not already done upon arrival in the camp—turn them into ashes. Those who decided to die an "active" death also accepted this "duty" but in defiance of the ignominy imposed by the Nazis. The

18. Elie Wiesel, *Night*, 33.
19. Améry, *On Suicide*, 128.
20. Ibid.

experience of freedom, or liberation, is of relatively brief duration, yet, irrespective of that, holds in itself the power to defy, to be "subject," to be what the "passive" death imperative seeks to eradicate. "At the moment when a human being says to himself he can throw away his life, he is already becoming free.... The experience of freedom is overwhelming."[21] It is not that one "has" what is called freedom but that one "becomes free" as one walks the way of freedom. In a manner of speaking, this confirms Sartre's statement: "It isn't what has been made of a human being that counts but what one makes of what one was made for."[22]

"Active" death, the last venture of life, here is an act of trust in the affirmation of the venturing that one has made with and throughout one's life. The radical character of defiance, in this context, is that it is an act of trusting that this defiance is meaningful in the presence of violated dignity and agency.

III

I understand "age of atrocity" to refer specifically to the Shoah and, accordingly, focused on those targeted by that atrocity. I narrowed the sweep of its intentionality to the undetermined number of those who took dying into their own hands. The distinction between "active" and "passive" death meant, *inter alia*, to distinguish between "murder," the criminal act of "passive" death in the innumerable diversity of the ghetto and the death camp all the way from the roundups, the transportation to ghetto and camp, to the killing there, on the one hand, and "taking one's life" as a free act of reaffirmation of one's being a subject, on the other. As I "face mortality in our work and ourselves" in the light of that distinction, I am guided by Emil Fackenheim's proposed 614th commandment: Do not give Hitler a posthumous victory!

The excerpt of Primo Levi's poem cited earlier names dimensions of the victory we are to deny: the failure to meditate on how the atrocity came about, the failure to tell one's children of it, the failure to remember: the refusal of *Zachor*! Other dimensions are Holocaust-denial, judging "active death" to be "murder" (calling it "suicide" does not avoid the implication of murder), and the ages-old anti-Judaism of Christianity.

Paralleling the decriminalization in numerous jurisdictions of death by free choice, I hold "active" death in the Shoah to be an act of the basic human right to claim and defend one's humanity and to be free—or

21. Améry, *On Suicide*, 133.
22. Ibid., 138.

freed—*from* imposed inhumanity and *for* liberty. Hitler's camps and ghettos suppressed and destroyed that condition of existence. In my judgment, to speak of the act of "active death" as "suicide" and a transgression of a "higher law" is a derogation of those human beings who chose that option, for it hands Hitler victory posthumously.

Secondly, anti-Judaism is a core-aspect, theologically speaking, of the Shoah. In the context of this paper, I focus specifically on "supersessionism," the notion that Judaism is a fossil now superseded by Christianity. A climactic manifestation of that aspect was *Kristallnacht,* the Nazis' signal that Judaism was to be eradicated.

Emmanuel Levinas's brief afterword to Zvi Kolitz's book picks up what to him is the heart of Yosl Rakover's testament. "To be a Jew is to be . . . an eternal swimmer against the roiling, evil current of humanity. . . . I am happy to belong to the unhappiest of all peoples in the world, whose Torah embodies the highest law and the most beautiful morality. . . . He [God] has delivered mankind over to its own savage urges and instincts. . . when the forces of evil dominate the world, it is, alas, completely natural that the first victims will be those who represent the holy and the pure. . . . I know that You are my God. For You are not, You cannot be the God of those whose deeds are the most horrific proof of their militant godlessness. . . . The God of other peoples, however, whom they call 'the God of love,' has offered to love every creature created in his name, and yet they have been murdering us without pity in His name day in, day out, for almost two thousand years."[23] There is no mistaking which religion is meant. Yosl's words, uttered in the Warsaw ghetto moments before his "active" death, are his defiance of the arrogance of church's supersessionist denigration of Jewish faith, a defiance that unmasks supersessionist anti-Judaism as a covert victory handed to Hitler.

If one can speak of a "categorical imperative" for facing mortality in an age of atrocity, it would be in Emil Fackenheim's formulation: Heed the commanding voice of Auschwitz! For him, "the commanding voice of Auschwitz" was integral to this plea that Hitler be refused posthumous victory. For this essay, the "commanding voice" is that of the women and men, the children and the aged, "before whom we stand" as we seek to remember them, obedient to "*Zachor,*" addressing us in and with their formulation of that imperative: Don't let Hitler have the last laugh, after all, by denying us our victory over him in how we, in our act of embracing death by our own hands, affirmed our humanity and demonstrated ourselves as moral agents, for that is how we denied him and his henchmen their sense of themselves as superior human beings and of us as inferior human beings. For we did

---

23. Kolitz, *Yosl Rakover Talks to God,* 82–83, 85.

not commit suicide; by our act, we restored the very indestructible humanity that Nazi racism sought to repudiate and destroy.

And it is in this imperative that we, reflecting on mortality in light of the Shoah, must keep those before whom we stand not only in remembrance but also in what we need to say in our understanding and ethics of mortality.

14.

Failing the Promise of Nuremberg

*or How the Germans' Inability to Mourn
Blocked Reconciliation*

FOR MEMBERS OF THE guild of theologians it is customary to begin with a prolegomenon—a fancy way of saying a few words before we begin to speak.

Two things make up my prolegomenon: *First,* my gratitude. I thank the organizers of this conference for graciously including me in the program. It is surely not to be taken for granted that someone should address this assembly who is the child of a man whose position in the multi-national IG Farben made him complicit in the Holocaust and the program known as "extermination through labor" carried out by that company. I am conscious that my very speaking here may cause distress to those present here on whom my people inflicted unspeakable pain and sorrow. I pray that I may not add to your ineradicable burden. *Second,* a brief word about where my reflections look for guidance. I have studied the reports of South Africa's Truth and Reconciliation Commission. I owe much to the work of three of its officials, in particular: Archbishop Desmond Tutu, who chaired the commission; Dr. Alex Boraine, vice-chair; and Dr. Charles Villa-Vicencio, director of research. All three had studied theology and are ordained clergy. Archbishop Tutu's firm conviction that there can be no reconciliation without forgiveness has won me over, even though I cannot turn it into a quasi-absolute precept. I fully embrace the following three points: If reconciliation is to have power and reality, and not be mere toleration resting on the unstable ground of the "forgive and forget" attitude, it has to exist in and with justice to victims. Secondly, this justice needs the moral fortitude of forgiveness so that it may be experienced as something that is able to keep the promise of new life. Third, if forgiveness truly seeks reconciliation through justice, the victimizers must have the ability to mourn and exercise it.

There were twelve trials in Nuremberg in addition to the one held before the International Military Tribunal, which dealt with the leading figures of the Nazi government. The twelve trials, conducted by United States Military Courts, are known officially as the "Trials of War Criminals before the Nuremberg Military Tribunals." Three of them dealt with leading industrialists of Nazi Germany for their conduct during the Hitler regime: the Flick Trial (number five), the IG Farben Trial (number six) and the Krupp Trial (number ten). The first and especially the second relate to my presentation. Each of them presented five indictments, two of which, almost identical in their wording, impinge on aspects of my father's work from mid-1941 onward. "War crimes and crimes against humanity through the plundering and spoliation of occupied territories, and the seizure of plants both in Austria, Czechoslovakia, Poland, Norway, France and Russia." "War crimes and crimes against humanity through participation in the enslavement and deportation to slave labor on a gigantic scale of concentration camp inmates and civilians in occupied countries, and of prisoners of war, and the mistreatment, terrorization, torture, and murder of enslaved persons."

The Flick Trial lasted from April 19 to December 22, 1947; of the six defendants, three received prison-term sentences, three were acquitted. The IG Farben Trial began on August 27, 1947 and ended on July 30, 1948. Thirteen of the twenty-four defendants were found guilty of one or both of those indictments and sentenced to prison terms ranging from one-and-a-half to eight years; ten were acquitted and one was removed from the trial for medical reasons. The names of many of the defendants I would have heard mentioned in my home at one time or another. Two were actually close neighbors: Christian Schneider (head of Department One, in charge of nitrogen and gasoline production; head of personnel department and a "supporting member" of the SS) and Walter Dürrfeld (head of construction of the Auschwitz plant and the Monowitz camp). I used to swim in the Schneider's private swimming pool, a three-minutes walk from my home, and the Dürrfelds were visitors in our home and we in theirs. After the German invasion and subsequent occupation of the Netherlands and Belgium and the defeat of France, Father was assigned by the IG Farben directorate to a team "overseeing" the chemical industries in those three countries, which actually meant absorbing those corporations into IG Farben, which was planning to structure itself into Europe's largest chemical concern. At a conference from August 31 to September 2, 1940, in Paris, IG Farben executives decided to grasp "the historic chance of adjusting the . . . economy [of those countries] to German requirements through appropriate encroachment on [their] economic system, [and that this chance] must be utilized completely and to the full."[1] The chemical industry in the three countries

---

1. *Trials of War Criminals*, 1452.

was to be organized as "partners" into IG Farben: to regulate French-Dutch-Belgian economic relations, to be "steered" by Germany, so that they may be "restored" on a sound basis and to be subordinate in every case to German interests. IG Farben was intent on building up a *Grossraumwirtschaft*—an economic empire—in the chemical field, to secure economic independence by securing ample supply for its own requirements; "to regulate the productive forces there accordingly by planning rational utilization of the existing production facilities, and to adjust them to the present requirements and to foreseeable requirements of the future in such a manner that, particularly, mismanagement of available manpower and capital may be avoided."[2] In developing an "economic optimum," the executives of IG Farben decided that the activities of the industries now under IG Farben control should be restricted to the domestic market of (the conquered countries), a policy that seems to have favored my father's subsequent fate.

His job was to implement that plan. But it needed the cooperation of the Hitler government. Dad's office was in Paris, but he traveled widely in those three Western countries. The efforts of Fritz Sauckel, whom Hitler appointed plenipotentiary general for labor mobilization on March 21, 1942, impacted directly on my father's work. Sauckel ordered that: "All prisoners of war from the West as well as from the East must be completely incorporated into the German armament and nutrition industries. Apart from prisoners of war, we must requisition from Soviet territory male and female labor beginning at the age of 15 . . . All workers must be fed, sheltered and treated in such a way as to exploit them to the highest possible extent at the lowest possible cost." The so-called "labor draft" functioned with moderate success in France through the Pétain regime until the end of 1942. But Albert Speer, in competition with Sauckel over the labor force, needed ever more workers, especially skilled ones. He proposed to Hitler "an excellent scheme for getting them. 'Through industry we could deceive the French by telling them that we would release for their use all prisoners of war who are [skilled workers], if they would only give us their names. They give the names and then we have them. Do that.'" Hitler obliged Speer, decreeing that "it is no longer necessary to give special consideration to the French, . . . recruiting can proceed with the sharpest measures."[3] But Fritz Sauckel complained about lack of cooperation; he said that "Speer had created a series of 'protected' armament factories in France from which workers could not be removed. . . . The most abominable point made by my adversaries is their claim that no executive had been provided to recruit in a sensible

2. Ibid., 1447.
3. Bernstein, *Final Judgment*, 210.

manner the French and Belgian quotas. Thereupon I even proceeded to employ and train a whole batch of French and female agents who for good pay went hunting for men and liquor them up... in order to dispatch them to Germany."[4] On June 27, 1943, Sauckel tells Hitler that he would make "available one million French men and women for German war production in France proper in the second half of 1943 and, in addition, of transferring 500,000 French men and women to the Reich before the end of the current year.... On August 13, he reports to Hitler that the deportations were to be kept secret, and that similar actions were to take place in Belgium and the Netherlands.... A program was established in Belgium for the employment of 150,000 workers in the Reich and, with the approval of the military commander of Belgium, an organization for compulsory labor corresponding to that of France was decided upon.... A program has likewise been prepared for Holland, providing for the transfer of 150,000 workers to Germany and of 100,000 workers, men and women, from Dutch civilian industries to German war production."[5] Even though much of Sauckel's effort did not achieve his desired and predicted result, due to logistical difficulties and intergovernmental agencies' competition, when V-E Day arrived "there were more than 6,000,000 foreign slaves on German soil."[6]

I remember well June 22, 1941, the day Hitler invaded the Soviet Union. Father called the family together to tell us the news; in the course of his remarks, he indicated that this would lead to Germany's defeat. He angrily chided Hitler for ignoring how Czarist Russia had dealt with Napoleon's invasion and predicted that Stalin would use exactly the same tactics of drawing the German forces ever more deeply into Russia, overstretching their supply routes and eventually letting winter exhaust them. Which is, of course, exactly what happened. Father said: "We cannot win this war." With that knowledge, he set himself to making sure that the chemical industries in France, Belgium and the Netherlands would be in a position to work quickly and efficiently for their own people again after the fall of Germany.

From mid 1945 until late summer of 1946, he was the director of another one-time subsidiary of IG Farben, the mining operation at Niedersachswerfen adjacent to the installations of the Junkers airplane manufacturers and the assembly works of Germany's missiles, directed by Wernher von Braun. The latter had been moved from Peenemünde, on the coast of the Baltic Sea, after the Allied's "Operation Hydra" had severely crippled those installations on August 17, 1943. My father visited Niedersachswerfen on eight

---

4. Ibid, 215–16.
5. Harris, *Tyranny on Trial*, 415–16.
6. Bernstein, *Final Judgment*, 210.

different occasions between September 1942 and September 1944, thirty-five days all told, seventeen of them after the move of the missile works into the tunnels of the Kohnstein mountain. For centuries, sodium sulphate had been excavated from that mountain. Then, in 1938, the IG Farben company Merseburg Ammoniak took an interest in that facility and began to supply materials needed for the war to the IG Farben Leuna factory.

The Niedersachswerfen operation, in both open-pit and underground mining, supplied raw materials needed in processes requiring nitrates, carried out in Leuna, where I was born in 1935, the third of my parents' eight children. (Leuna also produced gasoline by a synthetic process; nearby was the large Buna works where rubber was produced, also synthetically.) It took merely six days after the bombing of Peenemünde for the first deportees from France to arrive in Niedersachswerfen; Hitler personally approved the development of the subterranean complex of factories on September 10, 1943. In the course of their construction, three principal forced labor camps were established there with an additional thirty-two satellite camps. On April 11, 1945, all work ceased in those factories. The complex is known as "Mittelbau Dora," also referred to as Camp Nordhausen, had the highest rate of workers dying or being murdered in the "extermination through labor" program. The vast majority of the inmates died in the underground installations for the missile program.[7] Like Wernher von Braun, Father claimed to have known nothing of the extermination. But after our move from Leuna to Niedersachswerfen in June of 1945, he and Mother warned us children to stay far away from those men walking about in striped clothing. "They do not like us Germans," they told us.

On July 9, 1944, my father went to Auschwitz-Monowitz where IG Farben was constructing a large chemical plant and a camp for its workforce. It was the last day of the massive influx of 438000 Hungarian Jews in Auschwitz. The following eight days he visited six different industries in Czechoslovakia. All these dates came after the Allied invasion of Normandy. In Auschwitz, Father saw and conferred with Walter Dürrfeld who, together with Fritz ter Meer and Otto Ambros received the stiffest prison-sentences at Nuremberg: eight and seven years, respectively. They had been closely associated with Auschwitz III, fully aware of the dependency of the factory on the two Auschwitz camps for labor. Monowitz was itself a joint project of IG Farben, a shareholders' company, and the SS. IG Farben paid the SS a daily rate of three to four Reich Marks (RM) for every worker it supplied. IG Farben produced and paid for the construction materials for Birkenau. A horrible example of the military-industrial complex!

---

7. See for example Michel, *Dora*.

In late 1946, we illegally left the Soviet and moved to the British sector of Germany. Father was hired by a chemical company, itself a former unit of IG Farben. (That company, through its British subsidiary, came to supply the technology used in Iraq under Saddam Hussein to produce the poison gas used on the Kurds in Northern Iraq!)

There is another day that has remained vividly in my mind: we were living in Dortmund, West Germany, and Father was in Nuremberg for the IG Farben Trial. It was in the later part of the summer of 1947. For a long time, I had erroneously believed that he was among the twenty-four defendants. I can still feel the stomach-churning fear of what might happen to him, given his position in IG Farben. We learned later that a number of people with whom Father had worked in Belgium, France, and Holland had told the trial commission of his efforts to maintain the industries in those countries as healthy as possible and be ready after the defeat of Germany to resume full-capacity production for their own population. Apparently, this led to Father not being indicted.

Early the next year, my father's West German company sent him to work in Portugal as a consultant for the building of a chemical factory outside Lisbon; the Cold War had changed attitudes in the West toward German industrialists.

In 1952, my family moved to Canada and I had my first conscious meetings with Jews. But it was a while yet before I began to learn about the Holocaust, the involvement of Germany's industries, and the failure of the churches to resist that horror. Eventually I began to ask Father and Mother what they knew at that time about what was then becoming widely known. They denied any knowledge. Later, after my visits to Auschwitz, Dachau, Flossenbürg, Buchenwald and Mittelbau Dora, I became utterly unable to accept their assertions. I know now that they had known enough to know that they did not want to know any more.

On a visit to my family's home in Nova Scotia in the eighties, Father saw a copy of Joseph Borkin's *The Crime and Punishment of IG Farben* in my personal library. He read it briefly and then, dropping it rather demonstrably in front of me, said: "Jewish propaganda." I replied that Borkin was not Jewish and that he had carefully studied the Nuremberg sources relating to the IG Farben Trial. I failed to persuade him. He then said something that I had frequently heard in the first few years after World War II: Nuremberg was the justice of winners imposed on the losers. It was what Germans call a "*Justizirrtum*" (an error of justice), a notion propagated, for example, by Thilo von Wilmowsky in his assessment of the judgment rendered on his in-law Alfried Krupp by the Tenth Military

Tribunal Trial at Nuremberg.[8] It is uncanny that my father's perception was almost identical in language to that of a number of United States legal scholars and politicians, such as Chief Justice Harlan F. Stone, Justice William O. Douglas and Senator Robert A. Taft who contended that the trials represented "victors' justice." Justice Douglas put it like this: "We are not justified in substituting power for principle."[9] Those views had become known in Germany; I am certain that Father knew them. They helped block what I call "the promise of Nuremberg."

What do I mean by the promise of Nuremberg? I am not talking about something the Allies promised the Germans on condition that they do something in return. What I have in mind is what the process of indictment, trial and judgment as such could have accomplished in addition to bringing certain people to justice. This where my experience of and reflection upon the South African Truth and Reconciliation Commission enter. The offer there of amnesty stimulated a number of people to come forward and detail their complicity in and/or direct responsibility for crimes against humanity: torture, illegal detention, kidnapping, brutal killing and so forth. Some of them admitted their guilt, felt remorse and sought reacceptance into society, particularly by persons on whom they had placed had such horrible anguish and pain. Having been helped to acknowledge guilt, victimizers could enter into mourning and, through the transformation that mourning can accomplish, become participants in overcoming the past and rebuilding the present.

Mourning enables silence to be broken, truth no longer to be suppressed and reparation made. But my knowledge of how Germans—and not only they—thought about Germany's reparations for many years after Nuremberg is that it was reparation without mourning, without unconditional remorse. The ability to mourn is inseparable from an individual's ability to enter through empathy into another's reality. But the Nazis had destroyed that ability with their denigration and subsequent destruction of "the other."

I cite two passages from Alexander and Margarete Mitscherlich's pivotal study *The Inability to Mourn. Principles of Collective Behavior*.

> What is a collective to do when it finds itself exposed without cover to the realization that in its name six million people were murdered for no reason other than to satisfy its own aggressive urges? It has hardly any choice but to continue to deny its motives or else retreat into depression. . . . [Yet] depressive

---

8. Rogers, in *Second Generation Voices*, 293–94.
9. Borkin, *The Crime and Punishment of I.G. Farben*, 139.

reactions, self-reproach and despair over the extent of guilt were rare. The dead cannot be brought back to life. But as long we do not manage to free ourselves in relation to the living from the stereotyped prejudice embedded in our history... we shall remain chained to our psycho-social immobilism, as to an illness involving symptoms of severe paralysis. "The collective responsibility of a nation for a chapter in its development, "Georg Lukács writes, "is something so abstract and intangible that it borders on absurdity. And yet a period such as that of Hitler can be regarded as over and done with in our own memory only if the intellectual and moral outlook that filled it, gave it movement, direction and shape, has been radically overcome. Only then does it become possible for others—for other nations—to trust in the conversion and to feel that the past has truly passed." But one can "radically overcome" only on the basis of knowledge firmly anchored in consciousness, even knowledge that at first may be painful, since what happened could happen only when that consciousness had been corrupted. What censorship has excluded from our consciousness for decades as a memory too painful to bear may at any time return unbidden from the past; it has not been "mastered";.... The labor of mourning can be accomplished only when one knows what one has to sever oneself from. And only by slowly detaching oneself from the lost relations—whether these be to human beings or ideals—can a meaningful relationship to reality and the past be maintained. Without the painful work of recollection this can never be achieved. And without it, the old ideals, which in National Socialism led to the fatal turn taken by German history, will continue to operate within the consciousness.... Correcting false and restricted consciousness in this way, discovering our ability to feel compassion for people never before apprehended behind distorting projections, would give us back the ability to mourn.[10]

For me, the "promise" of Nuremberg lay in its potential to bring about in Germans, or give back to them, the ability and the full experience of mourning what the trials had made us see so utterly plainly and then act in accordance with that. Instead, the inability or unwillingness to mourn prevailed and put seemingly insurmountable obstacles into the path of acknowledging, of accepting without defensiveness or claims of ignorance, the guilt and shame that had come upon my country in the Hitler years. I heard much about our suffering during and after the War; I experienced the

---

10. Mitscherlich, *The Inability to Mourn*, 20 and 82–83.

twenty-eight horrendous air-raids on my home town and then, after May 1945, the severe deprivation of food and health care. And when the Cold War began and we again had enough to eat and we Germans had become useful to the Western Allies, the new opportunities, climaxing in the so-called *Wirtschaftswunder*, the economic miracle under Konrad Adenauer and Ludwig Erhard in West Germany, sidelined, or should I say blinded what mourning calls for.

The inability to mourn and its fateful sibling, morbid silence, mark my generation and, I believe, the second generation of descendants of perpetrators, bystanders, away-lookers and accomplices. And the protest against that silence and the inability to mourn it spawns also shapes my and my children's generation. Björn Krondorfer (born in 1959) writes: "I wanted [my parents] to realize how difficult it was to establish a trusting relationship between second generation Jews and Germans. I wanted them to acknowledge that they and their parents' generation had left young Germans with a heavy weight on their shoulders. I wanted them to take their share of the responsibility."[11] What Krondorfer describes as his parents' disposition, which is not unlike that of my parents toward Germany's past, is radicalized very accurately by Gottfried Wagner, as follows: "Based on my experience, I have now arrived at a criterion for the behavior of the German majority, which I would like to characterize as a 'disastrous separation of individual responsibility and private and public ethics after the Holocaust.' It forms an insurmountable potential of conflict for the repression, denial, and falsification of one's past."[12] Yet Wagner doesn't leave it there; he takes up the affirmation of Margarete Mitscherlich in her important study *Erinnerungsarbeit*, (The Labor of Remembrance): "The spiritual and intellectual liberation from false ideals and idealizations, from traditional prejudices is the pre-condition that an intellectual-spiritual development and new orientation can take place at all."[13] And that precondition underlies the very labor of remembrance, as I see it, in that we can confront "the great fear with great hope."[14]

Paul Mendes-Flohr specifies this "great hope." "The mourner seeks no explanation. Her lament is a protest both against evil and its explanation. Her lament refuses to allow the scandal of Auschwitz to be contained by explanation. The mourner's cry pierces and transcends language, the cradle

---

11. Krondorfer, in *Second Generation Voices*, 263.
12. Wagner, in *Second Generation Voices*, 351.
13. Ibid., 351–52.
14. The citation is by Ralph Giordano, the insightful German laborer in the project of memory. Ibid., 353.

of explanation. Lament thus, paradoxically, also bears hope, for in decrying what is—was—it implicitly but insistently affirms what ought to be. Resolutely refusing to accept the decree of fate, hope is borne by an unmitigated outrage, not by explanation.... There is ... a significant difference between personal loss and the commemoration of ... symbolic loss, ... certainly of the nature of the Holocaust. Whereas the mourning of personal loss ideally entails a 'working through' and thus ultimately a reconciliation with the loss, commemoration of a loss that has the moral and political dimensions of the order of the Holocaust does not—I dare say, should not—allow for such a closure. It would, indeed, be an immeasurable obscenity to reconcile oneself to the Holocaust—or *mutatis mutandis* any other barbarity resulting in the massive violation of human dignity and death." The labor of mourning and remembrance "serves to prevent the disgrace of closure, and hence sustains hope-against-hope that humanity will one day enter paradise. Until then, hope obliges us to resist resignation and concomitantly to resist evil."[15]

Let me transpose such affirmation of hope into my understanding of the promise of Nuremberg and its concomitant call upon me.

The promise of Nuremberg is also a theological one: Looking with open and sensitized eyes at the trials, and what they made known, helps us—in face of the stunning silence of the churches and the painful evidence of Christian theology's failure of responsibility—in setting out toward the necessary repentance and renewal of theology, take up with courage the imperative issued by the Holocaust for lamentation, for much unlearning and even more new learning and specific action.

I try to do the labor of mourning required of Christian theology. Mourning is a process of the soul, a spiritual process, where one slowly learns to bear a loss and work through it with the help of a repeated, painful process of remembering. The labor of mourning presupposes a particular kind of labor of remembering. It is not so much a matter of recalling facts and data as it is remembering forms of behavior, ideas about values, feelings and visions. The labor of mourning is a learning process in abandoning something and, as such, becomes the precondition for new ways of thinking, for new perceptions of reality, allowing changed behavior and the development of new identities of the self.[16] Seen as such, the labor of mourning and remembering attacks the much easier labor of suppressing and denying, the cheap labor involved in functioning as if the "unpleasant" past is now behind us and one can return safely to the customary occupation with what one had always done. In the domain of theology—to put the case pointedly—it was

---

15. Mendes-Flohr, *Catastrophe and Meaning*, 253 and 256.
16. Mitscherlich, *Erinnerungsarbeit*, 13–16.

a matter of making the Christian tradition "relevant" to the modern mind. But this effort made a leap over the years 1933 to 1945 without touching the ground, as if they were not "relevant" to the Christian tradition! But that won't do any more, especially because the so-called "eternal verities" had contributed to the extermination. Excluding the Shoah *as a decisive theological factor* renders theology after Auschwitz vacuous; it has no credibility "in the presence of the burning children" (Irving Greenberg).[17] As I see it, theology itself must abandon its narcissistic self-focusing not simply for the sake of having anything relevant to say to the post-Holocaust world, but for its very integrity and truthfulness. If theology is able to do that, it may fulfill in its domain the promise of Nuremberg and become a midwife to an approach to reconciliation.

I would just briefly mention three aspects theology has to abandon and to learn.

1. Theology has to abandon reading and interpreting the Bible without the direct participation of Jewish scripture scholars and, I think equally essentially, of rabbis who teach and guide their congregations today in the way of Torah. The result of their absence over twenty centuries was that Christian biblical scholarship and theology embraced religious and cultural anti-Jewishness.

2. Theology and the church in its preaching has to abandon the deceptive juxtaposition of Jewish faith and Christian faith, such as: letter vs. spirit, promise vs. fulfillment, law vs. gospel, old vs. new, tribal vs. universal. These are not only unbiblical and false but worse, malicious, in that they denigrate and quickly despise the faith of Jews.

3. Theology has to develop a positive conception of and disposition toward the Jewish "NO!" to Jesus of Nazareth as the promised Messiah. Unless theology can let go of spiritualizing messiahship into the forgiveness of and atonement for our sinfulness and hence into our salvation for eternal life, it fails to grasp the Jewish faithfulness to a far more universal or cosmic messianic hope in and striving for the healing of heaven and earth, the *tikkun olam* of creation.

Labor like that would take up the promise of Nuremberg. But even as such, it is not enough for turning the promise into reality. For it may remain too much in the reflective mode for forming new identity. Theology becomes reconciling when it moves forward against the original sin: anti-Judaism and its vicious cousin, anti-Semitism, the repentance for which is

---

17. Greenberg, *Auschwitz*, 23.

to fight that sin. Such repentant fight is to work for Jewish survival now. For Christians, messianic *tikkun olam* is the action that has grown out of the labors of mourning and remembering and has turned into the labor of mending the rent in the fabric of Jewish-Christian history.

The promise of Nuremberg is still that as the Holocaust and its perpetrators were before the bar of justice sixty years ago, the post-Holocaust world will take up the labor of reworking itself.

15.

Since Auschwitz Everyone Should Know that Things Worse Than War Are Possible

I. Introduction

I BEGIN MY PRESENTATION with a statement by a number of German historians who are involved in the study of the Hitler era and the destruction of European Jewry. In 1986, when the so-called "feud of the historians" (*Historikerstreit*) was at its height, they opposed other German historians who wanted to end the discussion of Germany's collective complicity in and guilt for the Shoah by relativizing Auschwitz. On February 8, 1991, the former issued a declaration, published by the respected weekly *Die Zeit*. I would like to cite the part that includes the title of my presentation.

> The Germany of our fathers made the attempt to annihilate Europe's Jews by gassing them. This genocide was brought to an end not by us Germans, but solely through the readiness of Americans, Britons, Russians and other peoples to go to war. Since Auschwitz everyone should know that things worse than war are possible. Today's German profiteers too have helped—knowingly or not—the Iraqi dictator to continue the murder of the Jewish people. The Government of Germany has not found a way to prevent this. Whether war is the only means of stopping the mass murderer from Baghdad, only the future can tell. However, in this hour, when Israel sees itself threatened yet again by gas, we know—irrespective of the necessity of an understanding between Jews and Arabs—where we must take our stand: the Jewish people now need more than German gas masks, German defensive weapons and German millions! It needs the solidarity of every German![1]

---

1. Kammerer, *In die Haare*, 140.

They made this declaration at the same time as many Germans associated with the peace movement took to the streets demonstrating against the Second Gulf War. "Never again war!" was the daily cry. It was uttered by the very people who, acknowledging Germany's crime of the Shoah, had cried earlier "Never again Auschwitz!" It was the very symbiosis of "Never again Auschwitz! Never again war!" that plunged Jewish-Christian relations in Germany into a deep crisis. Jews experienced painful isolation, betrayal and utter incomprehension, symptoms of the crisis.

II. Something Autobiographical

I interject some autobiographical references in order to make the location of my reflections more readily understandable. I was born in 1935 in Germany, part of the baby boom that marked the economic and psychological upswing my country experienced then under the rule of Hitler. My father was advancing well in his employment by the IG Farben conglomerate, holding responsible positions in research related also to the conduct of war. Our home life was marked by my parents' deep personal religious faith: we regularly attended public worship; Bible reading, prayer and singing hymns accompanied our family life like a *cantus firmus*. This had much to do with my decision as an eighteen-year-old to study theology and to seek ordination. I did not anticipate then that my subsequent post-graduate studies, which took me to the university where Karl Barth was my teacher and where I was together with other German fellow-students, would put me squarely before the Shoah, the silence of the churches, and the long tradition of Christian anti-Judaism. Not until I reached my later teens and my family's move from Europe to Canada did I meet Jewish people. My existence until then had been completely void of contact with persons who openly identified themselves as Jews or practiced the Jewish faith. I had only *heard* of Jews and then only in mystifications. It took a decade after our move to Canada when, as a result of my studies with Karl Barth and the Jewish philosopher Karl Löwith in Basel, I began to ask my parents questions in relation to the Shoah. It was the standard answer that I received: "We did not know." I speak of my parents as what we know as "bystanders" or, more accurately perhaps, as "away-lookers." Father visited Auschwitz-Monowitz at least once, consulting there with Walter Dürrfeld, head of the synthetic rubber production project there. Dürrfeld was a former colleague of Father's in Leuna, my home town, and his family and ours were quite close. I have no evidence to indicate that Father ever ordered or witnessed the death of Jews at the hands of the Nazis.

For more than four decades now, I have been supported, encouraged, and sustained by numerous Jewish friends. They give me room to enter into the shame I feel as a German in connection with the Shoah and, as a result, been enabled to reflect on my relation to my parents and my commitment to the Christian church. What is in me of them that taught me my values? This is the prime question, the answers to which often dismay, surprise and always challenge me. It is in relation to those two realities of my life that I experience a crisis calling me to look for different ways of being.[2]

III. The 1991 Gulf War

The search for such different ways put me in touch with a group of theologians, peace-activists and church people in Germany with whom I share not only that search but also a leftist political outlook. Many of them pursue the theological direction and ecclesiastical orientation associated with Karl Barth, Dietrich Bonhoeffer and Martin Niemöller. Several among those colleagues and by now close friends have participated for many years in an organization called "Arbeitsgemeinschaft Juden und Christen beim Deutschen Evangelischen Kirchentag," (Working-association of Jews and Christians under the auspices of the biennial Protestant Church Assembly). Founded in 1961, this Association called on the churches in Germany, as well as individual Christians, to face the Shoah *as Germans and as Christians*, to seek ways of personal and corporate contact with Jews and Israel, to examine the Christian tradition and its preaching for its anti-Judaism, and to learn in a wholly new way what being Jewish today really means. The association's work had borne good fruit; at least so it appeared. A strong presentation had been planned for the 1991 Assembly under the title "Not everything that distinguishes us also separates us." But the thirtieth anniversary celebrations did not take place. The scud-missile attack on Israel on January 18, 1991, and the existential threat it signified made it clear, in sudden and drastic ways, that the partners in the association as well as Jews and Christians elsewhere, were actually quite far apart and had been so even before the Gulf War. However pronounced the association's Christian members were in their pro-Israel stance, the second Gulf War and Iraq's missile attack became the moment of deep crisis.

What had happened was that solidarity with Israel now stood against the desire and search for peace which had driven hundreds of thousands of Germans into the streets again and again over the years, but especially in the eighties. Thousands of Christians attended the biennial Church Assembly

2. Rumscheidt, in *What Kind Of God?*, 51–63.

precisely because of the witness to peace to be found there and nowhere else. "Never again Auschwitz! Never again war!" What had long been asserted in the same breath, now stood in sharp opposition and "Never again war!" prevailed. A high-ranking prelate of one of Germany's regional Protestant churches wrote these words to co-workers in a letter that became public almost immediately: "Not even the readiness for another genocide, in particular of Israel, on the part of Iraq's Saddam Hussein justifies war."[3] But, in retrospect, such cynical pacifism, which can more readily countenance a second genocide of Jews than bombs on Iraq, brought together two central and *as such* laudable Christian faith convictions. One was given expression at the founding assembly of the World Council of Churches at Amsterdam in 1948: "According to the will of God, war is not to be." The other states that Christians are to be advocates for and engage themselves on behalf of the weak and helpless.

Having solidly affirmed the former, Christian peace-activists, leftist and liberal Christians in Europe and North America discovered through the latter conviction their sympathies for Palestinians as "the weak and helpless" or, as one could then begin to hear the still often repeated refrain, "the victims of the victims." The Working Association of Jews and Christians did make a presentation at the 1991 Assembly; however, it was no "celebration." A panel discussion addressed the fact that Israel was in danger and that the German Christian-Jewish encounter was in crisis.[4] Five of the six panellists are among my closest companions in the search for a new and genuine relationship with Jews today. I would like to present some of what was said at that panel in order to prepare for my observation on the contemporary crisis in Jewish-Christian relations.

IV. The 1991 Kirchentag Panel [5]

Two of the panellists are Jewish: Edna Brocke and Micha Brumlik; both live and work in Germany. They expressed that they had hoped for a clear and unambiguous engagement in Germany for the existence of Jews in *eretz Israel*. Instead, the silence of the West German Government and the citizens' demonstrations against the war—many of the banners exclaimed "No blood for oil!"—reflected in their view a flight from reality and an immersion into other deep-rooted psychological issues. The reality of the Middle East was left behind and the moving matter was Germans' own

---

3. Brocke, in *Kirche und Israel*, 64.
4. von Bonin, *Deutscher Evangelischer Kirchentag Ruhrgebiet*, 682–705.
5. Ibid.

preoccupation with the war they had lost half a century ago and the fears they felt about another war that could affect them. It was symptomatic of this when Germans said to Jews that the Iraqi scud missiles had not killed anyone directly, that "only" thirty-nine had been launched, causing only material damage. The very fact that Israelis had taken shelter in basements and, in some instances, seeking to escape the poison gas the missiles were believed to be carrying (supplied to Iraq by firms, among them both East and West Germans, one of which was a subsidiary of my father's company) had to seal window and door frames with masking tape, never entered into the discussion! The Green Party in the Federal State of Hessia refused to support that Israel should receive defensive missiles with which to intercept and destroy the Iraqi scuds; instead they concluded, in concert with many people elsewhere in the world, that the burden for the war having started in the first place really rested on the US and Israel. Why, one of the Jewish panellists asked, was there no spontaneous solidarity with Israel and Jews? Why, rather, solidarity with the people of Iraq? On January 4, 1991, the influential *Süddeutsche Zeitung* published the result of a poll on the question: from which country should the new Germany keep greatest distance in the next ten years? The majority of Germans put Israel in first place. Both Brocke and Brumlik concluded that, obviously, forty years after the Shoah the kind of solidarity Jews had hoped for was not to be expected; it is better, instead, not to rely on what seemed to be friendships or declarations of love, for they have proven themselves to be illusions.

I was not present at that panel; as I read and re-read the transcript even now, I am aware of a deep, deep sadness that Jews in Germany have to say such things to Germans; I am similarly aware of how false hope is when it is out of touch with reality. As a teacher in a theology school, I experience repeatedly from students, colleagues and, I admit, from myself what ideological power hope—one of the three supreme Christian virtues—can have and how it tends to distort reality.

What did the Christians Marquardt, Stöhr, Uhl and Weiss say during that panel discussion? Germans felt fear: fear that the poison gas and the environmental pollution could drift to Germany. The daily display on CNN of bomb and missile attacks awakened memories of raids on Germany during World War II, rekindling the fright of those days but also the old rage against the British and Americans who had conducted the attacks then and were doing so again now. In the midst of those self-focussed fears, few bothered to analyse the causes of the fear other nations, and especially Israel, were experiencing in those first months of 1991. When the war ended, the Germans' fear also ended and everything returned to "normal," to the "daily routine." But it was not and still is not "normal" in the Middle East.

The relation Germans and Jews and especially Christians and Jews had experienced before the Gulf War showed itself to be what Germans call a "blue sky friendship"—no clouds there to affect the nice feeling of being "together." The desire to shape a new way of thinking on the part of Germans and Christians failed. "Do we even have the possibility in our way of thinking of assessing the realities of the world as it exists today, especially in the Middle East, with any kind of appropriateness to those realities?" one panellist asked. For simply to co-opt and make our own the voices of opponents within Israel and among Jews to the concrete policies pursued by the Israeli government is utterly thoughtless unless one sat in one of those masking-tape-sealed basements, unless one has lost sleep from the nightmare that Jews faced the danger in the early weeks of 1991 of being gassed once again to death. It is cheap to make demands from a safe distance upon another people; it is even cheaper to declare that one is a pacifist and to deny all responsibility for others producing, selling and employing weapons. It is hypocritical to declare that one will not defend one's own existence under certain circumstances and then call on another people, threatened by the worst weapons of mass destruction, to do the same.

Germans developed a strong taste for the adage: let bygones be bygones; the desire to be rid of the past is as strong there as it is elsewhere. But, in the words of one Christian in that discussion, to put distance between oneself and one's history in this instance means also to put distance between oneself and Israel, oneself and Jews. And, if the problems created in the past refuse to go away, one can proceed to apply blame. In relation to the Middle East, one could hear voices in Germany saying that the Iraqi scuds are the logical consequence of the policies pursued by Israel toward Palestinians. Which, translated into plain language, means that those murdered decades earlier are now the guilty ones, the once-victims are now the victimizers. That schema allows those threatened with being or actually having been killed to be declared guilty by those who feel threatened themselves by whatever. And, thus, the schema and its effects make a deeper analysis of the Middle East conflict unnecessary because the answer is given already beforehand: a "post-fact" issue as it would be characterized nowadays.

What are we to do when we truly believe, on the one hand, that "according to the will of God, war is not to be," when the long-term goal is affirmed "war is not a means of politics," and, on the other hand, we face a situation in which the use of force cannot be excluded? In face of the struggles of liberation movements in the so-called "two-thirds world," including those of the Palestinian movement, Christians have shown "understanding" for those movements when they have excluded the use of military force. But what do we Christians do when we take something as beautiful as liberation theology from the Bible but ignore what goes with it there: the promise of land, the ongoing existence of the people striving for liberation and the responsibility resting on other nations for that people? This is not simply an issue of biblical exegesis or of theology but also—and even more so—a moral issue. Related to it is the fact that Jesus was a Jew, only a Jew and nothing but a Jew. What does that mean theologically? And does it have any consequences in relation to the modern state of Israel?

Let me interject something. Soon after the Six-Day War in 1967, I became embroiled in a "feud" in the United Church of Canada over the fate of Palestinians in the occupied territories. When I refer to the dangers that continue to confront the existence of the State of Israel, I am accused of being possessed either by a "guilt complex," or an "Auschwitz complex," or a "Holocaust syndrome." In essence, I am declared "sick," unable to order political realities correctly. So, next to "postpartum syndrome," "post-traumatic stress syndrome" and others, there is now a "Holocaust syndrome"! In face of such psychologizing, I ask: where else is such inventiveness going to take us? When confronted with human rights violations inflicted by Israelis on Palestinians, I do not deny, in fact I affirm, that they exist and need to be opposed. Every human being today has the obligation and the right to protest against human rights violations. Period! But when we talk morality, we must also address its credibility, its authenticity. (One Christian panellist asked: Do those who now vehemently raise their voices against Israeli human rights violations also raise them against such violations elsewhere? Or do they rather follow the abominable pattern of measuring Israel by moral standards applied nowhere else? Why is it, he wondered aloud, that Jews appear to be held to a moral virtuosity far higher than others, ourselves included?) Arguing that credibility here requires the recognition and affirmation of the right of the Jewish people to maintain a state in that land has also reaped me the diagnosis of psychological deficiency: having a complex or syndrome. Here my own deeply anxious, albeit still tentative conclusion converges with that stated by Edna Brocke in Dortmund, June 6, 1991. I quote her directly.

> [I] probably belong to a generation that had great hopes, I would now say great illusions, about the possibility to learn both in and from history, from the Shoah, from Auschwitz, and to enable new dimensions to emerge in the encounter of Jews and non-Jews. I really was taken by the idea, by the hope—today I would say: the illusion—that this event: *the Shoah,* had entered so deeply into people's consciousness that they would not just go back to their daily routines. The experience of how people in this country reacted to the hot war in the Gulf has disenchanted

me and I know now, in a way I had not felt before, that it is not so: *the Shoah has not made possible a really new approach between non-Jews and Jews.*[6]

I cannot dismiss her conclusion. This has to do with the theological or faith affirmations already mentioned. The panel addressed them as well. First, the affirmation that "according to the will of God, war is not to be." That statement allows for almost no modification, given the technology of modern warfare and its utter inability to meet even one condition of the so-called just war theory. The Christians in the Working Association made that point in their dialogues with Jews in Germany. At the time of the Gulf War, the dialogue raised the critical question: what is it with you Christians that you always know accurately what the will of God is and then, on the basis of this affirmation, establish your political orientation and action? Personally, I am persuaded by the affirmation the World Council of Churches made, but that critical question can't be silenced. How do I actually know that according to God's will there is to be no more war? The affirmation needs new examination and substantiation but Christians have thus far not done this. "Never again Auschwitz!" however, is radically pushing that examination and substantiation on us. The Shoah has made it necessary that we Christians distinguish between messianic hope for peace and the insight which reality provides, namely that the use of force, including and perhaps especially military force, is an imperative dictated by an existing situation. Here Christians tend to back off. Indeed, if the commandments of the Torah were kept, and if the visions of the prophets were actualized, there would be no more murder, false testimony, theft and war would no longer be conducted. But we are not there and this has a profound impact on Christians' deeply held pacifism.

Secondly, the moral demand of Christian theology that "Christians are to stand up for the weak and helpless." But by what criteria is another's weakness ascertained or measured and by what criteria is someone's weakness and helplessness judged to be more significant than that of another? How do we Christians actually know who at any given time is truly the weak and who, in comparison, is the strong? To put the point even more acutely: who are we Christians that we not only know but even feel ourselves always called to fight on behalf of the weak, that is, those whom we have defined as such? And who are we that we define someone as the strong? What looks like a positive, moral affirmation within Christian theology—and I do continue to hold it as such—has in practice turned into a casuistry of the weak and the strong, of those whose side we take and those whom we oppose.

---

6. Ibid., 692.

What has become very questionable for me now is this arrogance: we Christians not only always know who the weak and helpless are but we also take it upon ourselves absolutely to represent the side using what we take to be our fine skills. What does "weak" and "strong" mean here anyway?

V. The Contemporary Crisis in Jewish-Christian Relations

The sentence that makes up the title of my presentation helped me focus on what I name as a profoundly significant aspect of the contemporary crisis in Jewish-Christian relations. "Since Auschwitz there are worse things than war." I find that statement provocative not only for Germans but also for Christians everywhere.

I do not find myself at home in right-wing or fundamentalist Christianity, nor can I embrace the philo-Semitic, pro-Israel position that is espoused there; I am actually troubled by it. But I am yet more deeply troubled by something I encounter among a wide range of Christian people with whom I associate: what since the Enlightenment we have come to call our "autonomous reason" is characterized by the notion that we can know something better than victims can. We tend to project that we know better, for example, than Israelis what is good for their country and what surely is not. In addition, there is the attitude that our reason and our judgment, derived from within the horizon of our European and North American experience, function in the same way elsewhere so that people, let us say now in Israel, really can and should come to the same conclusions, judgments and decisions. We believe that, really, others need to see things the way we do.

The problem I face is that when we Christians and intellectuals criticize Israel, we function with a basic assumption: Jews are part of the community of reason shaped by the Enlightenment humanity of the Western world and people in the Middle East are not; their way of thinking is different. In practice, this means that we do not expect from the latter what we quite naturally expect from the former. This blasé arrogation on our part of knowing better in my view feeds the present crisis in Christian-Jewish relations.

Let me name that crisis in one sentence, with which I shall finish. When I reflect on how Christians within the context familiar to me address the Middle East conflict and, in particular the political practice of the State of Israel, I can no longer escape the conclusion that the Shoah has yet so to enter into our Christian consciousness that a truly new relation between Jews and Christians, between Jews and non-Jews, can begin to grow.

III. After the Shoah

16.

Poetry, Theology, and Ethics

A Study in Paul Celan

"... *der Tod ist ein Meister aus Deutschland*"

"Passing through the thousand darknesses of death bringing speech"

—Paul Celan

I

THE ABOVE TWO STATEMENTS by Jewish poet Paul Celan are brought together as an attempt to discern the call for a theology "after Auschwitz." I belong to a people who almost succeeded in their determination to "eradicate" in Europe those whom it designated as "the Others." My reflections on Celan's statements represent a theological attempt to bear respectful and nonviolent witness to the existence of those "Others." There is a dilemma in simultaneously claiming the Christian commandments, "Love God with all your heart, soul, and mind," and "Love your neighbor because she/he is like yourself." The disconcerting question that faces me is this: Can Christian theology so reconstruct itself after the Shoah, that in claiming the commandment "Love God with all your heart, soul, and mind," its construction of "Otherness" does not belie the second and equally important one: "Love your neighbor because she/he is like you?" In 1955, Theodor Adorno said that writing poems after Auschwitz is barbaric; is this also true for doing theology?

This chapter addresses the question by relating theology and literature and begins by elucidating what such a relation might be and what it looks like. It then examines Paul Celan's *Todesfuge*, from which the first statement is drawn. Finally, the poem is brought into conversation with, "theology."

II

At this point, three observations are necessary. First, the conviction that Auschwitz signals the collapse of Western value systems and epistemic structures is foundational for this chapter. Second, the symbiotic relation of ethics and aesthetics is so devastatingly affected by the reality of the death camps that it may be irreparable. Third, since the Enlightenment, theology, in its form as an institutionalized and academic undertaking, has distanced itself-to its detriment-from the aesthetic, and in so doing has undermined the power of the ethical.

Institutionalized theology in the Christian West, particularly in modern times, has reduced literature, as well as visual art, to the level of a decorative servant. Under the rigorous control of theology, it was, at best, to provide a subsidiary or complementary interpretation to theology. As it had done for other domains of the life of the spirit, the Enlightenment loosened the bonds of theology's tutelage over literature. This resulted in the development of literature into something of quasi-religious significance. It is constructive to recall, for example, how the work of Johann Wolfgang von Goethe was interpreted by historian and theologian Adolf von Harnack (1851–1930), or the place the poet's famous *Faust* came to occupy in anthroposophy.[1]

And this is no mere mystification on the part of people for whom "established" religion no longer sufficed; literature took over, reflected on the substance of theology, and secularized it. One thinks of the poets Hölderlin (1770–1843) or Rilke (1875–1926) and how the former became the focus for Martin Heidegger's twentieth-century philosophy of Being. It was Hölderlin who said, "but what abides is founded by poets." In my view, a false orientation in, if not the failure of, theology itself is the reason for literature becoming the "secular" bearer of religious substance. In the West, the religion that predominated for well over sixteen centuries was Christianity in its diverse denominations. Few of them can escape the indictment that they have failed the human being in the sense that they have held the human being in bondage. By this, I mean that religion was presented in a language of dominance most of the time. The most intense form of dominance is theology, a discourse among specialists often—and all too often—mysterious and esoteric, inaccessible to nearly the whole population. Much of regular preaching, too, was in the language of control: control both of the listening congregation and of the sacred. Even the reformative attempts to stop such domestication turned too easily into endeavors to coerce human beings into the petty

---

1. A highlight of Rudolf Steiner's anthroposophy was a full performance of Goethe's play *Faust* in Dornach, Switzerland.

orderliness of hierarchy, thereby enabling diverse secular and ecclesial orders of domination to maintain and strengthen themselves. The way the church presented religion, namely, by "predigesting" reality for people, has failed the human being, individually and collectively. What is named traditionally "The Word of God" is something "literary": it is a written and spoken communication. When transformed into a language of dominance, it becomes not what its substance is continuously asserted to be, namely, the liberation of people; instead, it cements their being in tutelage, blocking their coming of age. The Enlightenment's cry, *sapere aude,* dare to use your reason, persuaded its followers to substitute "the Good, the Beautiful, and the True" for "religion," if they did not see art as religion itself. However this development is to be judged, the Enlightenment bequeathed its Western children the basic conviction that the aesthetic is a means of humanization.

In a radio broadcast, aired in the late 1960s, Nobel Laureate Heinrich Böll (1917–1985) said this:

> Literature and art respect . . . human beings in their lostness. That is why [literature and art] can never be optimistic, whereas religion must be, thus [making] art and literature inhumane. [We human beings] are qualified by mourning, by love, and by transitoriness. [Literature] proclaims this perduring transitoriness. Creating . . . painting . . . composing . . . writing a poem or even prose . . . are themselves erotic processes that create relation; initially, an erotic relation between artist and artifact. . . . And the eros that comes into being here can, of course, also create a relation to human beings, possibly to God or the devil. . . . Now, it is my conviction that authors and artists, all creative people must enter into a relation of equality with the non-privileged, so that the art that is created does not become a domain for the educated elite for that only turns art into a pseudo-religious esotericism.

The cult of the genius, the "great men" (Adolf von Harnack is an example of this "cult") who characterized the West's nineteenth century and its pseudo-religion, needed to be resisted with the ethical imperatives of *equality*. To resist in such a manner, Böll continues, is

> the task of the twentieth-century artist to create. No more elitist notion!. . . Religion, the churches and denominations are bankrupt because what they wanted was dominance. They existed by authoritarian means, falsely believing that religion was transferable and could be passed on like an inheritance. [As a result of collapse of religion caused by this false belief, the aesthetic]

is put into a position that it really cannot defend: it becomes religion, that is, the only expression of the Word, barely audible and barely understandable, in the midst of the corruption of God's Word by its representatives. . . . It might just be that it is precisely a decidedly non-Christian, that is, anti-Christian, even blasphemous literature that leads forward into humanization and creates the human being who can be addressed with the Word of the God of which it is said that it became itself human.[2]

Without expressly saying so, Böll describes the process that became so utterly unmasked in the Shoah: the inability of religion to provide through its institutionalized and "scientific" media an ethics of resistance, that is, an ethics *for* human beings. For those media were elitist, readily amenable to the elitism of the planners and practitioners of the *Endlösung*.[3] This elitism is what I called earlier the false orientation in and the failure of theology. And while Heinrich Böll directly names the elitism of religion "established" in the church institution, he also identifies it, albeit in its varying form, in the aesthetic domain. Here he provides an insightful answer to the question of why it was in the nation of Goethe, Bach, and Beethoven that the Holocaust came into being. This creation of German will, organization, and technology starkly manifests the climax of a century-and-a-half-long process, namely, the utter impotence of aesthetics and religion to concretize themselves in an ethic of resistance, perhaps even to imagine one at all!

One dimension of this impotence is what was earlier called the language of dominance: the language of purpose, control, and possession. In such language, relationships are seen not in terms of equality but of hierarchy. Hierarchy presupposes separation of those "above" from those "below," the "privileged" from the "non-privileged." It is a language of dualisms. Its opposite would be an "anarchistic" one; it is close to what Böll refers to as non-Christian, anti-Christian, and blasphemous, the literature that may initiate humanization. It follows that stringent philosophical or scholastic conceptuality, as we know it in the Western tradition, is not expected to provide us with "anarchistic" language.

German feminist theologian and poet Dorothee Soelle argues that in shunning every attempt to impose "definitions," poetic language is able to render meaning audible and resonant precisely because of its narrative freedom and the plethora of linguistic means available to it. In particular, she names those used in mysticism: frequent repetition, comparison,

---

2. Soelle, *Almanach for Literatur und Theologie*, 97–98. Cited in text as *ALT*.

3. See the meticulous development of this point in Aly and Heim, *Vordenker der Vernichtung*.

exaggeration, hyperbole, antithesis, and paradox.[4] When theology and literature sever their relationship, both suffer. In that separation, theology seeks exile in "science," which, she argues, is finally something that is not of ultimate concern to human beings. What theology produced for the general population—rules and regulations, ecclesiastical ordinances, and catechetical pronouncements, declaring them to be for the good of the people—turned out to be detrimental to the existential nature of religion. The deep insights of theology—and indeed there are such—rarely found their way to the everyday world where human beings live much of their lives; rather, they were met with suspicion. This was less the result of the lack of interest in those insights than it was of the nature of theological language. Today, the language of dominance is being exposed as one that does not serve the emancipation and humanization of human beings, particularly the "non-elite." Thus the broadly "aesthetic," even in its weaknesses, is seen to be more credible and, for that reason, more decisive and significant.

I argue for a strong relation between theology and literature, for their mutual benefit. The separation of the domains of aesthetics, politics, and religion is the dogma of modernity, the modernity that Auschwitz exposed radically. Existing side by side in a spiritual "apartheid," a politics-free religion ends up venerating power and its idols, a religion-free politics decays into despising humanity itself, and an aesthetics-free politics and religion are mere utilitarian instruments of "principalities and powers" such as globalization, or the "new European order," depicted in Alyss and Heim's work referred to above.

> Theology and literature is a *cantus firmus,* a lead-tune, in my life. . . . [My theological interest in literature] was aroused by the numerous traces of religious language in fiction writing that does not regard itself as religious at all. . . . In the course of a secularization process, the language of Christian faith has come to be at the disposition of indirect, metaphorical speech. It has taken on most diverse functions, anywhere between blasphemy and sacralization. It is the emancipatory use of religious language in fiction writing that justifies not only the theologian, but also the literary scholar to ask about the theological implications of such acceptance and appropriation. (ALT, 207)

She speaks of the damage that the lack of poetry has inflicted on the theology of the academy. For poetry can make, and has made, visible the seriousness and playfulness, that is, the beauty of theology.

---

4. Soelle, *The Silent Cry,* 64.

> This kind of poetry is no luxury item; it is bread. It turns our planet, ever so beloved in spite of everything, more and more into home.... [P]oetry creates a boundary-dissolving freedom ... I really do not believe in the modern program of *poesie pure*. More precisely: wherever it happens successfully that the unmixed purity of the beautiful becomes sound and language, poetry is no longer "pure" and "for itself." Paul Celan's lyrical work serves as an example of how precisely, in most sparse, often hermetic language, the reality of the world of the extermination camp enters and the promises of tradition shine forth. When I learned Greek, the concept *kalonkagathon* became very dear to my heart. In my seventeen-year-old unintelligence, I wondered how the Greeks could take two words that for us have nothing to do with each other, and turn them into the one word: beauty-good. Where on earth would one find aesthetics and ethics in the same dish? ... In order really to do theology we need a different language. Poetry and liberation is a topic central to my life.[5]

Today many of us experience our language as horribly corrupted, serving ever more to obfuscate and stupidify than to emancipate. For example, the term *collateral damage* is a manifestation of the triumph of the Nazis' language of instrumentality, of death. It is particularly the vocabulary of feelings that has sustained serious damage, I think especially the feelings of anger, revulsion, abhorrence, and shame. They are for me at the heart of every reflection by a German and Christian like me, who tries to think at all after Auschwitz. If Karl Marx's observation is correct, that shame is a revolutionary feeling, then that word and others like those mentioned above need to be saved from the destruction of language. It is then that the destruction of human beings in language itself may be brought to an end, and we can begin anew to recognize ourselves in language, see again images of humanization, and become respectful of "the Other."

In one of her "eight theses on the criteria of theology's interest in literature," Dorothee Soelle states that theology needs to set itself apart critically only from that kind of art that denies what concerns human beings unconditionally and what, in so doing, denies the wholeness of the human being. For both theology and art, banality is a mortal danger. What is significant for theology in literature is what opens us, lifts us above the assurances of the known, confronts us with our own clichés, unmasks us, and transforms our relation to the world, as to the Other, thereby transforming us (*ALT*, 211). In other words, the symbiosis of aesthetics and ethics and

---

5. Soelle, *Against the Wind*, 151.

of poetry and theology needs to be rewoven if theology is to be reborn as a means of humanization, of finding and expressing the human being after Auschwitz—if this is even at all possible. For me, a child of Nazi Germany, if theology, my vocation, is to have any life whatsoever, the human being I need to find and hear above all is Jewish.

III

Paul Celan's *Todesfuge*[6] and its terse declaration that "Death is a master from Germany" situates me before the truth but in a place opposite to that from which Celan uttered those words. Celan experienced "the master from Germany" in the brutalization and degradation of his own family and people. As a German, not quite ten years old when Auschwitz was liberated by Soviet troops, I have "experienced" the master from my own home and native land and confront the *Meister* in what turns out to be a lifelong process wherein shame and humiliation have come to be decisive and possibly recreative feelings and motivations.

I do not here attempt a literary analysis of *Todesfuge*: John Felstiner has provided an excellent one in the chapter "A Fugue after Auschwitz (1944–1945)," to which I am gratefully indebted (*PC*, 22–41). However, I draw on his analysis to identify the literary, that is, the *aesthetic*, elements that summon theological reflection or imagination into an awareness of what Emmanuel Levinas calls "*la trace de l'autre*" which, understood in this context, is the trace and presence of the Jewish human being and a response that is respectful and nonviolent to the "Otherness" in which she or he is before me. In different words, I seek through *Todesfuge* to "do theology" in which, released by anger, revulsion, abhorrence, and shame, both personal and collective, an ethic may come into being that resists the "*Meister aus Deutschland*" in the service of life. I seek to say something here that I believe is embodied in the beautiful words *tikkun olam* (mending the world).

Paul Celan (1920–1970) *wrote in German!* It was his mother's language. "And can you bear, Mother, as *oh, at home,* once on a time, the gentle, the German, the pain-laden rhyme?" (*PC*, 24). It is also mine: the language that articulated the death of his people in Europe, the language in which "the word was made flesh and, having become flesh, was eventually turned into

---

6. Celan, *Gedichte in Auswahl*, 8–9. An excellent translation is found in Felstiner, *Paul Celan: Poet, Survivor, Jew*, 31–32. (Hereafter cited in text as *PC*). I agree with Felstiner's judgment that translating the poem's title into English, such as "Fugue of Death," "Death Fugue," or "Death's Fugue," loses the symmetry of the two words and how they make what belongs to death so visible.

heaps of cadavers."[7] Celan wrote in the language in which burned the fire that buried so many in "a grave in the air" (*PC*, 31). That language passed "through the thousand darknesses of deathbringing speech," which meant that his own writing also had to pass through those very darknesses (*PC*, xv). But "passing through," Celan's poetry also testifies to life: lost, taken away, clung to, longed for, and the like. "Like many people who lived through those years, he gave almost no factual testimony about them—which gives his poetry a testimonial charge" (*PC*, 22).

What first drew my attention to *Todesfuge* was not the statement "*der Tod ist ein Meister aus Deutschland*." When in a public lecture the German essayist Walter Jens spoke of the poetry of Paul Celan, he cited another line from that poem: "*dann steigt ihr als Rauch in die Luft dann habt ihr ein Grab in den Wolken da liegt man nicht eng*" ("you'll rise then as smoke to the sky you'll have a grave then in the clouds there you won't lie too cramped") (*PC*, 31). According to Jens, for Celan, that line was not poetic license, not a metaphor. It struck me upon hearing this how radically the fact of Auschwitz must have affected the Jews' sense of identity, when the preceding generations that gave them their roots are buried in "a grave in the clouds." For example, in Celan's sentence, Jens shows how Auschwitz had radically touched the foundations of the Jewish culture. It was then that I first asked whether Adorno's dictum, cited above, did not also apply to the pursuit I was preparing myself for: theology.

Felstiner interprets Celan's work as an attempt to uphold humanness (*PC*, 15). It is the attempt on Celan's part to go on living himself and not to lose sight of what is good, true, and beautiful; or, in the words of Dorothee Soelle, cited earlier, not to lose sight of what may yet turn our world into "home," the exact oppose of "*l'univers concentrationnaire*," the "concentrationary universe" of the Nazis (*PC*, 27).

> Out of those months that saw the war ending and its Jewish catastrophe revealed, Paul [Celan] wrote one lyric that drives far beyond private anguish, forming the benchmark for poetry "after Auschwitz": "Todesfuge" ... The *Guernica* of postwar European literature. ... The prolonged impact that "Todesfuge" has had stems partly from its array of historical and cultural signals—some overt and direct, some recondite or glancing. Practically every line embeds verbal material from the disrupted world to which this poem bears witness. From music, literature, and religion and from the camps themselves we find discomforting traces of Genesis, Bach, Wagner, Heinrich Heine,

---

7. Améry, *Jenseits von Schuld und Sühne*, 12, and Améry, *At the Mind's Limits*, x. Like Celan, Améry, was a survivor and also chose to end his life. (Cited as *JSS*)

> the tango, and especially Faust's heroine Margareta, alongside the maiden Shulamith from the Song of Songs. To realize these traces in translating Celan's verse can identify the poem with its indictment of so-called Judeo-Christian culture. *(PC,* 26-27)

According to Felstiner, by the latter part of 1944, Celan was apprised of the fact that Jews were forced to play dance tunes or to sing nostalgic songs, while other Jews were forced to dig graves. When the poem first appeared in print, it was in a Romanian translation; the magazine *Contemporanul* published it in May 1947 under the title "Tango of Death." Felstiner explains, "For Celan to call the poem 'Death Tango' was to annul the dance that fascinated Europe during his childhood—the essence of life as urbane, graceful, nonchalant" *(PC,* 28). Camp inmates, whose highest duty, according to Jean Améry, was to die *(JSS,* 12), spoke of "Death Tango" when referring to the music that was played when other inmates were taken out to be shot (PC, 30). The switch to "Death Fugue" relates such music, whatever it was in each concrete case, to the music of quintessential German composer Johann Sebastian Bach, whose *Art of the Fugue* was heralded by Oswald Spengler as the pinnacle of music in the Western world, in his morphology of that world's culture *Der Untergang des Abendlandes* (1918; *The Decline of the West* 1926–1928.) Moreover, by changing the title to *Todesfuge,* Celan also annuls Nazi claims about the superiority of the Nordic race and its blue-eyed, blond-haired people. Instead, the title spells out that death, like Bach and his *Kunst der Fuge,* and like Beethoven and his *Grosse Fuge,* is a master from Germany. In the body of the poem, Celan speaks five times of "your golden hair Margareta," a totally unmistakable allusion to Goethe's *Faust.* Like death, Goethe *ist ein Meister aus Deutschland:* the eye of death, of the master from Germany; "it is blue." Death and music, death and the mathematical precision and beauty of the fugue, death and order, composition as act of aesthetic creation, and death as act of creating the super-mensch: Celan's title alone, relentlessly spelled out in the subsequent text, reveals that the music played for the inmates' death marches to the gas chambers is even more the funereal dirge of a culture in *Untergang* which, translated literally, is "going under," into its grave. Celan both undermines and simply annotates: the purely descriptive elements of this poem undermine whatever elevated sense there is about German culture ordering life. This is depicted equally in the gloomy phrase, repeated three times, *"da liegt man nicht eng"* ("there you won't lie too cramped") *(PC,* 31). The same precision that formed Bach's fugues as well as the automobiles of Mercedes-Benz or BMW calculated the "housing" of inmates in those relentless rows of bunks that one may still see today in Auschwitz-Birkenau: there even death happened according to strict rules of order. The "grave shovelled in the air," the "cemetery" of those gassed in the "showers" and reduced in the crematoria to smoke and ashes is, of course, such that no one lies too cramped. But the "order" of the "final resting place" itself collapses here into the disorder of the very "no place" of the air, annulling even the "order" of death.

Finally, what is the object of the first statement cited in this chapter's epigraph: *der Tod ist ein Meister aus Deutschland?* As Felstiner points out, "*Meister* can designate God, Christ, rabbi, teacher, champion, captain, owner, guildsman, master of arts, of theology, labor-camp overseer, musical maestro, 'master' race, not to mention Goethe's *Wilhelm Meister* and Wagner's *Meistersinger von Nürnberg*, which carries overtones of the 1935 Nuremberg racial laws and the post-war trials. Any other choice but 'master' would lose the loaded sense of *Meister*" (*PC*, 39). The sentence is repeated four times in the last thirteen lines—themselves a fugue-like structure. The whole poem is a fugue, and the basic melody line is "death is a master from Germany." The repetition of *der Tod ist ein Meister aus Deutschland* carries those who hear or read it into the thousand darknesses of deathbringing speech.

For me, personally, the darkness of this deathbringing speech looms largest in the final two lines: *"dein goldenes Haar Margarete dein aschenes Haar Sulamith."* Felstiner leaves them untranslated. The golden hair of Margareta, the pure-blooded Aryan woman, is contrasted to the hair of Shulamith, "ashen," turned into ashes. "Instead of a promising Biblical parallelism, the figures of Margareta and Shulamith undercut each other—*dein goldenes Haar . . . dein aschenes Haar*. The German and Jewish ideals will not coexist. . . . Paul Celan's fugue runs out on [the Hebrew] name that resonates as strangely in German as it does in English, and which preempts them both. Darkened by ash, 'Shulamith' ends the poem holding onto what Nazism tried to erase: a rooted identity. Archaic, inalienable, she has the last word, not to mention the silence after" (*PC*, 40–41). Is Felstiner's conclusion true: that German and Jewish ideals will not coexist? Even though the Nazis did not utterly succeed in erasing the rooted identity of Jews, such an identity now does include that rootedness in the graves in the air. And is the silence after the last word the silence imposed by deathbringing speech?

IV

On that desperate morning of May 27, 1096, hundreds of Jews in the city of Mainz, having sought refuge in the Bishop's Court from the approaching hordes of the First Crusade, chose to end their lives *al kiddush hajhem*, "for the sanctity of the divine name." Soon after, in deep despair, a survivor exclaimed, "My eyes dissolve in tears. Torah, now that your wise women and men are gone, who will lift you up?"[8] Eight-and-a-half-centuries later, that question was repeated:

"Torah, who is left to lift you up?" In the presence of that question, Christians need to keep silent, although it is a question that they dare not let disappear from their horizon. A question to which they *do* need to seek the answer sounds more like this: Can entering into the guilt and shame of Christianity's complicity in anti-Judaism and anti-Semitism and its deepest, most horrible abyss in Auschwitz lead Christians to a conversion that may create a new and respectful beholding of Jewish "Otherness" and, in metaphorical language, a new turning toward Jerusalem?

In my epistemological endeavor, I am guided by Dietrich Bonhoeffer's insistence that understanding cannot be separated from the existence at which it was arrived. In addition, my theological hermeneutic was shaped by a small group of German theologians, of whom the poet Erich Fried, anti-fascist, Jew, and refugee from Nazism, once said that the fire that consumed the houses of God, albeit gone out long ago, still burns for them, even though they were not their houses of God.

Once the Christian concepts of repentance and conversion have been freed from the intentionality of sustaining the status quo of dominance, they may assist in the conversion of theology. In the face of the realism painted in Celan's *Todesfuge*, realism in and for theology can only mean turning back, changing ways and thinking on the basis of such turning and changing. In different words, to be converted, theology needs to incorporate anger, abhorrence, revulsion, and shame into its *method* and let them function destructively and constructively within itself. And that means that after it leaves the house of "scientific" and traditional institutionalized theology, its deepest insights may then also become accessible and helpful to the many who sought their new orientation in art rather than in religion.

> What are we to do. . . after Auschwitz? This continues to be the most haunting and, at the same time, the most impotent question. . . . Another question torments us as well: are we really at the place yet where we can discuss practical consequences? Is it not rather that Auschwitz is only just now beginning to enter our consciousness, that particularly we older ones are only just now ready to let the facts of Auschwitz enter our inner being, prepared only just now to look our guilt and complicity in the face? . . . But we do not want to relegate the question of what we

---

8. Hirschhorn, *Tora, wer wird dich nun erheben?*, 11

are to do to the end of the line. We want to begin with it. But we ought to realize that whatever we might possibly do today, after Auschwitz, does not remotely come close to what Auschwitz means for us today. For Auschwitz stands before us as judgment on our Christianity, on the manner of how we were and are Christians; furthermore—seen with the eyes of the victims of Auschwitz—as a judgment of Christianity itself Auschwitz stands before us as a call to conversion. Not only our behaviour is in need of change but our faith itself. In addition to ethical consequences, Auschwitz is to bring about faith consequences. Auschwitz constrains us to hear God's word utterly differently from how we heard it before Auschwitz. . . . What is to be done after Auschwitz presupposes nothing other than our willingness to become aware of what has become in our remembrance of the victims who remained in Auschwitz, what has become of those who, incomprehensibly, escaped the Holocaust with their lives and, finally, what has become of us ourselves, what has happened within ourselves, the people who were and are closer to the perpetrators than to the victims. . . . And that brings us to what Christians can and must do first after Auschwitz. Christians must keep open the wounds. More precisely: they must not blind themselves to the fact that the wounds bleed as before. . . . How long Auschwitz is the present, we do not know. We know only that we must be present to it for as long as it is the present— not only in the memory alone but in its surviving victims and in the daughters and sons marked by their having to survive. Without this, we flee from the present. To keep ourselves equal to the present: that is the first thing we ought to do after Auschwitz.[9]

Todesfuge enables such "capacity for the present" insofar as, through its invocation of "the grave in the air," it firmly holds the hearer and reader before the severe challenge that not everything that happened decades ago is now in the past. Through its concluding juxtaposition of Margareta and Shulamith, of *goldenes* and *aschenes Haar*, "a cord that makes discord, a coda with no closure" *(PC,* 40), it blocks any attempt at cheap and false reconciliation and forgiveness; here, "making up" is unmasked as an ideological weapon of an unconverted and unrepentant status quo. In fact, Celan shows how in themselves these two important theological/religious concepts are a subterfuge when wielded by the dominant elite.

Our century's murders of Jews, what gave rise to and what followed from them for which theology and church are

---

9. Marquardt, *Das Schweigen der Christen und die Menschlichkeit Gottes,* 9.

accountable, are the signs of our times that make every theology utterly questionable in a manner hitherto unknown. . . . Slowly, very slowly there emerges the reflection of how deeply Christians are entangled in guilt as a result of the anti-Judaic elements of the New Testament's preaching of Christ, through the way that preaching was interpreted in the church's dogmas and theologies and how in the course of a millennium and a half the church made practical use of those elements in the Western world and finally, through the church's failure to offer resistance against the crimes that rested on these elements and their interpretation. . . . As the Jews were abandoned, so was the action of divine election, the covenant and faithfulness of the God of Abraham, Isaac, and Jacob, the father of Jesus Christ; God was assaulted and denied in the center of his self-manifestation as the true and living God. But that means that Auschwitz has its own theological dimension. In its existence to date, theology is culpable and subjected to divine affliction. If we seek to remain theologians "before God," theologians before the living God, then we must not retreat before the doubtfulness of the theological enterprise posed by the historically given, concrete signs of our times. And that means: we have to fashion a particular consciousness from that doubtfulness.[10]

Such a consciousness begins when theology incriminates itself with Auschwitz, with what gave rise to and followed from it, and to take upon itself the weight of this incomprehensible and irreparable horror as an element constitutive of both its method and its substance.

Celan's *Todesfuge* rightly awaits the day when the Shoah becomes a component in and of Christian and theological identity. As I see it, a renewed endeavor of relating hermeneutically literature and theology, or in our specific discussion, Celan's *Todesfuge* and a Christian theology that shuns the contentment of the bystanders who saw the boycott of Jewish stores and workshops in April 1933, the passing of the Nuremberg Laws in 1935, and Kristallnacht in November 1938, and knew of the Shoah to which these events led with predictable logic, may perhaps allow theology to hope for something once again, if it may hope at all.

Heinrich Böll's assessment may be true that theology has failed the human being in the sense of holding in bondage and, consequently, dehumanizing the human being. If so, then theology stands indicted and convicted of having aided in eradicating the "traces of the Other," to use Emmanuel Levinas' phrase. The beauty of the others is destroyed by the totalitarian ethic of

---

10. Marquardt, *Von Elend und Heimsuchung der Theologie*, 74.

hierarchy, which ultimately cannot tolerate coexistence with others, whom it understands as alien, hostile, and less than human. But to reduce others to such contemptuous one-dimensionality and then to eliminate them is also to destroy one's own humanity. A theology instrumental in such development and reality may have no hope!

Doing theology "after Auschwitz" means finding a way to recover and restore our humanity, by rediscovering "the Others" as human, as beautiful. It may be that in repentance and conversion we can claim in "the Others" the neighbor, whom to love is to love one just like ourselves, whom to love is to love God, whom to love is to become and remain human.

My teacher, Karl Barth, taught us, his students, that we are human beings when we behold the other human beings and are ourselves, in turn, beheld by them, when we hear them and speak with them, when we stand with them and receive their standing with us. We are human beings when, not in coercion but in gladness, we are free to be and remain the companion of others.

# 17.

The Light of the Torah and the Children of "Hitler's Willing Executioners"

DANIEL JONAH GOLDHAGEN'S BOOK *Hitler's Willing Executioners: Ordinary Germans and the Holocaust*, published in 1996, raised anew, and in an extraordinarily sharp fashion, the justified question of whether German anti-Semitism was (and still is?) something specific to Germans that was preparatory to the Holocaust much more directly than anti-Semitic currents elsewhere. The fierce debate the book created in North America and Germany, which is itself perhaps more than the book itself, intensifies the quest for the theological roots of the "eliminatory" anti-Semitism in Germany which, according to Goldhagen, was the only place where it flourished and, contrary to him, in Christian Europe in general. I experience Goldhagen's challenge particularly acutely because I, born in the Third Reich in central Germany, am a son of an engineer of the large chemical concern IG Farben that played such a crucial role in Auschwitz. Until recently, I lived and worked in Canada at a theological school where I was frequently asked, and asked myself just as often, whether the Christian legacy of my parental home was the legacy of "Hitler's willing executioners."

My road into theology began in that home. Its direction changed abruptly and radically in a manner I could not have anticipated when I read Helmut Gollwitzer's book *Und führen wohin du nicht willst* (ET: *Unwilling Journey. A Diary from Russia*). It contains questions to Christians in Germany that I had never heard before, not to speak of having raised them myself. Should and may the confession of Jesus Christ, should and may Christian theology and the Christian church, go on in our "fatherland" as if the Germany of the National Socialists and its history, including all that it made happen, were simply and finally to be put behind and "shelved"? The neat separation of faith and politics in my parental home collapsed when I encountered Helmut Gollwitzer and with him Karl Barth, an encounter that helped me accept the primacy of biblical theology over dogmatics—at least the liberal dogmatics I had come to love so much at the time. I became "politicized." Was it a coincidence that these two factors came together? But whence the "antenna" with which I embraced those two theologians so avidly?

Eberhard Bethge gave his autobiographical reflections the title: *In Zitz gab es keine Juden* (There were no Jews in Zitz); that title describes my situation admirably. In the various places in Germany where I lived between 1935 and 1949, there were no Jews anymore. My first encounter with Jewish people occurred in Montréal when I was nineteen years old. My family had moved there in the early nineteen-fifties when my father was transferred there by a former IG Farben associate company. The manner Jewish students with whom I was together on a daily basis at McGill University from then on reacted to me made its mark on me. On the one hand, they made it unambiguously clear that they did not think me guilty personally for the terror against Jews but, on the other, and equally unambiguously, that in their view as a native German I was "born guilty" even though they did not know yet of the connection to IG Farben. (I came to know Peter Sichrovsky's phrase "born guilty" only later but I could empathize with much of what he describes.) I was captivated at the time by psychology—a colleague at the University of Minnesota, Patricia Hampl, calls that subject "the claustrophobic subject of this century and somehow *our* science" in her book, *A Romantic Education*—and I applied all those experiences to myself. But over the years the erroneous application taught me that in the liberal-theological stream of the faculty where I was studying I would find neither solution nor resolution. A year of post-graduate studies at the University of Basel and my personal relationship with Karl Barth brought about what I can call only a "conversion." There now was a possibility opening up for me to face the inescapable questions Gollwitzer put to Germany and to Christianity theologically instead of avoiding them altogether. There is an alternative for keeping on keeping on, an alternative to pretending that Hitler and all that is now behind us. A new beginning can be made on an indeed difficult journey and we Germans may also become different human beings.

When Helmut Gollwitzer and Friedrich-Wilhelm Marquardt turned eighty and sixty years respectively in 1988 and many people sent words of gratitude and good wishes, two ancient Hebrew verses helped me formulate my thoughts. "Those close to you, you test; like a father you keep awake their remembering," (Wisdom of Solomon, 11:10) and "Better than a fortress is a brother's protection; better than walls of a castle is that of a friend," (Proverbs, 18:19 in the LXX version). They truly deserved the titles I gave them: "Father Golli" and "Brother-Friend Friedel" both of whom I had come to know personally in 1982. My own father's silence about the recent

THE TORAH AND THE CHILDREN OF "HITLER'S WILLING EXECUTIONERS" 183

past, his "repression" kept me theologically and psychologically in a state of intractability; through him I found no access to that past nor to a different future. "With him I am disabled; in what I must do and be, I am 'fatherless,'" I wrote in the note to Helmut Gollwitzer. His "being-father to me" was particularly evident in a letter he wrote in response to my contribution. There, too, he "tested" me and kept my "remembering awake." He formulated my "intractability" as "a retrospective of a German of your generation from a bourgeois background."[1]

"Father Golli" introduced me to "Brother-Friend Friedel" whose book *Verwegenheiten. Theologische Stücke aus Berlin*[2] holds fast the demands of turning back and the *concrete* utopias they demand in truth and reality. Marquardt achieves this on account of his clarity about the absolute utopia, the necessary and promised new beginning in "setting out—being converted—confessing" (as Karl Barth wrote the evening before he died).[3] "When I speak of my friendship, of sympathy and gratitude for you, Friedrich-Wilhelm (a.k.a. Friedel) I do so out of great joy about a brother in discipleship who has become a friend and also out of great thankfulness for a friend who, on account of his steadfastness stands like a brother with others. And this proves how true Ben Sirach's beautiful statement is: 'A brother-like friend is a consolation of life.'"[4] These Father and Brother-Friend are for me persons for whom "the extinguished flames of the houses of God still burn even when they were not their houses of God," as the poet Erich Fried put it in a text dedicated to Helmut Gollwitzer.

The long detour through matters autobiographical and Dietrich Bonhoeffer's assertion implicit therein that understanding cannot be separated from the existential situation in which it was won, takes me back to Goldhagen's controversial theses that Germany was a land of willing executioners and how that challenges Christians and Germans.

This is not the place to provide more than a brief summary of Goldhagen's thesis. Numerous Germans, including many non-Nazis, many more than researchers were prepared to accept hitherto, brought with them into Hitler's Germany an anti-Semitism that predated 1933, often in very aggressive forms, and had been waiting for an opportunity to translate them into murderous action. Hitler did not have to court them openly but could indeed expect them actively to support him. Taking Tucholsky's juridically

---

1. See "For Helmut Gollwitzer on his Eightieth Birthday."
2. Some of the essays of that volume may be found in *Theological Audacities: Selected Essays*.
3. Busch, *Karl Barth*, 497.
4. Gniewoss, *Störenfriedels Zeddelkasten*, 29.

debatable assertion: "Soldiers are murderers" as a parallel, then Goldhagen's thesis: "Germany—a nation of murderers" is not altogether rash[5]. Even though Goldhagen has rather little to say in relation to the tradition of theological anti-Semitism, especially in German Lutheranism, and what he does say is derived from secondary literature, he nonetheless confronts us with the fact that the Holocaust was possible because, as Peter Haas puts it,[6] a new ethics was at work that declared the arrest and abduction of Jews not to be evil but, on the contrary, ethically acceptable and good. According to both Haas and Goldhagen, the Holocaust corresponded to the collective will of the majority of the population and the church as well. I cannot find anything in my parents' home that would indicate the opposite.

The debate about Goldhagen's book has become a phenomenon *sui generis* not only in Germany. On April 8, 1997, the United States Holocaust Museum in Washington held a major symposium; during it Goldhagen was subjected to a lack of fairness and ill-manneredness to such an extent, that a professor of the Catholic University of Washington protested and apologized to his doctoral students in attendance for having invited them to the event. Even when the conversation refrained from *ad hominem* judgments and stayed with the substance of the meeting, reproach and praise conflicted harshly. In Germany, people already spoke of the "Goldhagen affair" before the book had even been translated. Over one thousand copies of the American edition were sold within two weeks in Germany after it had appeared overseas. Elie Wiesel wrote that the book "makes a significant contribution to the understanding and the study of the Holocaust."[7] Andrei Markovits, at the Institute for European Studies at Harvard University, called it a brilliant book about the most delicate and until this day the most incomprehensible part of recent German as well as European history. At the opposite end, Ernst Jäckel of the University of Stuttgart declared that it is simply a bad book that, according to Professor Hans-Ulrich Wehler at the University of Bochum, operates in terms of a crude dogmatics of interpretation. But Berlin historian Wolfgang Wippermann thinks that Goldhagen has done our country and culture a great service. The Berlin newspaper *tageszeitung* quotes the Canadian sociologist Michal Bodeman and his judgment of the book: "pornography" while *Blätter für deutsche und internationale Politik* awarded Goldhagen the *Demokratiepreis* for 1997. Indeed, an "affair" about the right *answers* and

---

5. I thank Andreas Pangritz for this reference. And see Schoeps, *Ein Volk von Mördern*.

6. Haas, *Morality After Auschwitz*.

7. *The Observer*, March 31, 1996.

much less about what other non-specialists take to be Goldhagen's right *questions*. At any rate, the book was an enormous sales-success. Thousands of people ready for discussion came to Goldhagen events in every German metropolis. Josef Loffe, director of the department for foreign affairs at *Süddeutsche Zeitung*, speaks of "Goldhagen's willing listeners" and the well-known publicist Henry Broder wondered out loud about the "daily growing resistance in Germany against Hitler."[8] Listeners, among whom I count myself in far away Canada, may have asked themselves whether what Karl Jaspers wrote in 1947 was not right after all: it is escapist and a perverse excuse when we Germans try to justify ourselves by referring to the culpability of the whole of humankind. And finally, can one simply reject out of hand Marion Countess Dönhoff's concern that Goldhagen's book could reawaken the more or less subsided anti-Semitism.[9]

In connection with the beautiful verse of Talmud Berachot 17a "May your eyes shine with the light of the Torah" I ask: Does the light of the Torah also light the eyes of the children of Hitler's willing executioners? My question is not only a *question;* it is much more a *prayer* that the light of the Torah may light my, our eyes. In my tormented but also equally promising questions, thoughts like the following find an instant, positive echo:

> What are we to do . . . after Auschwitz? As always this is simultaneously the most haunting and most powerless question. . . . The question does torment us: are we there yet where we can talk about practical consequences? Are we not really only where Auschwitz is only now entering our conscience, where especially we older ones are open to letting the facts of Auschwitz enter our inmost selves, ready only now to face our guilt and complicity? . . . Still, let us not relegate the tormenting question of what we are to do to the bottom of the list. We want to begin with it.
>
> But we must know that whatever we can do at best today after Auschwitz does not even remotely come close to what Auschwitz concerns us today.
>
> For: *Auschwitz concerns us today as a judgment on Christianity,* on the way how we were and are Christian; yes, and more, seen with the eyes of the victims of Auschwitz, Auschwitz concerns us as a judgment on Christianity itself. And Auschwitz concerns us as a call to turn back. Not only our behavior ought to change but our faith itself. Auschwitz ought to lead not only to ethical consequences but also for faith. Auschwitz calls on

---

8. Schoeps, *Ein Volk von Mördern.*
9. *Die Zeit,* September 6, 1996.

us to hear the Word of God utterly differently than we heard it before Auschwitz.

What is to be done after Auschwitz ... presupposes nothing other than that we are willing to know what the victims that did not get out of Auschwitz have become in our memory, what became of those who, incredibly, escaped the Holocaust and, finally, what has become of us, and what in us ourselves, the people who were and are closer to the perpetrators than to their victims.... And this takes us to what Christians can and must do first: *Christians need to keep open the wounds.* More accurately: they must not deny the fact that the wounds are bleeding as before. ... How long Auschwitz will be present reality is something we cannot know. But we do know that we have to be present to it as it stands before as present reality; and not only in memory but in its surviving victims and their daughters and sons marked by their having survived. Without that we flee from the present. The first that we have to do after Auschwitz is to keep ourselves fit for the present.[10]

Marquardt's term "fit for the present" touches me in three ways.

1. On the one hand, remembering signifies the absolutely necessary refusal to hand Hitler victory posthumously by forgetting all about the victims of the Holocaust, as Emil Fackenheim, who became an important teacher for me, puts it. On the other, remembering is one's freely chosen presence to survivors and their children and children's children, a remembering and a presence that does not shun the challenges, including those that Goldhagen draped with scholarly tonality, but lets them stimulate response.

2. Marquardt's term demands that one refuse to be tempted by political, societal, global-market economical and other ideologies and self-interests into accepting that this Hitler and "his" Germany now, more than half a century after its demise, is finally behind us and "overcome." The Goldhagen "debate" tells not only the exact opposite. It unmasks an ideology which by ascribing priority to what it calls the "second" history of Germany, the years of the "communist" republic of east Germany, neatly delivers the time of Hitler's "Third Reich" into oblivion. Robert Leicht put it as follows: "Reunification has indeed answered the German question but not the many questions to the Germans.... Not everything that has happened has faded away."[11] It would appear

---

10. Marquardt, *Das Schweigen der Christen und die Menschlichkeit Gottes*, 9–15.
11. *Die Zeit,* September 6, 1996.

that Goldhagen himself has fallen prey to a similar self-delusion in his insistence that anti-Semitism has disappeared in the part of Germany that orients itself by the American West. In an interview with Dinitia Smith, he said that the Germans there are "like us," the Americans. I can take his questions to me and to my compatriots seriously only when I ignore such and similar statements.

3. Marquardt's term helps in noticing that with the fall of the Third Reich a particular theology has lost integrity and that there has to be a search for a wholly other theology. That also means that false and deceptive reconciliation, as the South African Kairos Document describes it, and forgiveness in the sense of *Wiedergutmachung*, compensation, deserve only to be rejected completely. In other words: being fit for the present means to strive for the conversion of theology in theology.

Friedel Marquardt calls such striving for the conversion of theology *Elend und Heimsuchung der Theologie*—The Wretchedness and Affliction of Theology—the prelude to his encouraging dogmatics.

> The murder of Jews in our century and the presuppositions and consequences thereof that theology and church have to answer for, are now the signals that render every theology questionable in a hitherto unknown radical manner. . . . Slowly, very slowly Christians begin to grasp how deeply enmeshed they are in guilt on account of anti-Jewish elements in their proclamation of Christ, in their interpretation of dogmas and their theologies of church, in the practical use the church made use of those elements millennia in the Western world and, finally, in their defenseless passivity that built on all this.[12] Faced with their historical culpability, Christians cannot take refuge in general theories of providence nor in what Karl Jaspers called "general culpability of all humankind." . . . As Jews were abandoned, the electing action, the covenant and the faithfulness of the God of Abraham, Isaac and Jacob, the Father of Jesus Christ were also abandoned and God was attacked in God's self-manifestation as true and living God and denied.
>
> Thus, Auschwitz has its own theological dimension. . . . In its existence up to this day, theology is burdened with guilt and has become an arena of affliction (*Heimsuchung*). If we seek to remain theologians "before God," theologians before the real God, we dare not ignore the questionability of the theological

---

12. Marquardt is the first theologian I know of who, as a Christian, is prepared to give public expression of despairing in the possibility of speaking of God and to make that methodologically a part in the formulation of dogmatics.

venture under the historically concrete signs of our time. And that means that we have to create a specific consciousness of that questionability.[13]

(And, finally, this striking assertion): "*Realismus heute bedeutet für mich Umkehr und Denken aus der Umkehr;*" Today realism for me means to turn back and to think on the basis of that turning.[14]

Marquardt and Martin Stöhr describe exactly what they call the "conversion of theology."[15] Among the many questions to be posed to Germans, in particular but not only to the theology and the church of Germans, is the sharp question of Daniel Goldhagen: Is German anti-Semitism not something specific that prepared for the Holocaust in a much more direct fashion than the anti-Semitic movements elsewhere? I hear that question as one from a Jew who still bears a burden who rightly still waits for us Christians and Germans, and us theologians, to begin to *burden* ourselves with "Auschwitz, its presuppositions and consequences and take upon ourselves the weight of this incomprehensible and never to be got over misery as an element" of our Christian, German and theological existence.[16]

When Friedrich-Wilhelm Marquardt includes despairing of theology and locates it hermeneutically into the "method" of his theological thinking, it does not mean that he has doubts about theology. But he knows that a theology that turns back will experience blessing (*Zuspruch*) and challenge (*Anspruch*) or in his own beautiful phrasing: a theology that turns back may hope for something if it may hope at all. The reply to the question: "What may we hope for if we may hope?" that he asks is, in connection with the challenge of Goldhagen, that the light of the Torah may—and even will—shine in our eyes too.

---

13. Marquardt quotes from a letter by H. J. Iwand, in 1959, to Josef L. Hromádka.
14. Marquardt, *Von Elend und Heimsuchung der Theologie*, 74-80.
15. Stöhr, in *Dreinreden*, 290-314.
16. Marquardt, *Eia, wärn wir da—eine theologische Utopie*, 577.

18.

Teaching the Next Generation

The Son of a Perpetrator Reflects

LET ME AT THE outset of my reflection express to you, as best as I can, even though I can articulate only inadequately what being in your midst on this day means to me, how powerfully moving, indeed, redeeming it is for me to address your Yom HaShoah commemoration. That a child of Nazi Germany, the son of an industrialist complicit in the machinery of the extermination of Jews, that a member of a church and a religion that nurtured anti-Judaism and anti-Semitism, that a person such as that is not only invited to be present to this commemoration of the children, women and men, the aged, whose murder his country, his fellow-citizens planned and then brutally, meticulously carried out, but should be the speaker at a moment of such significance, this is, from my perspective, comprehensible only as an act of magnificent humanity. I am in your debt, shall remain in your debt and, on my road toward the healing—if such is even possible—of the relation between Jews and Germans, I shall not walk without the gift of your presence to me.

The door through which I enter into my reflections is part of the essay-contest of the college this year. It is embodied in words of an ancient Hebrew prophet, Joel by name, who said, "Has anything of this sort happened in your days or in the days of your forebears? Tell your children about it, let them tell their children, and their children to the next generation" (1:2–3). A clear commandment is being uttered by that man to his generation some 2400 years ago, a commandment to remember and then to keep this memory alive in generations to come. Joel was not the first, nor was he the last, to utter that commandment.

The first time in my life I was given such a commandment in its specific connection with the Shoah was in the mid-sixties of the last century. I had moved with my family to the city of Toronto in Canada, where the largest number of Holocaust survivors in Canada live. One of those survivors was the late professor of philosophy at the University of Toronto, Rabbi Emil Fackenheim. Like me, he was born in Germany but, unlike me, had his citizenship and all his civil rights revoked, was marked "Jude"—Jew—and thus labeled "a danger to Germany" because of his being Jewish, was captured, sent to concentration camp, released and finally found refuge in Canada. At dinner one evening at a mutual friend's home I heard for the first time Fackenheim's phrasing of what he called "the 614th commandment": There is a commanding voice rising from Auschwitz: Do not give Hitler posthumous victory! His words stunned me; never had I heard anything like that before. He elaborated what that commandment meant to him. I shall mention two of his points only. Hitler's aim had been to eradicate Jews physically and, thereby, also eradicate them and their legacy from the memory of Europeans. Not to remember Hitler's Jewish victims would, therefore, contribute to Hitler's aim even after his ignominious death and the ruinous defeat of the Aryan Reich. Secondly, Hitler had a theological or religious aim for which he could draw on Christianity's centuries-old, persistent and nearly always pernicious anti-Judaism. I shall use words of the great Jewish teacher Rashi of Worms (1040–1105 C.E.). Aggrieved by the massacres committed at the outset of the First Crusade in 1095 C.E. against the Jewish population of the towns of Worms and Speyer, and after nearly all of the Jewish community in the town of Mainz voluntarily entered death *al kiddush hashem*—for the sanctification of the divine name—in 1096 C.E. before the 12,000 or so crusaders had the chance to "avenge the death of their Redeemer" in their religious fury, Rashi wrote, "When Israel will no longer exist to sing your praises, then your name will vanish from every mouth and throat." Indeed, one of the few Jews of Mainz, who did not go to death with his fellow Jews, was to write a few months later—his name was Eliezer ben Nathan—"Torah, who will now lift you up high?" That the Torah would not be lifted up high ever again and that the name of the God of Abraham and Sarah, Rebecca and Isaac, Israel and Rachel would cease to be praised, that, too, was Hitler's aim. "Do not give Hitler posthumous victory!" is what, in Fackenheim's words, is commanded to us, our children and our children's children. Remember!—tell!—teach!—learn! And thus defeat those aims of one who professed his own blasphemous, idolatrous religion. Emil Fackenheim and, with him, other rabbis: Richard Rubenstein and Irving Greenberg, and many other generous Jewish persons, like Barbara Appelbaum, Professor Barbara Lovenheim and Angie Suss Paul, all of this city of Rochester, have walked with me, supporting, counseling, consoling. They all have what is so well described in the Book of Proverbs, in the remarkable translation known as the Septuagint: Better than a fortified city a brother, a sister protects you; like the lock of a fortress is the friend" (18:19). In my efforts to remember and to understand, to tell of what I know and to prevent that knowledge from falling into oblivion, these persons and others have become, in the words of another biblical book, "a father, a mother who test me and who keep my memory awake because they are close to me" (The Wisdom of Solomon 11:10).

My father and mother, however, did not seek to keep awake the memory of the Shoah. What they knew they did not tell me; when asked they replied: we did not know. Dad and Mum were devout Christians, loving and caring parents to us, their children, upright citizens of Germany and, later, of Canada. Father held an upper-middle-level executive position in the powerful industrial conglomerate known as IG Farben. From 1941 to early 1945 he had oversight of the chemical industries of France and the Low Countries and, after the Allied invasion in June 1944, Poland and Czechoslovakia. He knew from that work the extensive use of forced labor by IG Farben in its factories. Before the German conquest of Western Europe, he had worked in a factory near Leipzig where gasoline and rubber were produced by means of synthetic processes. The factory that was built in Auschwitz-Monowitz to produce those same products drew for its workers on the concentration/extermination camps that we know by the name Auschwitz. The expertise developed in the factory in Leuna near Leipzig was transferred to the new factory, including the man in charge in Monowitz: Dr. Walter Dürrfeld, a close friend of our family in Leuna, the town where I was born. The concentration camp in Auschwitz provided plenty of cheap labor, enough to have the administrative office of Monowitz calculate how many calories workers needed a day to stay alive and keep working for three to four months; after that, given the plentiful supply of replacement workers, they could be left to die, that is, to be gassed. My father knew of that forced labor workforce; his industry worked in close cooperation with the SS. IG Farben supplied building materials for the concentration camp at Auschwitz-Birkenau in order to accelerate the construction of the factory. It also paid the SS three marks (RM) a day for each manual worker and four RM for each specialized one. They had to work ten to eleven hours a day in the summer and a minimum of nine in the winter. Eventually, IG Farben built its own camp at Monowitz to have its workers closer at hand and not have to transport them every day from Birkenau Camp and back. My father's industry invested five million RM in that camp: the first concentration camp initiated and financed by a private company! The medical facilities were deliberately kept small so that sick workers could be eliminated rather than cared for. There was a mutual agreement between the factory administration, headed by our family friend Walter Dürrfeld, and the SS that all "weak inmates were to be got rid of," meaning a one-way trip to the gas-ovens of Auschwitz-Birkenau. IG Farben determined that no more than six to seven percent of the workforce could be declared "weak": regular selections assured that all beyond that figure were gassed. The reason for that low figure was that the industry was not willing to pay the SS the daily rate for "weak" workers. Dürrfeld, whom I knew to be a loving husband and father, a man of intelligence and hard working, was present at those selections and assisted in them. He, however, was interested in keeping workers in order to get the construction job completed speedily. Still, forcing workers in a weakened state also meant certain death—by exhaustion, the beatings and torture they were subjected to. Asking one day what was being done with those selected as "too weak to work," an SS man by the name of Schoettl said: They're going to our obligatory commando called 'ascent into heaven.'" Dürrfeld knew what that meant. Of the 35,000 inmates that were forced by my father's company into slave labor at Monowitz, 25,000 or as many as 30,000 were victims of the "extermination trough labor," practiced by that name by IG Farben.

As far as I can determine, Father was at the Monowitz installations once; I am not aware of any participation on his part in the selections or in any direct action to have a slave worker "destroyed."

I began to ask questions about Jews, the camps and the forced labor squadrons, which I saw as a boy of eight and nine in my home town, after I began to study theology. I had begun reading German theologians who raised the subject of the guilt of Germans and especially of the churches and their silence in connection with the Holocaust. By that time, my family and I had already been ten years in Canada. I had Jewish classmates and friends. So, I asked my parents about this and heard the same reply: we did not know. But I kept asking until one day my mother took me aside and said that I had to stop this because I was making father very upset with my probing. I immediately went to see him and said that my quest was not to determine guilt, to judge him but, rather, to find out whether I, too, had inherited values that could allow such a duality as was manifest in many Germans and Christians: hard workers, loving parents, upright citizens, regular church attendees and lovers of culture, on the one hand, and participants in the destruction of human beings, in the extermination of Jews in particular, looking on them as sub-humans, on the other. My question was and still is: What is in me of them that taught me my values? I then told Father what I had come to conclude: in Hitler's Germany, Germans knew as much or as little as they wanted to know. What they did not know, they did not want to know. But they always knew enough to know that they did not want to know any more. He became very angry, so much so that I was scared. He said after a moment or two that if I ever raised the subject again our relationship was over. I gave him my word that I would never do so again, a promise that I have kept until his death in 1991. But I have had to live my relationship of love for Dad ever since knowing that he knew but was not going to tell me anything.

There is an important book that Barbara Appelbaum drew to my attention recently. It is by Mona Sue Weissmark, entitled *Justice Matters: Legacies of the Holocaust and World War II*,[1] published by Oxford University Press in 2004. In it, the author describes and analyzes an "experiment" of bringing together children of Holocaust survivors and children of Nazis. She wanted to see how the intersection of their pasts and the painful legacy history has put on them works out. What happens when children of victims come face to face with children of those who had made them victims? For me the question of why victims and perpetrators so very often don't speak of what they experienced or know to their children is essential.

In an autobiographical section—Weissmark is herself the daughter of parents who survived Auschwitz, Dachau, and Buchenwald—describes how her mother, after much, much hesitating, would answer questions about the Holocaust and her own experiences in it, would provide details and then abruptly say: Enough already with the questions. We have to do things now. I now quote directly: "... [I was] trying to manage the horrors that contained my mother's and father's history. I wanted to hear more, but as usual, my mother pushed aside the past for what was, for her, the far more important task of making sure it didn't intrude my childhood."[2] But the past was always there nonetheless, crying out for an answer.

Looking back, I recognize a similar feature in my parents. I believe that inwardly they acknowledged the burden that rests on Germans as a result of the Holocaust and their complicity, however direct or indirect, in it. Their desire for their children to grow up without that burden, to mature into productive, moral and cultural adults, held them back from letting us into what they knew. And so, that perhaps laudable parental attribute stopped them from doing what Joel commands, "Tell your children about it, let them tell their children, and their children the next generation." But there is more to it than that. Mum and Dad, too, wanted to get on with their lives in the post-war world without the dread of air raids, hunger, cold, police surveillance and, instead, with the joy, calm and harmony of family life, children, grandchildren, and all that meant pushing into non-remembrance, into oblivion, the abyss of recent Germany, the Hitler past.

It was up to me to search that abyss, face it and enter it. My mother died in 1972; at that time I lived with my spouse and our children in Windsor,

1. Weissman, *Justice Matters*.
2. Ibid., 4.

Ontario, across the river from Detroit. My wife Barbara and I had established a pretty close relationship with the Jewish community there. Several friends paid tribute (as I want to put it) to Barbara, my late partner-in-marriage, and me by having several trees planted in memory of my mother in Israel. That gesture deeply moved me, yet I did not tell Father about it, not knowing how he would respond. But here is where I find a direct personal application of Joel's question, "Has anything of this sort happened in your days or in the days of your forebears?" The answer is NO, it has never happened before in my family. Those trees now join the ancient prophet and his commandment to tell the children so that they will tell it to theirs. In January 2003, we lost Barbara; cancer, that cruel, cruel enemy, took her from the side of me, our children and our grandchildren. Peter, our oldest son, works in a law-firm in Nova Scotia; several of his law-partners are Jews. They attended the memorial service for Barbara; some days later, they told Peter that trees were being planted in Israel in memory of his mother.

From the land where Joel lived, the land where Abraham and Sarah, Rebecca and Isaac, Israel and Rachel were at home, from the very soil in which Jewish existence is rooted, irrespective of where Jewish feet walk, from there comes the commandment to me that Emil Fackenheim phrased, "Do not give Hitler posthumous victory!" Remember! Do not act as if the Hitler past is now over and done with, to be forgotten. Speak, so that a new beginning can be made on a road that is, indeed, difficult. Speak, so that—now directly related to me, my church, my people—we may become different. Speak, remember, speak again, remember anew so that a conversion, and with it renewal, is made possible.

To you all, present here today in this college, this city, I am grateful. The ancient sage Jesus-ben-Sirach once said, "The brotherly/sisterly friend is one of life's consolations." I want to tell you, my sisterly/brotherly friends that your presence now and here, but also in times and places to come is, indeed, consolation, encouragement and inspiration to go on the labors of memory.

19.

White-Collar Crimes Against Humanity

The IG Farben Auschwitz Story

LADIES AND GENTLEMEN,

It is an honor for me to be in your presence tonight and to have the privilege of looking with you at one aspect of the abyss of the darkness associated with what we commonly refer to as "the Holocaust" or "the Shoah." I am grateful in many ways and for a number of reasons which, I hope, will become clear in the course of my presentation, that I may be here with you. But at this point I want to say a particular word of thanks to Professor Richard Rubinstein who, as a mentor, critic, and friend, has enriched my life in many ways. His late partner-in-marriage, Dr. Betty Rogers Rubinstein, and he have been instrumental in giving my own confrontation, as a German and the child of parents complicit in the Nazis' assault on European Jewry, both foundation and direction. I would like to express this in different words drawn from sacred scripture: "You put to the test those close to you and, like a father, you keep memory awake in them," and "Better than a fortified city does a brother protect, like the bars of a castles is a friend" (Wisdom of Solomon 11:10 and Proverbs 18:10 respectively, in the Septuagint translation). Thank you, Richard.

My presentation is in three parts: In the first part I will tell you in terms of autobiography how this German, born during the reign of Hitler, learned to face his country's, his church's, and his family's involvement and complicity in that darkness. The second part is to present something about my father's employer, IG Farben, and its place in Hitler's politics and war. The third part addresses directly the factory and camp of IG Auschwitz. A conclusion will sum up where the road of confronting the Holocaust has and is still taking me.

III. AFTER THE SHOAH

I

I lead into this part with something I read in the *Harvard Divinity Bulletin*:[1] In the article entitled "An American Jew in Poland: Grappling with a tragic living history," author Jordie Gerson, former Hillel Campus Rabbi at Yale and University of Vermont, describes a trip to Poland of a group of American, German, and Polish graduate students; they visited Warsaw, Lublin, and Majdanek. Close to the end of their stay, Gerson had a conversation with one of the Germans. Descending from the mausoleum in the Majdanek camp, he says to her: "My people, the Germans did this. . . . The Jewish people lost their lives here, but we, the Germans, we lost our dignity." Later, now among themselves, the American Jewish students debrief in a pub with, as Gerson adds, a lot of Vodka; one of the professors, called Yoki, asks them: "You know what a Hasidic rabbi once said about the Shoah? . . . He said: "It could have been worse. We could have been the murderers."

As a German I cannot and should not speak about the substance of the Hasidic rabbi's words; but I can speak about the German's statement; in fact, make it mine: My people, my church, my family, we did the "worse," we were complicit in the extermination of Jews, we were the murderers.

I was born in 1935, three weeks before the promulgation of the Nuremberg laws, at that time the climax of the Nazis' disenfranchisement of Jews in Germany. Hitler was at the height of his popularity among my fellow Germans but was also admired, even hailed, in Great Britain, France, and the United States, to name just a few countries. Unemployment was a thing of the Weimar Republic; the shame of the Versailles Treaty after World War I had been erased; industry was working at full capacity; the country's armed forces were formidable once again; in one word: We Germans felt that we were "somebody" in the world again, thanks to Hitler. He had made Germany "great again."

My father, born in 1900, was conscripted in 1918 and saw some action in Serbia. After World War I, he entered university and graduated with a PhD in chemistry in 1927; he was hired immediately by IG Farben as a researcher in the company's Leuna factory, where fuels, rubber, medicines, as well as plastics were produced synthetically. The war had severely curtailed Germany's imports of crude oil and natural India rubber. IG Farben had developed processes that produced those and other materials, such as nitrates, that eventually became essential for military purposes. Among dye stuffs, medical products, chemical fertilizers, a company that would eventually become part of IG Farben also produced the poison gas that was used on the

---

1. Gerson, "An American Jew in Poland," 10–11.

Western front during World War I. My father worked for IG Farben from 1927 until his retirement in 1965; his firm provided his pension income until his death in 1991. After the fall of France in 1941 in World War II, IG Farben persuaded the Nazi government that it alone had the competency to run the chemical industries in the countries Germany had occupied: France, Belgium, and Holland, in Western Europe as well as those in the East. My father was part of the group that took charge of those industries in the West, being in charge meant annexing them and putting them into service for the German military operations and readying them for the "thousand-year Reich" and for competitiveness in the anticipated world market once the war was won. Father's office was in Paris from early 1942 until after the Allies' landing in Normandy in mid-1944. During those years, we saw relatively little of him as well as during the twelve months when the American, British, and Canadian air forces flew twenty-eight major bombing raids on Leuna; 6,552 allied bombers dropped a total of 18,000 tons of explosives on Leuna, also killing a large number of the forced laborers working in Leuna. By April 4, 1945, the factory ceased to function completely.

I grew up in a devout Christian home; I have no recollection of ever hearing at that time any anti-Semitic expressions from my parents; by 1935, Leuna was *judenrein*—any Jews who had lived there or worked for IG Farben had left either voluntarily or else had been forced out. It was at school that I heard the anti-Semitic stuff the Nazis wanted us to learn; in church anti-Judaism was joined with anti-Semitism. I absorbed it and that stuff became part of my mental frame of reference. My home was silent about anti-Semitism and anti-Judaism. One day our teacher, a Nazi, who wore his brown shirt and Swastika armband fairly regularly, had instructed us that we were to tell him if we ever heard anything critical about Hitler or favorable about Jews; once at home, I told this to my mother. She probably decided to keep what she thought about all this to herself lest she endanger not only us at home but also my father, who in his executive position was much more exposed. But it could also be because her Christianity clearly held faith and politics well apart that she kept silent. My conclusion, many years later, was that my parents were what I call "away-lookers," a term I prefer to "bystanders."

I did not know any Jewish person until I was eighteen-years-old, one year after we had left Europe for Canada where IG Farben, no longer known then by that name but in essence alive in its subsidiaries, had set up office in order to continue its work in North America that had begun in the mid-nineteen-twenties, chiefly in New Jersey. Montréal has a vibrant Jewish population and a large number of Holocaust survivors. At McGill University, I began to meet Jews and had to unlearn, as I made more and more contact with them, all the negative stuff about Jews my school, country, and church had instilled into me. Eventually I had a wonderful relationship with a Jewish woman; it was that relationship that—after the following incident—set my feet onto the long and excruciating road of confronting my anti-Semitism and anti-Judaism. I wanted to bring Sally home to meet my parents; the occasion was one of our family's happy New Year's Eve parties at home. I spoke to Mum and Dad about her; after a while my father said *"Du bringst uns doch keine Jüdin ins Haus!"*—You're not bringing a Jewish woman into our house, are you? That day, well over a decade after the end of the Nazi years, I discovered that anti-Semitism is a poison that has longevity. I wondered whether I also had it lurking inside me still. The relationship with Sally ended because I feared that I could possibly hurt her badly were it to erupt from me when I held her in my arms. I carry the hurt of the break with her still this day.

Among my father's colleagues was someone with whom more than a relationship between colleagues developed; that man's family and ours shared a friendship that lasted beyond the end of World War II. Our families exchanged visits to each other's homes. The last time I saw Mr. Dürrfeld and some of his children was in 1958 at his home in the Ruhr River area in West Germany; he was then a member of the executive board of one of IG Farben's subsidiaries. The same year my father graduated with a PhD, Walter Dürrfeld graduated with a PhD in Mechanical Engineering and was also immediately hired by IG Farben and sent to Leuna. In 1941, he was placed in charge of constructing IG Auschwitz-Monowitz. It was planned to be the largest of the company's numerous factories. More about him part III.

II

What was IG Farben? A general sketch has to suffice for now.

My first direct experience of the IG's diverse factories was in Leuna from 1935 to 1945 where we had to put up with the environmentally utterly unfriendly chemical emissions, particularly those of the production of synthetic fuels. We lived about three quarters of a mile from the factory in the town that neighboring communities irreverently dubbed "the stink pot." Then from mid-1945 to late 1946 we lived near Nordhausen, in the Harz Mountains region, where IG Farben was mining the raw material for its nitrate products: explosives and chemical fertilizer. On the grounds of that factory was the mountain in which two major German war industries were producing the so-called "miracle weapons" of Germany: the Junkers jet fighter planes, and rocket-propelled ballistic missiles (Wernher von

Braun's brain child). At first the Americans and then, in August 1945, the Russians were busy removing whatever they could of those installations for their own use; what we saw were the forced laborers who had survived the dreadful exploitation and extermination by the German officials. My father was on the list of German industrialists to be taken to the Soviet Union; we managed to escape for Western Germany in December 1946. Two of my uncles served as managers in industries that provided raw materials for the chemical sector of IG Farben; one of them later became my stepfather.

In the 1880s an American named Goodyear developed vulcanized India rubber and an Irishman named Dunlop used it to make inflatable tires. As the car industry expanded, the demand for India rubber grew exponentially and the German chemical industry explored the possibility of producing synthetic rubber tires. Three German firms got together and joined with Continental Rubber to make tires. Four years later, when World War I had broken out, the German imperial government ordered tires for the army and that meant that new facilities had to be built. The step into war production had been taken; the firm of Bayer, the makers of Aspirin, anchored that development. But even before that war, some people were thinking of a closer alliance of the big chemical firms: Bayer, BASF, Hoechst, and Agfa;[2] the war gave the impetus for fusing the companies and expanding their factories. As a result of the war, they had lost large parts of their external markets and after the war, German industry realized that its prewar position in world markets was lost. Those developments caused the birth of IG Farben in 1925. It became the second biggest German enterprise behind Germany's United Steelworks. It had 155,000 employees and became the fourth largest of the significant chemical concerns of the world next to Dupont, Imperial Chemical Industries, and Allied Chemical and Dye Corporation. Next to fuels and rubber, IG produced nearly all dyes made in Germany, fertilizers, magnesium, pharmaceuticals and polymer-chemical products. IG Farben cooperated with a number of American companies, giving them licenses to produce IG Farben-patented materials; among those US companies were Standard Oil and Dupont. The latter honored its agreement with IG even during World War II, making the requisite payments into Swiss bank accounts.

Things developed rapidly in 1933, after Hitler's assumption of power in January that year. The German government wanted to become as independent as possible of imports of raw materials, seeking to meet needs via synthetic processes. Research in relation to synthetic rubber went into high

---

2. Farbenfabrikenwerke Bayer; *Badische Anilin-und Sodafabrik*; *Farbwerke Hoechst*; *Ag für Anilinfabrikation*.

gear as did the demand for tires that could withstand the tough conditions of military operations; production of 72,000 tons a year was demanded of IG Farben who then began thinking about building a new factory to meet that order. Something interesting took place then: in 1935 Hitler threatened IG Farben that, should the company be unwilling to produce the demanded amount of synthetic rubber quickly, he would "order" that the new factory would be constructed, but not by IG Farben. IG feared that it would lose its monopoly and agreed to invest a huge amount of its own resources into that project. At the same time, Hitler also pushed IG into tripling its production of fuels, but for that he gave the company a sweetheart deal. One of the three envisaged rubber producing factories was to be built close to the Leuna works. All this meant a continually deepening dependence of Hitler's government on IG Farben and IG Farben's on his government. Pressure was exerted on IG Farben's executives to join the Nazi Party; a large part of the upper echelon managers joined in the Spring of 1937. Among them was our nearby neighbor in Leuna, Dr. Christian Schneider, whom I saw fairly often in Leuna's swimming pools with his family. The names of other executive members I remember my father mentioning at home were Carl Krauch, IG Farben's chief liaison with Berlin, Heinrich Bütefisch, Otto Ambros, Walter Dürrfeld, all of whom played significant roles in relation to IG Auschwitz.

The idea of the Auschwitz location occurred to Friedrich ter Meer, chair of the IG board, after the 1938 Munich Conference at which Britain and France had acceded to Hitler's demand to "bring the Sudetenland home into the Reich." And, wouldn't you know, one of that country's largest companies was located in that part of Czechoslovakia: the Aussig Verein, Europe's fourth-largest chemical firm; it could surely also be "incorporated" into IG Farben and so it was. This was yet another factor that drew IG Farben into Hitler's militarization and war efforts.

Another thing needs to be mentioned: the fusion of profit and politics.[3] We have already noted the fusion of IG Farben profit and Hitler's military aims. Here the term politics refers to the Nazis' *Drang nach Osten*, the drive toward the East and the envisaged enlargement of *Lebensraum* for Germany. After the rapid conquest of Poland in September 1939, IG management looked on that country as the new great manufacturing base for IG and planned, together with the minister for economic expansion, the "economic development of the Eastern region." Expansion of industry eastwards implied growth of German settlements there. An industrial complex as envisaged by IG Farben and the concomitant expansion of Germans eastward would mean establishing a bulwark of German culture and ethnicity.

3. See Wagner, *IG Auschwitz*, 37.

At the IG board meeting of January 11, 1941, Otto Ambros proposed that the factory be built in Oświęcim, Auschwitz in German, and presented a favorable report prepared about that location by another of my father's Leuna colleagues, Josenhans (with whose spouse my mother worked as a nurse's aide.) The envisaged area had a sufficient water supply, was safe from flooding, and its even ground made it ideal for constructing the factory and offered room for possible expansion. The town of Oświęcim was not much to write home about; its 7,000 Poles and 4,000 Jews could be expelled to make room for German workers, as there was a concentration camp for Jews and Poles nearby; every German who comes here is a colonist. During the meeting, the camp we know as Auschwitz One was mentioned as a source of workers for the construction of the factory: The seed for industrializing the extermination of Jews had been planted! It was decided that Jews were to be kept in the Auschwitz concentration camp as potential workers rather than have them sent to other places. Josenhans' report states that according to SS chief Himmler, the camp was to be enlarged so that the inmates could be available for IG Farben's plans. The board decided formally on February 6, 1941, to build IG Auschwitz-Monowitz, also called Auschwitz III, and to draw on the camp for its "ordinary" workers. The decision made Himmler an integral part of the IG Farben project: His and Hitler's plans to create the larger living space for Germans in the East meshed neatly with their determination to destroy the European Jewry in the plan of a private company to build a factory that would meet both the needs of the Nazis' racial and military politics while serving the company's need for profit.

Himmler was ecstatic because for some time he had wanted to interest private enterprise in the labor-potential of "his" camps. Very soon after the IG board had made its decision, he went to Auschwitz I and ordered the camp's commandant Rudolf Höss to enlarge it to accommodate 30,000 inmates, 10,000 of whom were to be at IG Farben's disposal. In addition, a prisoner-of-war camp was to be built near the village of Birkenau with room for 100,000 prisoners. That camp is known also as Auschwitz II. The SS contact person was Karl Wolff and the IG Farben's was my father's colleague Heinrich Bütefisch, himself a member of the SS since 1939. In 1941, our Leuna neighbor Christian Schneider appointed Walter Dürrfeld technical director and in 1944 chief executive of the entire project.

In order to assure that a sufficient workforce was always available to IG, the firm agreed to make building materials available to the SS for its planned construction of Auschwitz II. By 1941, such materials were very hard to come by as nearly all of it was needed by the armed forces. A memorandum dated April 5, 1941, states that only with the support of that camp could IG begin planning and building the factory. The SS immediately transferred inmates from other camps to Auschwitz II. It is accurate to state that without the materials IG Farben made available to the SS, the extermination camp Auschwitz-Birkenau would have come into existence only much later, if at all.

At the official ground-breaking ceremony of the Monowitz-factory, Otto Ambros praised the project as "a model of the German colonization of the East," made possible, as he wrote a few days later, through the beneficial cooperation of the SS. The town of Oświęcim was cleared of its population and "relocated" to camp Auschwitz I and construction began on April 21, 1941, one day after Hitler's birthday, in the area where the village of Monowitz had been before it was razed to make room for IG Farben's huge project.

III

The white-collar crimes against humanity to be addressed now differ from those committed in Auschwitz-Birkenau in that no gas chambers and Cyclone B gas were used in the process of "the extermination of inmates through labor." What that camp and the IG complex had in common was that, as Jean Améry puts it, the inmates' highest duty was to die; the destruction of Jews was just as much an aim at IG Auschwitz-Monowitz as it was at Birkenau.

Many historians speak of the inhumane treatment of the inmate workforce as "slave labor," e.g. Daniel Goldhagen. I do not use that term, preferring "forced labor." The term "slave" is inappropriate for the inmate workers at IG Auschwitz. The inmates were not slaves, they did not perform slave labor and the people of IG Farben were not slave owners. A comparison to the slavery in the United States is helpful here. A slave holder invests in the energy resources of the workers in order to reap maximum profit from them; a minimum of the essentials for life have to be provided in order to assure optimal and long-lasting interest yield on invested capital. But the SS was in no way interested in keeping inmates alive and its primary aim was not financial profit. Precisely because the issue for the SS was ultimately the destruction and not the economic exploitation of Jewish inmates, their life expectancy under the conditions of forced labor could be as low as a few months and, as happened when the tens of thousands of Jews of Hungary arrived beginning in May and June 1944, a few weeks. To describe "extermination through labor" as slave labor is tantamount to an apology of both SS and IG Farben.

Among the diverse components that make up the white-collar crimes against humanity committed by IG Monowitz, I would like to look more extensively at the so-called "care" of the sick and the process of selection associated with it.

I begin with the housing of the Monowitz camp inmate work force. A regular block-building housed 168 sleeping places in the now familiar two- or three-decker wooden structures. At least two, at times even more bodies had to share one sleeping place. Given that there were no separate eating or living facilities in those buildings, the deliberately planned scarcity of space became ever more aggravated: One's half or third of the bed was not only where one slept but also where one ate and tried to dry one's wet clothing during rainy or snowy weather. The stench that filled the entire block heightened the feeling of claustrophobia. The air was unbearable: bodies reeking of sweat that had not seen soap or water for weeks on end, filthy clothing that could be changed only every six to eight weeks, the odors of inmates sick with diarrhea or other infectious diseases or with open wounds, and all that compounded by the stench of the urinals placed near the doors. Even with the windows open, inmates would experience lack of oxygen during the night losing even more sleep, thus getting little if any recovery of energy for the next day. As one can imagine, the risk of infection was not only very high but also part of the desired destruction of inmates. The SS doctors, alert to the high danger of infectious diseases spreading to the whole work force, warned the Monowitz management of this only to be rebuffed: there was to be no further investment in inmates unable to work. The food made available for the inmates wasn't conducive to providing the energy required for construction work: The so-called "Buna-soup" was a kind of ready-to-cook instant soup (as we would call it today) with a few onions or something of similar taste; since fat was hard to come by the soup was "fat-free." Some of the office personnel reported that the soup was a thin liquid with vegetable leftovers or potato peels and wood shavings. Walter Dürrfeld is said to have tasted this soup in the presence of inmates, presumable to assuage his conscience, but he could not persuade even his driver to try this revolting concoction. Given the meager calorie intake, the average weight loss of a forced laborer was between four and nine pounds a week. Here is a picture of how that impacted on the work inmates had to do: There was much concrete-construction for the building material which arrived by train; 120 workers had to unload 40 rail-cars in the span of three hours, lugging the 100-pound bags on the double from the station to the construction site. Often those bags weighed more than the man lugging it. And then, even when it was 30- to 35-degrees below zero, no decent clothing for such weather and work was provided. When inmates tried to warm up, they were driven back to work with beatings for, so the argument went, every minute used to revive one's frozen body was costing IG Farben more money. The inmates had nothing but economic value; under the existing conditions they had worn themselves out but that was of no interest to the company my father worked for. The IG left the worn-out human beings to the SS for "disposal": trucks hauled them to Birkenau where under the supervision of SS medics they died by the thousands in the Cyclone B gas chambers.

The consequences of this were most visible in the "infirmary." It is pretty accurate to say that sooner or later every inmate became a patient. When Camp Monowitz was opened in November 1942 next to the factory under construction, the infirmary consisted of one building where only inmates with minor injuries or illnesses were treated by two or three inmate-doctors. More serious cases were sent over to Auschwitz I. Competent medical care of the exhausted, sick or injured inmates was initially not envisaged for the infirmary. Only fifteen beds were set up at first. The consequences of such bad medical care were horrid: Of the roughly 4,000 human beings who were housed in Camp Monowitz at the turn of 1942/1943, only half of them were alive by February. The inmate-doctors were instructed by the SS and IG bosses that they could admit and treat only patients who could be expected to be ready to return to work within fourteen days. Inmates later testified that the supply of medications was utterly inadequate, even though Bayer was part of IG Farben; for example, about twenty aspirin tablets were available per day for 180 patients! But the ever-growing number of people dying from exposure to the Auschwitz winter couldn't be dealt with medication anyway. The wooden shoes provided for the majority of the inmates were of no use to keep feet warm, and there were not enough bandages available to protect the sore-infected feet once an inmate was back at work, making any treatment practically pointless.

The daily selections outside the infirmary served the purpose of reducing the number of patients. Inmates were selected for their ability to work, those not able were selected for "disposal" to Auschwitz I and II. And so this procedure supplemented the selections immediately after the deportation transports rolled into Birkenau when the aged, the weak, and women with children were sent to be gassed right away. Whoever could not work for IG Farben had definitively forfeited the right of his or her life and the short delay in his or her murder was over as the result of this "second" selection.

An SS doctor appointed in March 1943 to Camp Monowitz, Horst Fischer by name, quickly grasped that living conditions there and the demands on the inmates could only lead to extremely rapid physical deterioration. There was no way to avoid increasing the quota of admissible patients. But the IG management refused to accept Fischer's conclusion; it was not prepared to enlarge the infirmary's facilities, make any improvements to the inadequate housing or offer better nourishment and clothing. Instead, to deal with the causes of the flagging ability of the inmates to work as demanded, Dürrfeld put pressure on the SS: He limited the period of time he would pay the SS for each worker it sent to Monowitz to fourteen to twenty-one days in cases of illness. His rigorous action was possible, of course, seeing that there was no lack of inmates in Auschwitz at that time; new transports rolled in steadily from all over Europe. The number of patients to be treated was fixed at five percent of the people the SS sent to work which meant that the SS would have to cover the costs of an inmate patient unable to work for any time beyond Dürrfeld's limit. To avoid that possibility, of course, was to select unable workers for what was called "operation ascension to heaven" in Auschwitz I and II and for the SS to replace them with able-bodied workers. During those selections in Monowitz, high-ranking SS officials, and at time Dürrfeld himself, directly participated in them; they did not trust one another, either had his own idea who were the "right" inmates to be chosen to work and who were those "right" for gassing, for "disposal." The number of Jewish inmates in Camp Monowitz was never under seventy percent and from early 1943 onwards nine of ten inmates were Jews; shortly before the camp was liberated by the Soviet army on January 27, 1945, it was ninety-three percent. It was racist-ideological convictions that shaped the way IG managed Monowitz and its Jewish workforce. The longer the machinery of the destruction and eradication of European Jewry operated, the less interested the SS became in selecting only those really unable to work. The initial intention to maintain an able-bodied workforce for IG took a backseat to the murder of the ideologically foremost enemy: the Jews. Between November 1942 and September 1944, 7,295 inmates—those whose names had been recorded—were sent from the Monowitz infirmary to Birkenau or Auschwitz I. But that number covers only those whose names were recorded in documents recovered after the end of World War II. Literature about IG Farben Monowitz speaks regularly about twenty to twenty-five thousand gassed Monowitz inmates.

Conclusion

Not one iota of what I have told you have I learned from my father! Our conversations, from their initially relatively unclouded atmosphere in the mid-sixties to their abrupt and fractious ending in 1972, would eventually always lead to his assertion that he knew nothing at that time about what IG Farben and, in particular, his colleagues Walter Dürrfeld, Heinrich Bütefisch, Christian Schneider, Carl Krauch, Otto Ambros, Josenhans, and others, were involved in. I realize in retrospect that I had asked my parents only what they knew *during the war itself*; I failed to ask what they had come to know since the end of the war. It is only now that I have learned more about the reintegration of those men into West Germany's industry, how they and others of the higher ranking people of IG Farben returned to prestigious and well-paying positions in the various companies that resulted from the break-up of IG after the war, helped very much by the heating up of the Cold War. As I now reflect on my father's contacts with several of them, how they worked together again, I have to conclude that he knew a good deal but was not prepared to tell me what.

A brief digression now. When the first IG Farben trial opened in the summer of 1947, by which time we had by then been able to leave the Soviet-occupied sector of Germany and had settled in the British sector, I felt that a sense of apprehension about that trial had descended on my parents. I was too young at the time, only twelve-years-old, to discern the real underlying reasons for that. What I do remember, however, is that there was fear that Father might also be indicted and tried. And then when the news came later that fall that Father would not be tried how utterly relieved Mother was. I can now conclude only that there were reasons for the apprehension, that is to say, that my parents knew what IG Farben had been involved in. When I later raised the subject of the 1947/1948 trial with Father and, in particular, the eight-year prison sentence imposed on Walter Dürrfeld, (who was released after only three years!) he retorted that what Nuremberg manifested was nothing but a political act that arose directly out of the war psychosis and which outraged any sense of justice; it was "victors' justice."

Although my father never expressed his views on what IG Farben's legal and/or moral responsibilities were toward those whom the firm he had worked for so many years of his life had abused, starved and gassed to death, I have a pretty good sense of what he thought about how that issue should be addressed. Nazi victims, those who survived and possibly their descendants, should properly be reimbursed or compensated by means of government agreements or laws, since it was the state that had been responsible for the crimes of the Nazi regime. The concept that IG Farben had been complicit in Auschwitz as in other of its factories and should therefore also be liable was entirely foreign to Father. He and his colleagues had only done what was their job, their duty.

In the end, IG Farben and its successor companies—among them my father's last employer, Hoechst—paid 30 million Deutsche marks to victims through the Jewish Claims Committee. I did not find that out from my father, but from the literature published after he died in 1991.

What then has sustained me in my exploration of this story and keeps me keeping on? What lets me live with the truth that I am a son of a perpetrator, that is, of a man complicit through his work in the horror of the Shoah, the child of a nation that cannot get around the fact that in its name murder became rampant, a participant in the faith-community that drew on its core-values and beliefs not to resist but to go along?

In answer to those questions, I will turn to and end with personal experience; for me it is powerfully symbolic. My mother died in 1972; at that time my family and I were living in Windsor, Ontario. I had by then been in regular contact with the Jewish community in that town in connection with my deepening research into the Holocaust. By a circuitous route I learned several weeks later that several Jewish families had trees planted in Israel in memory of my mother. Three decades later, my partner-in-marriage, Barbara, was taken from us after her battle with cancer. Our oldest son, Peter, works in one of Nova Scotia's largest law firms. A number of days after the memorial service, attended by several hundreds of people from Halifax and elsewhere, Peter came and told me that his Jewish colleagues had caused a number of trees to be planted in Israel in memory of his mother and to honor his father for his work on the Holocaust.

For me it is an utterly rich and certainly miraculous gift that Jews, knowing very well what my father's employer and his own work were part of, what Germany had done to their people and the legacy of all that, chose the very soil of *eretz Israel* to plant trees, new life, in memory of a German mother and of the spouse of a German struggling to come to some terms with his parents, his people's, his church's complicity. It is from trees in Israel and from those who had them planted that I can draw the energy to keep on keeping on.

20.
Professional Ethics after Auschwitz

1: Introduction

APPROACHING THE SHOAH, APPROACHING our topic today, I am aware of the ineradicably impact of my native land, its spiritual, cultural and political traditions, and also my own family's muted but palpable anti-Semitism, its bystander silence; and perhaps most existentially, I experience the shame resulting from all this. I am very grateful for and acknowledge with profound appreciation the extensive critical reflection of theologians of the United States and many other countries outside of Germany; I welcome their numerous, helpful and instructive contributions to the Annual Scholars Conferences. But I need to add another factor about my hermeneutics. I claim for myself what Professor Dorothee Soelle said of herself when addressing the 1983 Assembly of the World Council of Churches, Vancouver: "I come from a country and nation that smells of Cyclone-B gas." It is this inescapable truth that has steered my reflections consistently to the *theological* reflection of fellow Christians in Germany who themselves acknowledge and bear this burden. I name with gratitude the late Helmut Gollwitzer, Bertold Klappert, Friedrich-Wilhelm Marquardt, Luise Schottroff, Martin Stöhr, the late Leonore Siegele-Wenschkewitz and Michael Weinrich. They are part of the contextuality of the thinking, mourning and acting I have to do. Together with very significant Jewish friends in North America, they direct the focus of the theology I attempt to do "after Auschwitz."

2: Ethics—My Operational Basis

The ground-breaking study of Professors Margarete and Alexander Mitscherlich, *The Inability to Mourn*[1] depicts the Nazi's ethic as one that operated without any ability to suffer and to mourn; one of its primary prin-

---

1. Mitscherlich, *Die Unfähigkeit zu trauern*.

ciples or "categorical imperatives" was that suffering ought not to affect one's being. It was an ethic *without* "an other," without a "you" who could lay claim on oneself and, as a result, create the restless conscience that is capable of remorse and mourning and creates the capacity for conversion. To analyze the rationality and principles with which this ethic functioned, using only the moral category of evil, is to find it an inadequate tool. The Mitscherlich's recognition of this inadequacy is reflected in their book's sub-title, *Principles of Collective Behaviour*. *The Inability to Mourn* is complemented by the important work of Professor Peter Haas, in particular his book *Morality After Auschwitz. The Radical Challenge of the Nazi Ethic*.[2] These two studies have persuaded me that it was, indeed, an ethic that functioned in the planning and implementation of the Holocaust, in the perpetrators, in those who stood by and those who looked away. And because it was an ethic, I cannot avoid scrutinizing my own ethic, uncovering "what is in me of them": the generations of my parents and of their forebears. An ethic *after* Auschwitz is, indeed, a categorical imperative for their succeeding generation for it is deeply questionable whether "morality *before* Auschwitz" is salvageable. I need only name the "virtues" of *Arbeit, Sauberkeit, Effizienz, Pünklichkeit, Gehorsamkeit*—work, cleanliness, efficiency, punctuality, obedience—to show the futility of upholding a pre-Auschwitz ethic. For it is precisely from these that the Nazi ethic derived its rectitude. It is these "virtues" that were proclaimed in huge letters on the roofs of the death-camp barracks, between the gas-chambers and on the walls of the IG Farben factories. It is beyond the scope of this presentation to summarize Professor Haas's illuminating theory of ethics. But I do want to identify those of its features that continue to provide focus for my task of searching for and building what our topic calls "professional ethics after Auschwitz."

Study after study demonstrates the horrible fact that Nazi professionals—lawyers, doctors, theologians, teachers, high-ranking government and military officials—did what they did with commitment and determination. Non-professionals did likewise: they operated trains, herded people into cattle-cars, constructed camps, built ovens, etc. They were not merely "following orders." In all they did, they manifested that they perceived value in it. This is where Peter Haas speaks of the human propensity to redefine evil. He says, "Under the influence of . . . the Nazi ethic, vast numbers of people simply came to understand evil in different terms and . . . acted upon their understanding."[3]

---

2. Haas, *Morality After Auschwitz*.
3. Ibid., 2.

For me our subject is not about exploring what evil is and how it is to be defined in light of Auschwitz. My question is, in face of that utter evil, how do people come to understand the ethical obligations to which they submit and which they then carry out?

Professor Haas analyzes how the Holocaust demonstrates the dual effect of a successful ethical system: it empowers people to dehumanize, torture and kill, and then, as a matter of ethical routine, to deny any guilt. It is, indeed, difficult for ethical sensitivity to concede that an ethic was at work in the Holocaust, that the perpetrators and those who stood by or looked away had notions of right and wrong. Ethical-theological reflection after Auschwitz needs to resist appealing or returning to orthodoxies. What Auschwitz represents is a radical crossing of ethical thresholds precisely on grounds of a system of ethics. I am persuaded that the categories of right and wrong, of good and evil did function in the system that planned and executed Auschwitz and that this very reality has irrevocably altered the landscape of ethical thought. For that system did have the important components an ethic must have in order for it to compel people to commit themselves to it and to live by it. According to Professor Haas, those components are: coherence, non-self-contradiction and intuitive correctness. I quote him at some length here in order to show that ethics is not so much something that has specific content, such as inviolable, eternal verities. Rather, ethics advances

> individual or group values or interests: a collection of beliefs and values that apparently work against a community's survival or welfare will ultimately be rejected by that community as improper. On the other hand, an ethical system that is logically coherent and that also appears to advance the foundational interests of the community has at least a chance of gaining widespread acceptance and becoming normative.... [T]he Nazi ethic was able to gain adherents precisely on the grounds that it provided a scheme of behavior which was deemed by Germans to address appropriately the problems they imagined to be of greatest threat to themselves and their culture.... We begin with certain inherent predispositions to think in terms of the diametrically opposites of good and evil but then define specific instances of good and evil as we confront the world through a certain cultural and social setting. It is through ethical discourse, then, that we move from implicit values and convictions to conscious thought and analysis. If an ethic can generate and sustain a coherent and internally reinforcing evaluative discourse, and if it produces results that seem to conform to and address the

needs at hand, people can be motivated to adopt and conform to whatever evaluations it generates.[4]

We thus face an ethic that did not define the arrest, brutalization, deportation, selection and gassing of Jews as wrong but, in fact, as ethically tolerable and even as good. My own experience of Walter Dürrfeld was one of someone thoughtful, intelligent and caring, who, at the same time, tolerated the exploitation and mistreatment of Jews in Monowitz and their utter destruction in Birkenau. Professor Haas's laconic summary of such persons is: "It is not that they had lost the ability to behave ethically; they simply evaluated certain activities in a different, yet still ethically coherent way."[5] Auschwitz and all the innumerable other places were possible because they were ethically defensible; they reflect the human power to re-conceive good and evil and then to shape society in light of this new conception.[6]

3: Formal Factors of Ethical Discourse After Auschwitz

Now, if it is through ethical *discourse* that we arrive at analysis and application, if through such discourse we come to evaluate activities said to be good or evil, right or wrong, then what factors will need to impinge on that discourse *after Auschwitz*? In what follows, drawing on the work of Professor Martin Stöhr, I name factors which I cannot do without in imaging and formulating an ethic for Christian theology after Auschwitz. The list is by no means fully comprehensive, nor are the factors named in order of priority.

1. It has long been a feature of Christian theology in the academy to strive for "objectivity"—whatever that nebulous ideal means at any moment. This has meant and, unfortunately, continues to mean that the real experiences of real human beings and what they mean to them are ruled out as essential components of theological scholarship. This means that Auschwitz is not a *theological* factor. The truth of the matter for me is that *Christian theology and church do not discover Jews, their history and their fate nor the necessity of dialoguing with them except through full and open embrace of the fact of Auschwitz.*

2. As a result, *theology and ethics have to encounter suffering at their very foundation; the ability to suffer and to mourn has to become a constitutive component for them.* It cannot be a matter of indifference

---

4. Ibid., 5.
5. Ibid., 7.
6. Ibid., 9.

to theology and all its sub-disciplines that Auschwitz is for millions of people, believers or not, the *Sitz im Leben* of their belief or their unbelief. Despite the clear intent of eradicating the Jewish people from actual history, despite Christian theology's intent of eliminating the Jewish people from salvation history, this people has been neither utterly eradicated nor cut off from God.

3. Both in the Diaspora and in Israel, the Jewish people have experienced a new beginning in continuity with its past and in hope for its future. What the Epistle to the Romans calls the root that bears Christianity (Rom 11:18) is alive, which for Christian theology means that *the power to define what Judaism is and what Jews are does not belong to Christian ethics and theology.*

4. The courage of embracing in intellectual freedom the critical study of the Bible is minuscule in comparison to the courage required now of Christians *to look unflinchingly at the tradition of Christianity and what it caused and then to make a new beginning that does not establish one's position by negating others.*

5. Doing theology and ethics after Auschwitz will need to determine why the churches obsequiously depended on and accommodated themselves to the power and ideology of the Roman Empire and, specifically, why German churches embraced traditions of government that despised politics while being obedient to worldly power. *The freedom of the Christian will have to be thoroughly reconceptualized if Auschwitz is not to be denied.*

6. But much more has to be addressed than why Christians were susceptible to prejudice, contempt, and the idolization of the state or ruler. *What is the substance of the Christian faith that contributes to the hostility toward Jews?* Three points need addressing here:

   a. the charge of deicide against Jews, embodied in scapegoat theories and legends of the "wandering Jew" and used to legitimate Jewish suffering;

   b. the definition of Christianity through negations of Judaism in such juxtapositions as: letter and spirit, promise and fulfilment, law and gospel, revenge and love, old and new, tribal and universal;

   c. the historical Christian idealism that spiritualized faith at the expense of its actualization here and now and the concurrent historical materialism which proposed that Jewish suffering as well as Israel's disenfranchisement by Christianity resulted from the Jews' refusal to acknowledge Jesus the Messiah. God's punishment for this was the destruction of Jerusalem, the sign of God's disavowal of Judaism.

7. The deadly ropes placed on the necks of Jews were spun from many threads of Europe's intellectual and spiritual history, as well as of its economic and political traditions. To acknowledge and document this blocks Auschwitz from being turned into a generic case-study of the negative consequences of prejudice and the horrors of excessive nationalism and racism, into an example of what "original sin" might lead to or what neglect of social responsibility by science, economy, and church can create. *The victims' dignity calls for more accurate exploration of what happened, what specific factors sustained Auschwitz and what deadly threads are still—or once again—being spun for our action.*

8. *The State of Israel is an essential aspect in an ethic and theology after Auschwitz.* The Scylla of the fundamentalism that looks upon the establishment of Israel as an indicator of God's eschatological timetable has to be avoided as much as the Charybdis of an understanding of that state that negates any and all connection with the tradition of Jewish faith and life. This counteracts the perceptions of Jews as a *race* (in the meaning of that term given by the Enlightenment and since) and of Judaism as one of the *world religions* (in the meaning housed in today's secular university departments of religious studies and in documents of the Vatican and the World Council of Churches). Instead, it opens the perspective on Judaism as a *people* living in that state and in Diaspora, which in its real, actual existence is relevant for Christian theology and church.

9. *The positive meaning of the Jewish majority's No! To Jesus as Israel's Messiah has to be made known.* In that No! there resides a faithfulness to a far more universal messianic hope for the renewal of heaven and earth than what Christian proselytization and Christian actualization of its faith manifests. Auschwitz has thoroughly undermined the traditional Christian understanding of Messiah.

10. *The compelling voice of "Remember! Do not forget!" warns against co-opting Auschwitz,* the Holocaust, and its concentration-extermination camps for what is said to be "analogous" events. If one believes our media, the world is infested with "holocausts." But clearly, the point is not that Auschwitz and Hiroshima, Buchenwald and Dresden, Soweto and Vietnam, Cambodia and the Gulag Archipelago, Rwanda and Iraq, Kosovo and Chiapas are to be ranked in terms of numbers of

victims, to be compared one to another as to who suffered more and when one no longer needs to speak of one since another is more recent. *Auschwitz needs its own language if one is truly to hear what that place and event says. I am convinced that Jews alone can and should fashion that language.*

11. Finally, the victims of National-Socialist power have the right—beyond their death!—not to be demeaned in their dignity yet again by being turned into demonstration objects for pedagogical or ethical clarity. *These victims have the right to participate in and influence our decisions after Auschwitz.*

4: Ethics for a Theology After Auschwitz

I understand my task as a participant on this panel to reflect specifically on my profession, that of theologian. Thus, I shall not address the problem of *Christian* existence after the Shoah but the problem of *theological existence* in face of that defining event. (I borrow this term from my teacher Karl Barth who coined it when compelled to be clear about doing theology in the Nazi Germany of the thirties.)

The dictum "Buchenwald lies next to Weimar" also holds true for Christian theology. Peter Haas shows persuasively that one and the same person could declare judgment in the name of God on the obstinate Christ-killers and Messiah-deniers on whom Christ's blood is to be visited and then listen enraptured to a Mozart mass or Bach cantata. People did dearly love their children after having moved into houses from which the Jewish owners and their families had been expelled, a procedure euphemistically called "Aryanization." This is where the Nazis provided the glue that brought and then held together what already existed and did not have to be invented by them. Much of the Nazi ethic was not originally National Socialist; much could be derived from theological tradition.

My premise in this section shares the conviction Professor Haas states in the Epilogue of his *Morality After Auschwitz* where he discusses Jewish theology and the rethinking of ethics and looks at the work of Richard Rubenstein, Eliezer Berkovits, Emil Fackenheim, and Elie Wiesel. "We witness in these people a developing intellectual tradition that takes seriously the demise of Western ethical credibility and even conceptions of God in the wake of Nazism and tries to find a new basis for constructing a way of understanding good and evil." Enlightenment Western civilization is under indictment, in particular the Enlightenment notion that at the center of moral concern is the individual rather than the community, its welfare and survival. For human *community*, so these thinkers argue, is a value in its own right and is to be pursued everywhere for its own sake.[7] I am in concurrence with this conviction, for which reason I believe that Christian theology and church have to re-fashion profoundly the relationship to Judaism. This, I would propose, is fundamental to a professional ethic for theology after Auschwitz. As I have already hinted, in this task the voice of victims—the dead, the survivors their children, and their children's children—must be an essential, if not *the* essential, component.

"What are we to do after Auschwitz?" This is now much less an *ethical* and much more a *theological* question—to be precise: an *ethical* question about the very being of theology. I remind you again, if I may, that I speak as a theologian and Christian of German origin. And for me this means that asking what *actions* ought to be done after Auschwitz does not come close to what Auschwitz *means* to theology and Christian faith of Germans—but also of those who live in the house of Western Enlightenment tradition. Auschwitz concerns us as the very judgment of Christianity, of how we were and are Christians. Not only our demeanour is to change, declares this judgment, *our faith itself is to change.*

Professional ethics for Christian theology after Auschwitz presupposes nothing less than that we are prepared to recognize what has become in our memory of the victims who remained in Auschwitz, what has become of those who for miraculous or other unfathomable reasons have escaped the Shoah, what it means to live as someone descended from victims murdered and victims survived and, finally, what has become of us who were and are closer to the perpetrators than the victims.

The topic of our panel needs to be guarded against a reading that puts Auschwitz wholly into the past and, consequently, into a category of horrors to be compared, measured, and subsequently put behind oneself. The wounds of Auschwitz are still open: it is not up to Christians to *keep* them open, but they dare not deceive themselves and assume that they have stopped bleeding. Such a claim provokes the almost automatic response: For how much longer are Christians supposed to face Auschwitz? Is it not time by now to let the dead bury their dead? Is it not the church's task to bring about reconciliation, to resolve conflicts, especially conflicts of conscience? Is not forgiveness of sin the most profound element of the church's message as well as its task in society? Does not love really cover up a multitude of sins?

Theology and church need to offer firm resistance against this ideology. As long as the nightmares of those who escaped Auschwitz have not

---

7. Ibid., 215–16.

stopped recurring, Auschwitz has to be faced. As long as the peace that Christians desire to make with themselves is exposed as mendacious by the deep unrest of the Shoah's victims, bearing in their bodies, souls and spirit the indelible stigmata of their victimization, Auschwitz has to be faced. One of the primary tasks of professional theological ethics is to remember and to make known that there are still numerous men, women, children, and children's children who have vowed never to set foot on German soil because the sounds from a German mouth makes them shudder, who may be prepared with their heads to forgive but unable to do so with their hearts, who may feel that going to Germany or associating knowingly with a German is a betrayal of the victims. And how can I make peace with myself when I must be avoided by my people's victims? It could be a very important task for Christians to learn and to teach how one may live as a human being who is shunned by others. An ethic of being shunned would be a step into conversion and a genuine practical source of help for Christians to whom triumph, power, and self-assuredness are necessities of existence.

I raise my next point with specific reference to the scandal in the 1990s involving the ruling Christian Democratic Union government in Hessia/Germany which—faced with irrefutable evidence—admitted that its treasurer, Prince Casimir zu Sayn-Wittgenstein, had lied when he said that millions of Deutsch Marks (DM) had been received by the party from bequests of Jewish families. The truth was that those monies had come from illegal accounts the party had opened outside Germany, namely in Switzerland and Lichtenstein. The Government of Israel protested saying that this lie served anti-Semitic prejudices. Behind the Prince's personal and the party's corporate mendacious deception is the calculated resolution to bury and forget Auschwitz, a sign of new indifference or universal coldness toward the Shoah and its victims. Blatant, all too blatant the refusal to let Jews feel that they are needed in Germany!

Christians—or anyone else for that matter—do not know how long Auschwitz will remain in the present; what Christians must know is *that they have* to be present to it as long as *it* is present. Present not only in memory but in its surviving victims and the children that are marked by the survivors' lives. If it is at all appropriate for me to borrow a sentence from Emil Fackenheim, then I would assert that the commanding voice of Auschwitz tells Christian theology and church to become and then remain capable of being present to Auschwitz. Earlier I have tried to name some aspects that I believe such capability requires.

Professional ethics after Auschwitz needs to address the issue of "collective guilt." Rather than reject it and, consequently, force the administration of justice into the narrowest imaginable confines of judgment, namely *individual* criminal law, a clear and sustainable basis for what a court in Canada's British Columbia last year named "vicarious liability" has to be worked out.[8] When Professor Daniel Goldhagen speaks of "willing executioners," he points, I believe, in a direction that has to be followed: *in* every perpetrator and every killer in Auschwitz and *behind* them stood those who raged at brother and sister Israel, at brother and sister communist, at brother and sister homosexual and gypsy, a brother and sister member of the indigenous population, refusing to be reconciled and, thus, walk along with them and offer prayer to God. In and behind the planners, doers, observers, supporters of Auschwitz, in and behind everyone who looked away, stood the anti-Jewish Christian, the tradition of anti-Judaistic interpretation of Scripture, every anti-communist slogan and every ounce of xenophobia, which in German is called *Fremdenhass*. Here is the imperative to become sociologically serious about the Sermon on the Mount, from which we learn how deeply every crime is rooted in a context that is itself criminal. And it is that context that imposes vicarious liability and collective guilt.

Let me conclude with an extrapolation for theology from Theodor Adorno's observation that it is barbarous to write poetry after Auschwitz. Jewish thinkers have reflected profoundly and with anguish on the question of where God was in Auschwitz. Christian theology appears unable *not* to fall back on a theology of the cross as an "answer" to that Jewish question. In 1980, Pope John Paul II went to Auschwitz; he prayed there and wept but he also interpreted Auschwitz as the Golgotha of our time. In every victim he saw the repetition of the sacrifice of Jesus Christ. Such an approach may be unavoidable but I want to resist it: the key of a theology of the cross fits too neatly, is too readily at hand. For every theology of the cross includes resurrection as its final word. Without resurrection from the dead, Jesus's death is nothing. Where is resurrection in Auschwitz? What Christian theology still has to learn from Jewish theology is that with its answers it may indeed walk over the dead bodies of the Shoah's victims and not hear their voices. Not to learn this and to speak nonetheless after Auschwitz is barbarous.

---

8. Charges have been laid by more than five thousand former students at residential schools for First Nations children against Canada's federal government and four mainline churches. The charges are of physical, mental, and sexual abuse, and cultural genocide. The individual acts of teachers, administrators and other members of the schools' staff are not the crime as much as the system that conceived, legislated, financed, and operated those schools between 1849 and 1963.

21.

Children of Perpetrators

The Generations After Auschwitz

*"Sometimes I wish my eyes hadn't been opened,
Sometimes I wish I could no longer see."*

—Carole Etzler

TWENTY-FIVE YEARS AGO, I was present at a public discussion about a book with the evocative title *After Auschwitz*. The event took place in a Toronto synagogue; two Rabbis were the primary discussants: Emil Fackenheim and Richard Rubenstein, the book's author. The invitation had come from Rabbi Stuart Rosenberg; he thought that the event would be of value to me, a minister at a local United Church of Canada congregation, a German and a Christian, drawn into the then current controversy between the editor of the *United Church Observer* and the Jewish community over Israeli-Palestinian relations since the Six-Day War. I had already come to know Emil Fackenheim and was deeply touched by his moral passion; his plea not to give Hitler a posthumous victory had, and still has, the power of authenticity.

Richard Rubenstein was unknown to me; when the evening was over, I left dazed by the force of his challenge to the very possibility of theology after Auschwitz. I had not yet heard of Theodor Adorno's dictum that there is something barbaric about writing poetry after Auschwitz. I do not know how contemporaries whose vocation is to poetry deal with Adorno; I knew that evening that Rubenstein had irrevocably altered what I had hitherto expected, or even wanted, my vocation to theology to become. *After Auschwitz*—a phrase which, coupled with the logical power and passion that mark Richard Rubenstein, ineluctably moved me toward what Carole Etzler sings of in her song: "Sometimes I wish my eyes hadn't been opened, sometimes I wish I could no longer see." In a manner of speaking, I can say that I wished I had not met this man, the relationship to whom I have come to call friendship.

He has made me see, or perhaps more accurately, hear: a bellowing silence. Six million Jews dead, gone: I never knew you, but how present you are to me in the silence of my parents. It is that silence which marks my generation. Indeed, it is the protest against that silence which makes us a generation, especially to ourselves (to adapt a most insightful statement by Patricia Hampl from her meditative autobiography *A Romantic Education*).

It is my belief that there is no other German generation which had a childhood as brief as ours; the silence, or the denial, and the concomitant refusal to remember, made us lose our childhood in cynicism, depression, or aggressiveness.

> What is a collective to do when it finds itself exposed without cover to the realization that in its name six million people were murdered for no reason other than to satisfy its own aggressive urges? It has hardly any choice but to continue to deny its motives or else retreat into depression.... (Yet) depressive reactions, self reproach and despair over the extent of guilt were rare.

So wrote analysts Alexander and Margarete Mitscherlich in their study, *The Inability to Mourn*.[1]

I owe it to Richard Rubenstein that I have had to enter into the struggle that leads to mourning, enter into the silence and denials of parents with my eyes open, into what I wish I did not have to see. But "Psychology, which is somehow our science, the claustrophobic discipline of the century, has made us acknowledge the value of remembering—even at the peril of shame."[2] Over the past two and a half decades since we first met in Toronto, he and I have compared our remembering, how it differs in form and quality even though much of its substance is the same. What the dead speak and how they, therefore, are present to him marks him and his Jewish generation; what the living shroud in silence and how those dead, therefore, are absent to me marks me and my German generation.

In the following I want to try to describe my experience of being of the perpetrator nation. I have to tell something of myself, of the relation between father and myself, which I broaden into a look at current German literature on children and grandchildren of perpetrators. I will add observations on how I perceive the relation of Jews to me as a member of the German nation and conclude how I view my religion after Auschwitz.

---

1. Mitscherlich, *Die Unfähigkeit zu trauern*, 30. English edition: *The Inability to Mourn*, 20.

2. Hampl, *A Romantic Education*, 6.

Who Am I?

I was born in 1935 in Leuna, a town where the IG Farben conglomerate produced chemicals and gasoline. By mid 1944, when British and American aircraft could fly to Central Germany and back without refueling, we became subject to major air raids: nearly thirty in ten months. Father was an engineer and held an upper middle-range executive position in IG Farben. Until the Allied landing in Normandy, he had responsibilities for industry in Holland, Belgium and France; after that his work shifted to the East, to Poland and Czechoslovakia. Returning home one day from there, his train was held up on the outskirts of Leipzig; it was late fall 1944 and another horrible air-attack on that city. When father arrived home, much to our relief, he told us what the raid on Leipzig had done; I can still see his eyes now. To mother's question of where he had been, he replied that he had seen Walter Dürrfeld, a colleague and a friend of the family. I had played with the Dürrfeld children after they lost their home in an air raid and had been taken in by our next-door neighbor. What I did not know then, but came to know later, was that Walter Dürrfeld had been the head of the IG Farben complex at Auschwitz.

In 1952, we moved to Canada; IG Farben, in its postwar configuration, reestablished itself in North America. It was then that I made my first acquaintance with Jews. I began to learn what denial of guilt sounds like when the interlocutor is a relative of victims. I attempted to speak to my father and, for that matter, to my mother about the Holocaust, what they knew of and whom they knew in Auschwitz. I felt that I needed to know what my father had done there in mid 1944, his only visit, lasting four or five days. His response, and regularly ever after, was that "we did not know." After my meeting with Richard Rubenstein my questions took a more urgent form; the response, becoming similarly more urgent every time, was that the matter now should be laid to rest; Mother added that I was causing father grief. She died in late 1972, and father in early 1991; both took their silence to the grave.

Father and I

An ancient Jew once said: "Those who are close to you, you test; like a father, you keep awake their remembering." I found this in a noncanonical writing of the Septuagint, in The Book of Wisdom, 11:10. To that believer's heart the father-link to memory is crucial. A modern Jew tells the story of his miraculous survival; he lives because he was born and sheltered in the remarkable village in Haute Loire, Le Chambon-sur-Lignon. In his story, Pierre Sauvage repeats what Eva Heritier, a young woman who had played with him when he was about a year old, said about her parents. Sauvage wants to say the same about all those fathers and mothers who had saved 5000 Jews: "May we be able to resemble them, if only a little bit. May we become the reflection of their image."[3] Before such words, the wisdom, affection and vision they reflect, I feel deeply how much I wish my eyes had not been opened.

In the mid-eighties, I began to find out that other Germans of my age feel the same. In 1986, I met the Canadian filmmaker Irene Lilienheim-Angelico at a showing of her film, *Dark Lullabies*. She wanted to find out how children of perpetrators see themselves and how she would react to them. She went back to her native Germany, the country which had sent her parents to Dachau. They had survived and had soon left, with a baby daughter, for Canada. In her film she asks perpetrator children of the first and second generations this question: "How do you understand the world which you inherited, a world which, victimizing me, I cannot understand? What is in you of them who taught you your values?"

The pivotal scene for me is the conversation she has with Harald Lüders, a German film-maker, somewhat younger than I. The following reconstruction is a moving part of their talk:

> Even though your extended family is no more, you have rootage in the past. You can go into that past and feel close to those people even though they are dead. I envy you for that positive linkage to the generations before yours; I envy you for having a memory to be kept alive. For me, for many Germans, it is the opposite. I do have extended family, but the connection with the past is a broken one. For only when I am free from father will I have more power to do what I believe in. I must renounce what my history passes on to me; it is a memory not to be embraced.

Others in the film say things like: "The memory I bear destroys the very happy times I had as a little child"; "I need to become my own person, live my life; then and only then can I come to deal with my father's life"; "I have been cheated out of my history; destroyed is the feeling for the place I called home."

What do people become when they face that past is what she asks; she is not alone in that, however. A number of studies address themselves to the question: Niklas Frank, *Abrechnung*; Siegfried Gauch, *Vaterspuren*; Peter

---

3. These words were written in a letter to Pierre Sauvage by the daughter of Emma and Henri Heritier, Eva, after Mme Heritier's death and are read by him towards the end of his remarkable film, *Weapons of the Spirit*.

Härtling, *Nachgetragene Liebe*; Christoph Meckel, *Suchbild*; and Brigitte Schwaiger, *Lange Abwesenheit*. In a more analytical vein: Peter Sichrowsky, *Schuldig geboren*, (available in translation as *Born Guilty: Children of Nazi Families*); and Dorte von Westernhagen, *Die Kinder der Täter: Das Dritte Reich und die Generation danach*. In all of them, it is the past that is the present; the attempts to deal with it manifest what I would call disturbances, if not deformations, of the soul. These studies, with the possible exception of Frank's, do not condemn, but rather seek to understand why father had become a perpetrator. I perceive in all that same heavy inability to break free from father, which I know too well myself. What strikes me particularly is that this burden is there for children of both those who actually took the lives of Jews and those who "only" put up with it or looked the other way. Von Westernhagen poses the problem succinctly by asking: As we grew up, did we not have to despise our parents simply to establish self-respect? And yet, at the same time, did we not have to love them unconditionally, the way all children must and actually can for a time, so as to learn how to give love and form moral integrity ourselves later on?

This literature depicts problems of identity formation: from compulsive adoration of parents to crippling hate or flight into vocations which seem to promise a silencing of the past through flagellation or other atonement. In relation to value formation, the spectrum ranges from utter callousness to veneration of heroic power; from idolizing democracy to dualistic, "us-them," "friend-foe" constructions of reality; from the aggrandizement of father into a metahistorical figure to the search for surrogate parents.

> In addition, those studies seek to determine what kind of parents persons turn out to be when the relation to the preceding generation is experienced in such a problematic way. Here the normal process of growing away from parents takes on peculiar features. More often this "growing" is much more a deliberate breaking away in directions that permit exposing and reciting "what is in us of them." I find it highly suggestive that this breaking away is seen also as a rejection of one's personal historical rootedness. What in psychological writing is often described in language of pathology is described here in language of history: not a generation *uprooted* but one *uprooting itself* from history. Härtling cites the phrase of Paul Celan: "In the air, your roots remain, there, in the air."[4]

Sichrowsky quotes a man named Rainer:

---

4. Hartling, *Nachgetragene Liebe*, 6.

Yes, [father] played games with me and read to me and consoled me when I scraped my knees when I fell off my bicycle. But what about later on when, full of dismay and inner doubt, I didn't know where I belonged? When his war-crimes drove me ... from pillar to post? *When I tried to become a different German than he? Where was father then?* ... He could have explained to me why he had submitted ... I heard nothing from him, not a word. And that's why I hate him, because in addition to messing up his life he missed the opportunity to let me profit from his experience.[5]

Another asks: "Do you know what it means to live without a past? I extinguished my past.... How lovely it would be, a life without a past."[6] An answer to what it is like to live without a past is given by Meckel:

"*It is to be filled with longing for memories that do not exist, for conversations you have never had.*"[7] Or this devastating comment: "Here is the unconscious reduction of a person's self, the brokenness which tortures the children who could not know that such father-existences, such despotism without platform or power, characterized the whole generation. Their love of father made protest difficult. For years and years there was perplexity and anxiety."

"There was no air to breathe; laughter took flight. The children were no match for the psychic dilemma of father. They looked for a fatherless world for themselves, they asked for a bit of joy and found that they needed the whole world."[8] As I see it, everything at this juncture is projected into the future; there is an uncharted immigration, both promising and threatening, into that whole world which, in reality, is nowhere specifically or, at least, always elsewhere. It is a threatening but also promising emigration from the now which cannot bear the burden of the past, from the now and from the world which not only cannot trust the solidity of bonds with parent, but which he feels compelled to break them.

In 1967, Alexander and Margarete Mitscherlich published their classic study *The Inability to Mourn: Principles of Collective Behaviour*. They speak of a process called *de-realization*. One of its features is the insistence that no German grew up actually believing that their or their forebears' deeds needed to be excused since, as everyone knew, what was done had been commanded. Another is associated with the long-time leader of the

5. Sichrowsky, *Schuldig geboren*, 29 (emphasis added). English edition: *Born Guilty: Children of Nazi Families*, 68.
6. Ibid., 67–8; English edition, 56–7.
7. Meckel, *Suchbild*, 87.
8. Ibid., 89.

Christian Social Union Party, the late Franz Josef Strauss. He disliked all who were skeptical about the knee-jerk "but I was only doing my duty" response. Angered by their persistence in probing the question of guilt, he spoke of them as degenerate and masochistically perverse and called them "atonement Germans." I grew up with the feature of de-realization which became an imperative: the duty of children is to leave this alone, for children cannot understand what it was really like then. Another, bitterly cruel feature was the recent *Historikerstreit*:

> The issue of controversy was whether the darkest and bloodiest period of recent German history, namely the "Final Solution of the Jewish Question" might be compared to other genocides or the elimination of opposition on the part of other regimes and whether the Holocaust is not even related to such monstrous deeds of our history. To speak of "relation" introduces the danger of "relativizing"; the attempt to make connections can inadvertently lead to minimizing a crime heinous beyond compare and, subsequently, become the first step towards erasing corporate guilt and responsibility.[9]

Sitting in judgment on parents is not an option of psychological maturity; it only weaves accusation and self-justification into one. The Mitscherlichs show the prevalence of narcissism in both perpetrators and their children; in relation to my "generation" they demonstrate the atrophy of the ability to focus on others to result from the inability to deal with the parents' past. Germans like me, they say, seem unable to take note of others because we have not yet come to exist as "others" ourselves. In self-indulgent focusing on shame, loss of integrity or, conversely, on innocence, mature ways of dealing with the burden of guilt are blocked just as effectively as they are by the efforts to keep guilt feelings at bay. And all such labor poisons life, because it keeps at distance precisely those who, because they can be "others" to us, can allow the labor of mourning to begin.

One of Sichrowsky's interviewees claims that the world would be a much simpler place if one could just get rid of the past. If only one could accuse father, put him on trial, get him to confess his guilt for having done what had been commanded and pronounce judgment or grant absolution! But the burden of children is more than a matter of dealing with father's transgression: It is metaphysical.

What I mean is this: The child may have experienced the relation to father as loving and caring. Yet father was given to collective ideals that were utterly inhuman and which, after the defeat in 1945, were declared to

---

9. Sauter, *Glauben und Lernen*, 5.

have existed in the minds of a few mad people only. The price of such denial, and of silence, is that the relation becomes burdened with deep mendacity. The children's identification with father grows ambiguous, resolvable only through frank discussion of the past. But the less the parent-child relation fosters open discussion of feelings and problems, the more troubled the normal process of growing away from parents becomes as children grow up. Maturing includes giving up certain ideals and dependencies and the concomitant mourning of their loss. But giving up is also critical assessment, the sober examination of "that which is in us of them," the testing of one's openness to and readiness for others. Whenever parents do not allow separation through discussion, the next generation has really little scope for action; either it perpetuates that parental mendacity in personal and public life or it breaks away from the past without the labor of memory and learning. The result is inner emptiness, what older generations lament as "the lack of ideals," or the embrace of ideals the outward manifestation of which may include ill-directed anger and aggressiveness, what older generations lament as "terrorism." What emerges is a false self or one with a character-mask; what looks like a position void of ideals or filled with revolutionary ones (as father always put it to me) is, in actuality, a repetition of the previous generation's identification without the awareness that this is what is happening.

To me, Paul Celan's phrase "rooted in the air" bespeaks the absence of the labors of memory and mourning. Security is of the future since there lies freedom from father. Adding to the difficulty is that forgiveness is closed off as a means of healing.

Simon Wiesenthal's book *The Sunflower* makes the persuasive case that only victims can forgive. But they are dead. "We never knew you," my generation says, and we cannot grant forgiveness to the perpetrators on your behalf. And even if forgiveness could mend the broken bond to father, it cannot restore the matrix of generational identity. Being held by memory in and to the past from which to venture forth in search of self, borne by mourning and love, appears to remain an option for the Dachau child Irene Lilienheim-Angelico, but not for Harald Lüders or me, the children of Hitler's Germany.

Belonging to the Fatherland

This problem of the post-Holocaust relation to father reflects itself as well in the relation to the "Fatherland" and to the "Father" of Jesus Christ.

Auschwitz infected every axiom of German civilization that had to do with the fundamental presuppositions of the polis and its interhuman life. Auschwitz repudiates every civilization that in its thinking and acting presupposes a minimum of anticipatory trust. It does so because socially nurtured trust in the very social orders, which are a precondition for life and survival, were perverted at the most basic level. The German writer Friedrich Wilhelm Foerster once observed that virtue had hired itself out to vice, spirit entered into the service of madness, and humility aligned itself with arrogance. Fidelity had made a pact with treachery, and conscientiousness gone to work for malice. Thus it was, he added, which had given rise to that dreadful solidarity of the upright with the infamous, and had secretly given strength to Germany in those days. *How could a nation which nurtured Goethe, Beethoven and Planck give its bosom to that brood of vipers?* This is what many ask who struggle with the enormity of Auschwitz. I have no answer to give. I wish that I did not have to search for one.

For years, I devoted myself to what in my language is called *Wiedergutmachung*, which means everything from reparation to atonement. It is an effort rooted in what I now believe is the naive conviction that one group of people has power to make up for others' crimes. Whatever good Germans can do for Jews may be good, but it is no *Wiedergutmachung* as such.

It was a particularly painful lesson for me to learn this. As a youngster, I had known no Jews; they were already absent from my context. Instead, they were mythic figures who lived in the speeches of the men whom I heard expatiate on radio. My teacher painted them with the now familiar hues and they were present in the quite nonhostile language of my parents. Jews were objectifications. When I began to meet and study with Jews in Montreal and Toronto and desired to make up for what my fatherland had done to their people, I believed that the openness I showed, with the eagerness to make up, would create a reciprocal conciliatory process towards me personally and towards my people, seeing that, after all, not all Germans were bad. I was sure that I was preparing the ground for both sides to enter into it. Then I learned that Jews could not initiate reconciliation with me or my nation; what eluded me was the reason my efforts seemed so fruitless. Then I came across a text which taught a painful lesson:

> I felt uncomfortable chanting a Hebrew prayer in front of a room of Germans—I felt I might be bringing something holy into a profane place. But I also felt something even more uncomfortable: the sense that those people had truly listened and responded to what I had said in just the way I wanted. The idea that perhaps a dialogue had actually taken place, that I felt the

stirrings of relationship with a group of Germans, was frightening. Was I betraying my family? Perhaps now that practically no more Jews live in Germany, (their) attitude towards us will change.... Maybe my real wish is for Germans to show that they also have to struggle and suffer, from the generation who were Nazis to my own contemporaries.... Seeing Germans as real human beings, not as mythic figures, entering into relationships with them, is frightening. To stop objectifying and start humanizing Germans threatens the deep commitment I have never to betray my family or people.[10]

I now know that after Auschwitz, the reconciliation I see for Jews is potentially the betrayal of family and people. I believe today that Germans ought not to be about "reconciliation" with Jews: so much has Auschwitz perverted this noble value of civilization and religion! Instead, Germans ought to strive for something else:

> (No one can) bring the dead back to life. But until . . . Germans manage to free (themselves) in relation to the living from the stereotyped prejudice; embedded in (their) history . . . (they) shall remain chained to (their) psycho-social immobilism, as to an illness involving symptoms of severe paralysis. "The collective responsibility of a nation for a chapter in its development," Georg Lukacs writes, "is something so abstract and intangible that it borders on absurdity. And yet a period such as that of Hitler can be regarded as over and done with in our own memory only if the intellectual and moral outlook that filled it, gave it movement, direction, and shape, has been radically overcome. Only then does it become possible for others—for other nations—to trust in the conversion and to feel that the past has truly passed." But one can "radically overcome" only on the basis of knowledge firmly anchored in consciousness, even knowledge that at first may be painful, since what happened could happen only because that consciousness had been corrupted. What censorship has excluded from German consciousness for . . . decades as a memory too painful to bear may at any time return unbidden from the past; it has not been "mastered"; it does not belong to a past that has been grappled with and understood. The (labor) of mourning can be accomplished only when one knows what one has to sever oneself from. And only by slowly detaching oneself from the lost relations—whether these be to other human beings or ideals—can a meaningful relationship to reality and to the past be maintained. Without the painful

10. Heschel, *Christianity and Crisis*, 391–92.

work of recollection this can never be achieved. And without it, the old ideals, which in National Socialism led to the fatal turn taken by German history, will continue to operate within the consciousness.... Correcting false and restricted consciousness in this way, discovering a capacity to feel compassion for people never before apprehended behind... distorting projections, would give (Germans) back (their) ability to mourn.[11]

Real guilt waits for those who take it up knowing that it is theirs, but such acceptance and knowledge cannot be forced upon people. The matrix of this process is the relationship between the guilty and their victims. Relationship with the six million victims is possible for Germans today only, I believe, in the faithful commitment to what Emil Fackenheim so eloquently calls "the new commandment": *Do not give Hitler a posthumous victory.* I do not wish to undervalue what has been done in German legislation and in synodal decisions in terms of protection, recognition, and dialogue; I am troubled by what I can interpret only as the absence of the desire to enter into a relationship with Jews that is helpful to the process of Germans taking up guilt. If the pronouncement of the Yad Vashem Memorial in Jerusalem is correct, that remembrance is the secret of redemption, then the widely repeated declaration that "a country as successful as Germany has the right not to hear about Auschwitz any more" does turn the fatherland into something "profane," unrepentant, and unredeemable. The fatherland must, instead, first become a land where fathers "keep awake the remembering" so that the children will be enabled to take up the burden of guilt into their labor of mourning so that a relationship with Jews has any chance of growing again. Or is the relationship irreparably destroyed?

The Faith of the Fathers

I call myself a Christian; I am baptized and, since 1961, a minister. My baptism as an infant strikes me as a cultural event.

Shortly after my confirmation at age fifteen, another cultural occasion, I began thinking about becoming an academic in the discipline of theology. I became aware of what is called a *personal* faith only about the time when I came face to face with my antisemitism; oddly, that was after my ordination.

I had begun making contacts with survivors and their children; living in Montréal and Toronto made that possible given the sizeable Jewish population there. Among those with whom I was privileged to work were

---

11. Mitscherlich und Mitscherlich, *Die Unfähigkeit zu trauern*, 82–83. The citation includes a quote from Georg Lukacs' *Von Nietzsche bis Hitler*, 21. English edition 66–67.

Emil Fackenheim, Susannah Heschel, Gunther Plaut, Stuart Rosenberg, Richard Rubenstein and, as of a short time ago only, David Blumenthal; some have given me the gift of friendship. This gift, which is also a demand, has sent me back also to my Christian heritage. For me the promise of the relationship with Jews is closely knit to a sense of fright, for it is as if I lived in a dead religion.

I have heard it said that because Jews live under the commandment not to forget the victims, many of whom had the prayer: "Hear, O Israel" on their lips as they were bullied into death-chambers, this prayer remains on Jewish lips today. To let it fall from memory would be to let something holy die. As a person who is not Jewish, I can only bring respect and reverence to that. It is utterly different, I believe, when one reflects upon the fact that perpetrators repeated the "Our Father" even after their "work."

Did the petition "and forgive us our trespasses, our debts" not get stuck in their throats? Therefore, *to raise up into memory the factuality of this sacrilege* is to watch something holy die. "*Nach Auschwitz ein Gedicht zu schreiben, ist barbarisch,*" wrote Theodor Adorno; for years now I am unable to repeat the classic Christian prayer without the sense of something barbaric on my lips. Christians who made Auschwitz function have sullied the lips of other Christians who are themselves unable to cleanse them. After Auschwitz, Christian theologians speak with unclean lips, write with unclean hands. This, it seems to me, is an inescapable conclusion with which any effort to determine what theology can be like today must begin. One thing has become very clear to me already: Christian theology without the direct participation of Jews is hollow, false—an insight itself highly ominous. As a theologian I face someone like Susannah Heschel who repeats the accusation against my people and who is unable to offer forgiveness to perpetrators and their children. But precisely forgiveness and reconciliation are what some of those people seek; I certainly do. Both forgiveness and reconciliation are central aspects of the faith of our fathers. But it is not Susannah Heschel, or others like her, who somehow obstinately refuse to grant what I, and others like me, seek earnestly; it was people of the faith of our fathers who contaminated forgiveness and voided reconciliation. Christians now face no one who can forgive them, said Dorothee Soelle.

When I seek meaning, value, and identity within the house of the Christian tradition now, after having met survivors and their children, all I feel is that the spirit has departed and left only dry bones in the house. And yet, the task of burying those bones, that religion in its familiar 1800-year-old, historical manifestation holds promise. It promises the absence of all which first came from father in bonds of love and affection, from the fatherland in rich heritage of ethos and culture, from the faith of the fathers in sacred story and drama but which now, all of it, breaks the heart. The burial of the bones promises the chance of "being German other than father was," the chance of living in a land that can forget about being *das Vaterland*, the chance of moving on into faith that is not the faith of our fathers which showed itself so dead in the Shoah. I believe in that promise more than in anything else even while I have no language yet to tell what an alive faith will be like for me. But the promise has what in my native language and is called *Zuspruch und Anspruch*, promise and demand. The promise is a future when Germans and Jews, Christians and Jews, will experience a relationship that will not threaten to break faith with family and people, on the one hand, and not elicit heart and soul breaking denials of love for fathers, on the other. The demand is what Jews call *tikkun*: the correction of reality. A Christian parallel to *tikkun* is found, I believe, in Dietrich Bonhoeffer's term *praying and doing justice*.

For him, to do justice in the *polis* was necessary so that praying did not retreat into self-sufficient piety while prayer was needed, so that doing justice did not turn into ideological arrogance. In my context here, the labor of *mourning* would not be the *labor* of mourning if taking of guilt upon oneself were not also active struggle for Jewish survival. The Confessing Church in Germany had to learn that offering resistance to the Nazis by confessing the name of Christ led to an overemphasis on prayer which, in the end, found itself consumed by pessimism: It discovered too late that confessing the name of Christ should have taken the form of resistance to the Nazis as this would have kept prayer active in the correcting of reality. To mourn and to repent for Auschwitz is not sufficient: If mourning and repentance are to achieve concrete results and attain the status of values of civilization, they must be part of the praxis that is about mending the rent that is antisemitism. But as such they are resources for both prayer and doing what is just. To do justice could be the antidote against Christian prayer as nothing but pious hypocrisy, like repeating the "Our Father" after turning on the ovens in the death-camps. Prayer might keep the doing of justice from succumbing to resignation and silence, crucial steps towards Hitler's posthumous victory. It may well be, therefore, that the labor of correcting reality, of *tikkun*, holds the possibility of my religion entering anew after Auschwitz into truth.

22.

Rebuilding Christian Faith After Auschwitz

An Autobiographical Reflection of a Perpetrator's Son

LADIES AND GENTLEMEN,

Please, allow me at the very outset of this address to give expression to my sense of how greatly I am honored by the invitation of the Westchester Holocaust Education Center and by your presence here tonight. That someone with a biography like mine should be part of a Holocaust Center's teaching and learning endeavors, and that women and men like you should actually decide to come and hear what I am to say is, in my view, something no one like me should ever take for granted.

I know from personal experience that the physical presence of a German, not to speak of German being spoken, can and does trigger reactions, feelings and recollections of anguish, horror, deepest pain, revulsion. I acknowledge and do not refuse to accept that I have been, and quite likely continue to be, a medium for Jews and some other people of becoming yet again reconnected with all that resides in the word Auschwitz. I have learned that desiring to contribute something toward forms of human relationships with others, but with Jews in particular, that embody respect, hospitality and genuine openness to others' "otherness," I can have no other starting point than to admit that—belonging to the family, nation and church that I do—I am representative of the problem, if "problem" is even the word to be used here. I know that simply by being who I am, I potentially re-open or keep open wounds in people in the three, soon to be four, generations of those whom Hitler, in the name of and with the ready participation of the German—my—people, intended and nearly succeeded in utterly destroying. This is one pole, so to speak, where I must begin in all my reflections on the Holocaust: the radically open confession that, being this human being, I am burdened with being German after, or better since, Auschwitz.

But there is a second pole, from which I set out. The burden I bear can be expressed as a commandment. Three years ago, at the Annual Scholars Conference on the Holocaust and the Churches, I was a member of a panel that addressed the topic of "Professional Ethics After Auschwitz." One of the panelists' parents was in the audience; they were introduced as survivors. The mother sat in the back, the father in the front row. About twenty feet separated me from this gentleman and we looked directly into each other's eyes. When my turn came to speak, I said spontaneously that, in the presence of persons who have seen, heard, felt, suffered, and survived my people's destruction of their people, their families, children, parents, I should remain silent and, in so doing, pay respect to their pain and, perhaps more importantly, to the sacred memory of those who perished in the Shoah. Several calls from the audience, including this gentleman-father, urged me to go on. After the presentation, a number of people came to speak with me; one, a woman several years older than I, stood before me, rolled up the sleeve of her sweater and showed me the tattooed number. Then, she hugged me. Only after that did she speak. "I give you a commandment," she said. "Speak! You must speak!" Her commandment is a blessed burden: it sets me free to acknowledge the burden of the first pole I spoke of, a miserable burden. Her commandment, a truly magnificent gift, has closed any escape into self-pity, guilt-paralysis and mere attention to my own self. She has set my feet on a road where others like her, and others of whom some are present here this evening, have drawn me into discussion and offered the very thing I was taught as a child and did indeed learn never to expect or ever to accept: friendship from Jews.

May I repeat that I feel deeply, deeply honored by being allowed to be here now.

One more quick word before I begin to speak. Even though I spent more than half of my life in the university, I am not here to present an academic talk. If I had to choose a term to describe the state of mind—but also of the heart and soul—I am in when I do reflections like these here, I would choose the term "mourning." And in the state of mourning, the lines between "objective" and "subjective" are ever so blurred. I, for one, cannot opt for "objective" language when it comes to the Shoah; rather, I chose speech appropriate to conversion, mine, not yours! More of this later.

> Sometimes I wished my eyes hadn't been opened,
> Sometimes I wished I could no longer see.

These lines by Carole Etzler Eagleheart open the autobiographical section of my address. Here I shall relate some details of my life, in particular, the relationship to Father.

I was born into a middle-class, bourgeois family in the Germany under Hitler's rule just as the infamous "Nuremberg Laws" were promulgated. It was a time when the tyrant's star was bright and still rising on the horizon of many, many Germans. The Christian faith of my parents (Mother came from the so-called "free church" tradition of German Pietism and Father from the Lutheran Church) exercised itself in terms of "personal inwardness" and "individualistic ethics," seeing no essential or necessary relation to politics, economics or industrial activity. Father was employed by the huge conglomerate and multinational IG Farben. In the course of time he climbed the executive ladder. In Leuna, where we lived, he worked as a researcher in the factory's chief products: synthetic gasoline, chemical fertilizer and the production of nitrates essential for the manufacture of explosives. Nearby was the synthetic rubber production plant of IG Farben, called Buna, whose offspring was Auschwitz-Monowitz, headed by a close family friend, Walter Dürrfeld. The first girl I remember being "smitten" with was one of the Dürrfeld's daughters. Until the Allied invasion of Normandy in mid-1944, Father's job was to oversee and direct the rehabilitation of the industry in France, Belgium and The Netherlands so as to assure their optimum contribution to Germany's war effort. After the invasion, Father was transferred to the East, with a similar assignment for the industry in Poland and Czechoslovakia. As far as I know, he took only one trip to Auschwitz-Monowitz to see Walter Dürrfeld. Dürrfeld was tried, convicted and sentenced at Nuremberg; after his early release, the contacts between him and Father resumed.

By the time I attended nursery school, the town of Leuna was already "free of Jews," as it was put cynically. I met no Jewish person until my late teens after the whole family had moved to Montréal, an industrial transfer made by Father's then-employer, another firm related to the former IG Farben. Until then, Jews were mythical figures to me, the objectifications of my people, its schools, churches, governing authorities. A classmate in my final year of high-school was a Polish Jew, a survivor. When I think back to my conversations with him—this was in 1952–53—all I can remember is that what he heard from me was sheer anti-Semitism and the denial of any guilt. Some change took place when, a year later, I entered McGill University and encountered many more Jewish fellow students. I am aware of how little hostility I met openly from them. A significant moment took place one Saturday morning. Between Mathematics and English classes, the student with whom I shared the bench in our alphabetically ordered class and I always went to play poole. That Saturday, he banged his knee against the poole-table and muttered something to which I responded: "I didn't know, Norman, that you spoke German." He looked me right in the eye and told me that he had spoken Yiddish. And he added: "So, what are you going to do now, Martin?" I had grown fond of Norman by then, but was unaware of his being Jewish. We continued playing poole every Saturday thereafter until our different schedules no longer made that possible. What I did learn that morning was that I had to change. I learned from him what the denial of guilt or complicity sounds like when the interlocutor is someone who lost family in the Holocaust. In Norman's presence, I became aware that my defensive posture, which included the alleged shout of the crowd outside Pontius Pilate's palace: "his blood be on us and on our children!" was vacuous. Even though I began to develop several good personal relationships with Jewish students, both female and male, at McGill University, I did not yet move on to speaking to my parents about that other cynical term "the final solution of the Jewish problem." Then—it must have been in the late fifties—another significant thing happened. My family spent every New Year's Eve together and we older children were allowed to bring a friend to the evening's celebrations. I told my parents that I had invited a woman, whose name I then mentioned. My father said—I will repeat his words first in German—"Du bringst uns doch keine Jüdin ins Haus!" "You're not suggesting that you want to bring a Jewish woman into our house!" I was in love with Sally and the rage I felt at Father's words helped open the door to talking about Germany's recent history. What had he done when he visited Walter Dürrfeld in Auschwitz III? What did he know about the Jews and their families in Leuna and why they had all gone? What did he know of the use of forced labor by IG Farben industries and of Jews in particular? You will have surmised by now that what I came to hear was consistently from both Mother and Father: "We did not know."

For several years after my graduation, the opportunities to talk about all this became relatively few as Father worked overseas and I myself had moved. But in the late sixties, I could resume my questions. At that time, I had been present to a public discussion in Toronto between Rabbis Emil Fackenheim and Richard Rubenstein. I had come to know the former quite well. The topic was Rubenstein's recently published book *After Auschwitz*. That night I learned something from Richard, who is now an irreplaceable friend for more than thirty years. He made me hear a bellowing silence. The six million women and men, old, young, in the prime of their lives, and all those children: gone! I knew none of them but in the silence of my parents they are somehow present to me. My mother died in 1972 and my father in 1991; they took their silence to their graves.

Toward the end of his remarkable film *Weapons of the Spirit*, which tells of the rescue of Jews by the people of the Haute Loire village of Le Chambon-sur Lignon, Pierre Sauvage records what a woman says about her mother and father who had saved Pierre's parents and himself. "May we be able to resemble them, if only a little bit. May we be the reflection of their image." When I apply these words to Mother and Father, whom I deeply loved and for whom I pray that they may rest in peace, from whom I received great riches of culture, the love of nature, and a personal sense of the divine, I hear Carole Etzler's words cited a moment ago: "Sometimes I wished my eyes hadn't been opened."

Another important film for me is called *Dark Lullabies*. It was made by Irene Lilienheim-Angelico, the daughter of Dachau survivors. She was born in the town of Dachau, some months after the end of World War II. Her family moved to Canada at the first opportunity. The film shows her returning to Germany, wanting to talk with perpetrators' children, to discover how they understood themselves and how she reacted to them. One of her questions probes my conscience all the time: "How do you understand the world you inherited, a world which, victimizing me, I cannot understand? What is in you of them that taught you your values?"

What is in me of my parents who taught me my values, some of which I named a moment ago? What is in me of them whom I loved and still do, my mum and my dad? That is what I wanted to find out when I tried again and again to get them to break the silence clothed in the mendacious "We knew nothing." Could I trust my relationship with Jews then and now? Was my love for Sally infected with something? Did I have to stop loving my parents? Is my memory of them perhaps itself an exercise in delusion? It is not my intent to burden you with psychology; rather to indicate that, in exploring not only my ability for inter-relationships and my subsequent reflection on and interpretation of them, I had to learn that the presence of others to me, in this case the presence of Jews who knew that I am German, is the one essential condition that allows responses to my self-reflection to emerge. Let me cite the way Gottfried Wagner—the composer Richard Wagner's great-grandson—puts it in his autobiographical work *Twilight of the Wagners*. He draws on words by the Vienna-born, British philosopher Karl Popper. In a chapter entitled "Father's Last Letter," Wagner notes how essential critical discussion with others is for us to see ourselves, our ideas and values from different angles so that we may judge them with any kind of objectivity. Then he quotes Popper: "The sensible, the critical approach can only be the result of the criticism of others and one can achieve self-criticism only through the criticism of others."

Let me name some who have been critics of me and who have helped me immensely on my road. I have already spoken of Richard Rubenstein and Emil Fackenheim; with gratitude I add the following: Marilyn Nefsky, Susannah Heschel and her gentle mother, Sylvia Strauss Heschel, Gunther Plaut, Zev Garber, Steve Jacobs, Albert and Evelyn Friedlander, Richard Leibovitz, Barbara Appelbaum, Sheldon Grebstein and Irving and Blu Greenberg. That through them and others my feet have been placed on a different road from the one I trod in the first two decades of my life is abundantly clear to me. What amazes me continuously, even as I rejoice in having it, is why they, Jews all, have embraced me with a friendship that is priceless?

Der Tod ist ein Meister aud Deutschland

That is what Paul Celan, the poet, said: Death is a master from Germany—that is, the land of my forebears, my "fatherland." When we sing the National Anthem in Canada in its French version, we sing: "*O Canada, terre des nos aieux, ton front est ceint de fleurons glorieux, car ton bras sait porter l'epée, il sait porter la croix . . .*"—"O Canada, land of our forebears, your brow is resplendent with glorious achievement; because your arm can bear the sword, it can bear the cross . . ." In those words, my chosen country of residence exudes a "patriotism," a love of "fatherland" that, as you will surely understand, makes me feel great discomfort. Every country sings of its forebears' glorious achievements; surely, what we call "national anthems" are not the place where we recite their atrocities. As a German, whose every axiom of my "fatherland's" civilization is infected by Auschwitz, I can sing words like those French ones just cited with reluctance and, I am afraid, that this holds for every national anthem I know. The very problem of my post-Shoah relationship to my father, my father's generation and the one preceding it, touches deeply upon the relationship I have to the "land of my fathers, or forebears" as it also does—as I shall elaborate later—to the "faith of my fathers" in the "Father" of Jesus Christ.

When I say that Auschwitz infected—may I even say "infested?"—every axiom of German civilization, I have in mind particularly the very presuppositions for living in the human community, in what in Greek is known as "polis." Auschwitz showed that and how socially nurtured trust in the very orders that are pre-conditional for life together and for survival had been perverted at the most basic level. I can do no better to describe what I mean than by quoting the German Friedrich Wilhelm Foerster: "Virtue had hired itself out to vice, spirit entered into the service of madness, humility aligned itself with arrogance. Fidelity had made a pact with treachery, conscientiousness had gone to work for malice. Thus it was that the dreadful solidarity of the upright with the infamous arose, secretly giving power to Hitler's Germany." Why? Why? Why? is all I can utter. But I have no answer, no explanation. I do know, however, that death is a master from Germany, my home and native land (to borrow a line from the English version of Canada's National Anthem.)

Let me transpose the substance of Paul Celan's phrase from his deeply eloquent *Todesfuge*; my theological colleague and now close personal friend, Dorothee Soelle, once began an address to the Vancouver World Council of Churches general assembly by saying: "I come from a country and a nation that smells of Cyclone-B gas." How can I love my homeland, the land of my fathers? It was Emperor Charlemagne who granted manumission to my ancestors in the year 801 C.E.—that's how far back we can trace my paternal forebears. How can I love, or honor, the traditions that are my heritage? But I do. I do want to claim the gifts to all humankind of Beethoven, Bach, Mendelssohn, Mahler, Schoenberg, of Goethe, Schiller, Heinrich Heine, Bert Brecht and Kurt Weill, of the inconsistent Thuringian peasant and teacher Martin Luther, while also at the very same time keep before me the ineradicable impact of that country's spiritual cultural and political tradition, my own family's muted but palpable anti-Semitism, my country's deafening bystander or away-looker silence, and my shame. Karl Marx helps immensely here when he analyzed shame to be also a constructive, re-creative, even revolutionary emotion. He helps me from becoming mired in the finally utterly ambiguous sense of "guilt." Let me add in passing that I do not reject the notion of "collective guilt"; it has deep heuristic value for reflecting on or exploring the burden of being German after the Holocaust. "Burden": the destruction of European Jewry was not only planned in the country I call my native land, but put in place there. "Burden": how could the very same people and nation that nurtured the composers, poets, writers and theologians I named a moment ago, the scientists Max Planck and Werner Heisenberg, give its bosom to the brood of vipers that made something unthinkable become reality? Auschwitz throws up such questions. I have no answers and I wish I could provide one different from that of Paul Celan: *Der Tod ist ein Meister aus Deutschland*. Still, I mourn, seek to repent for the reality that created the questions.

I have no quotation to place at the head of my third section on the "faith of my fathers," except, perhaps, to recite the often-sung church hymn: "Faith of our fathers, living faith, we will be true to thee till death." But let me begin with a look at a tragic event of times long past yet so very present.

On that desperate morning of May 27, 1096 C.E., hundreds of Jews in the city of Mainz, having sought refuge in the Bishop's court from the approaching hordes of the First Crusade, chose to end their lives *al kiddush hashem*, "for the sanctity of the Divine Name." Soon thereafter, in deep despair, a survivor exclaimed in lament: "My eyes dissolve in tears. Now that your wise women and men are gone, who will lift you up high, Torah?" Eight and a half centuries later, after the hordes of the Holocaust implementers had done their worst, a question and lament like that is heard again: "Who is left to lift you up now, Torah?"

In the presence of that question, Christians must keep silent, although it is a question they dare not allow to disappear from their sight. A question to which they do need to give an answer sounds more like this: Can entering into the guilt and shame of Christianity's long complicity in anti-Judaism and anti-Semitism and their deepest, most terrible abyss in Auschwitz, lead Christians to a conversion that may create a new and respectful beholding of Jews and lead, in metaphorical terms, to a new turning toward Jerusalem?

In retrospect, I realize that I should have put a question mark after the first part of my title: "Rebuilding Christian Faith after Auschwitz?" In a moment, I shall refer to several areas of Christian faith where I would "re-build," each of them require radical openness of Christians to Jews. But no Christian can or ought to take it for granted that Jews are anxious to be part of rebuilding something that turned its very core symbol into the sword that was turned against Jews for centuries, as James Carroll has shown so persuasively.

I call myself a Christian, or perhaps less grandiose: a follower of Jesus. I was baptized and, since 1961, am an ordained minister. My baptism as an infant strikes me now as a cultural event only. Shortly after my confirmation at age fifteen, another merely cultural event, I began thinking about becoming an academic in the discipline called "theology." It was not until I came face-to-face with my own anti-Semitism that I became aware of what I would hesitatingly call personal faith convictions. Let me tell you how this happened.

Not only did Christian faith in Germany generally fail to create an ethic and subsequent actions of resistance, it also failed to prevent perpetrators from praying the "Our Father" after their murderous labors. Once this began to dawn on me, once it became plain that the words "and forgive us our trespasses, our debts" did not get stuck in their throats, something holy died for me. Theodor Adorno's claim that to write poetry after Auschwitz is barbaric, has transformed itself for me into believing that the repetition of that prayer on my part is tinged with and somehow carries forward an unholy barbarism. Christians who made the Shoah happen have sullied the lips of subsequent Christians who are themselves unable to cleanse them. To rebuild Christian faith is possible for me only on condition of acknowledging that doing theology after Auschwitz can happen only as an act of confession, mourning and repentance striving for conversion. It is essential that mourning is in the first instance for the victims and only then for what was done by the perpetrators in the name of Germany, if there is to be hope for a new beginning between Jews and Germans, when Jews may feel that the conversion sought and lived out by Germans is trustworthy. We are presently experiencing again a new, huge upsurge of anti-Semitism; it has come out of "remission," showing how deep the corruption of consciousness still is and how very, very hard and painful the necessary work is to eradicate it. I share the conclusion of Edna Brocke, an Israeli living in Germany where she is the director of the Center for Cultural Encounter in the Old Synagogue in Essen. In a panel discussion in 1991, open to the public, she said that she belongs to a generation that had great hopes, more accurately great illusions, about the possibility to learn from Auschwitz then enable new dimensions to emerge in the encounter between Jews and non-Jews. She had really been taken by the idea, indeed the hope that the Shoah had entered so deeply into people's being that they would not go back to their daily routines. It turns out, she said, it was an illusion, for it seems that the Shoah has not made a really new approach between non-Jews and Jews possible.

I turn now specifically to the conversion of Christian faith and its often obstinate baby: theology. To become converted, this disciplined reflection has to incorporate into its methods the anger, revulsion, abhorrence, shame and guilt elicited by the Shoah and then let them function both destructively and constructively. That is to say, an academic activity will have to make part of its very methods factors rejected to this very day as irrelevant to the scientific pursuit. I want to cite a somewhat lengthy excerpt from an address of one of my theological teachers from Germany, the late Friedrich-Wilhelm Marquardt, given in 1979.

> What are we to do . . . after Auschwitz? This continues to be the most haunting, and, at the same time, the most impotent question. . . . Another question torments us as well: are we really at the place yet where we can discuss practical consequences? Is it not rather that Auschwitz is only just now beginning to enter our consciousness, that particularly we older ones are only just now ready to let the facts of Auschwitz enter our inner being, prepared only just now to look our guilt and complicity in the face? . . . But we shall not place the question of what we are to do at the end of the line. We should begin with it. But we ought to realize that whatever we might possibly do today, after Auschwitz, does not come remotely close to what Auschwitz means for us today. For Auschwitz stands before us as judgment on our Christianity, on the manner of how we were and are Christians, and more yet, seen with the eyes of the victims of Auschwitz, as a judgment of Christianity itself. Auschwitz stands before

us as a call to conversion. Not only is our behavior in need of change, our faith itself is. . . . Auschwitz constrains us to hear God's word utterly differently from how we heard it before Auschwitz. . . . Conversion touches the very being of Christianity as we have understood it thus far. . . . What is to be done after Auschwitz presupposes nothing other than our willingness to become aware of what has become in our remembrance of the victims who remained in Auschwitz, what has become of those who, incomprehensibly, escaped the Holocaust with their lives and, finally, what has become of us ourselves, what has happened within ourselves, the people who were and are closer to the perpetrators than to the victims. . . . And that brings us to what Christians can and must do first after Auschwitz. Christians must keep the wounds open; more precisely: they must not blind themselves to the fact that the wounds bleed as before. . . . How long do we need to do this? As long as the nightmares of those who escaped the Shoah haunt them in their sleep. As long as the peace that we want to make with ourselves is shown to be a lie by the utter "un-peace" of people who were victims in Auschwitz and for the remainder of their lives bear the indelible character of victimization in their bodies and souls. One of the first tasks of Christians and churches consists in telling our people untiringly that there are still thousands of victims who must avoid us, who have sworn never to set foot on German soil again, that are shaken by fear of seeing a German face or hearing sounds from a German mouth. . . . How can any of us be at peace when one is to be avoided like a sore on humanity? An important Christian teaching could be on how one can learn to live as a human being who is avoided by human beings. . . . How long Auschwitz is present, we do not know. We know only that we must be present to it for as long as it is present—not only in memory alone but in its surviving victims and in the daughters and sons marked by their having survived. Without this, we flee from the present. To keep ourselves equal to the present: that is the first thing we ought to do after Auschwitz.[1]

I am quite aware that many Jews insist on being seen not as victims only or as victims at all, that instead their strength and accomplishments are to be noted and saluted. But the moment Christians adopt that perception, they simply play into the hands of those who want to have all that Shoah thing put behind them and who tell people like me that we have

---

1. Marquardt and Friedlander, *Das Schweigen der Christen und die Menschlichkeit Gottes*, 9–13.

an Auschwitz complex or, as it was put to me recently, a "post-Shoah syndrome," that we lost our nerves.

I signaled earlier that "rebuilding the Christian faith" could for me not be a matter of elucidating what Christians should and can now *believe*, give assent to and then formulate into a creedal statement. "Rebuilding" after Auschwitz has for me the aim of renewing the relation between Jews and Christians and all that that implies. I cannot claim that this view meets with widespread agreement among those Christians who consciously want to "rebuild" the faith of the church these days. I name now some obstacles I believe need to be removed permanently if such a renewal is to have a chance even to begin to happen.

1. Christianity and its institutions have claimed to have authority and power to define what Jews are and what Judaism is.

2. Christianity has defined itself and its positions through the negation and denigration of Jews and Judaism. It has done this by proposing, among other things, a series of juxtapositions such as: letter and spirit; —promise and fulfillment; law and gospel; revenge and love; tribal and universal; old and new; material and spiritual, and so forth. In each of these the first factor is said to depict the Jewish "religion" and the second the Christian "faith." And then it is said that the Jews' refusal to acknowledge and accept Jesus as the Messiah promised them led God to disavow Judaism, signaling it through the destruction of Jerusalem by the Romans in 70 C.E.

3. Christianity and often the Church are as such exculpated; it was, instead, individual Christians who were guilty of the crimes of the Holocaust.

4. Christian faith regards itself as untouched in its essence by Auschwitz, by the murder of all those children alone. This sense of unaffectedness was given classic but cynical expression by Otto Dibelius, a highest-ranking Protestant bishop in West Germany, when, in his farewell sermon in 1966, he said: "Since Auschwitz, some folk have just lost their nerves, that's all."

Views and attitudes like those have to be eradicated. In their place, there need to be factors I hold essential for the renewal of relations between Jews and Christians.

1. Christian faith and church will not meet Jews, know their history and fate, see the necessity of seeking dialog with them unless and until they openly embrace the fact of the Shoah. For me this also means that

the suffering of the victims and the responsibility of the perpetrators become constitutive for every kind of Christian self-reflection.

2. Even though this is done regularly, especially in political debates, Auschwitz cannot be turned into a generic case study on what prejudice, racism, nationalism, original sin, or the neglect of social responsibility can lead to. The dignity of those murdered in the Shoah demands a more nuanced and accurate examination of what happened, what specific factors led to and sustained the Shoah and which of those factors are operating again now. Christian faith owes those whom the Holocaust eradicated a clear confession of how it helped the destruction of Jewry.

3. Whatever decisions Christians take as a result of acknowledging their complicity, the victims, their surviving relatives and their children have the right to influence those decisions. Their voice, however it becomes present, dares not be ignored when Christians ask: What are we to do after Auschwitz? Encounter with Jews, in my view, is to be a crucial *Sitz im Leben* for the rebuilding of Christian faith. But let me be very specific about how I see that encounter. I do not believe in repeating the "harmony model" that I experienced twenty years ago when we got together with Jews to explore what we have "in common." I now see a far greater need to address the "differences" so that Christians begin to learn from Judaism and Jews. I think such learning is a far more appropriate task for Christians than what is propagated far and wide under the name of "Christian-Jewish dialog"; as I experience it now. It has become—I am afraid—an empty commodity. To advance Jewish-Christian relations in which Christians show respect for the "otherness" of Jews and the beauty of that "otherness" is the aim of the rebuilding I seek to do. For here it is that I have begun to learn not only that, but also, how Christian faith convictions come to grief before Jewish self-understanding, that and how ancient Christian affirmations founder on real, living human beings.

4. Among those affirmations is that Jesus of Nazareth is the Messiah promised to Israel. What is to be done with the Jewish NO! to that affirmation? I have not abandoned that component of Christian faith, but I know very clearly that Christians will have left Christian anti-Judaism behind them only when they succeed theologically to do something positive with the Jewish NO! to Jesus Christ. Let me add as an aside that I resist, oppose, looking with Pope John Paul II for "Golgotha in Auschwitz" and to recognize Auschwitz as the Golgotha of our time. This is not a positive procedure simply because Christian

faith already has the answer to Golgotha, knowing what needs to be said after Golgotha. For what Christians say to Jews about the "new reality" that is said to have been inaugurated after Golgotha, about what became "different" through Jesus, is crushed by Auschwitz. The impact of Christian co-responsibility in the Shoah and the experience of a true, living encounter with Jews now both question Christian tradition profoundly. When Richard Rubenstein met Dean Heinrich Grüber, a man who befriended and helped Jews during the Nazi era, and was told that somehow Auschwitz was God's will, Rubenstein reports that this was a turning point in his own convictions, namely that no one can and should believe in a God who not only permits but even wills this. I now understand an answer like Dean Grüber's that seeks to squeeze meaning out of Auschwitz, such as: this is the rod of God's anger with his people, as nothing but a way of evading the necessary re-orientation, the conversion of theology and faith.

5. The last essential factor I name—there could be more—for the renewal of the relation between Jews and Christians (which, let me repeat again, is what I mean by rebuilding the faith of the Church) is the return of Israel to its land and the establishment of the State of Israel. I have a long way to go yet to grasp the full implication and impact of this. It is my great, great hope soon to make my first visit to Israel; a promised fellowship for studies at Yad Vashem awaits an opportunity to be taken up. What I have to address is—as signaled earlier—my problematic relation, as a German, to "land"—fatherland, what the Nazis called *Boden*. But I know enough already that precisely that land, Israel, is where many saved from the Shoah exist and work to make that land fruitful, hospitable. I also know that, at its core, Judaism is no "religion" as such but an actually existing people whose existence has an identity connection with that land. And that identity is not mediated by some form of theology or philosophy but by real, living human beings witnessing to the connectedness between the people today and their biblical forebears. This has implications on how I read the Bible. It requires a new way of reading it. Talmud and Midrash, the Jewish tradition of Halakhah begin to be seen as having the right to speak when I interpret the scriptures and when I rebuild the Christian faith.

Let me conclude with three vignettes. I want to signal that however convinced I am of the truth of Edna Brocke's conclusion that the Shoah has not yet made possible a really new approach between non-Jews and Jews, I also feel something else. While I was teaching at the University in Windsor, Ontario, my mother died. Jewish neighbors and colleagues had trees planted in Israel in her memory and to express their relationship to me. And earlier this past month, after the death of my dear wife—may she rest in peace—colleagues of my son in Halifax had trees planted in memory of her in The Yad Lanoflim. Second vignette. In the past four years, once in London and once in New York, I was guest in the homes of well-known and respected Rabbis for the Sabbath meal and prayer: Albert and Evelyn Friedlander in London and Yitz and Blu Greenberg in New York made it a point that it was precisely that occasion to which they asked me to be in their home and at their table. Trees in Israel and Sabbath hospitality are to me a healing of the soul. Finally, in the late Spring of 1994, I went to Auschwitz with a very dear friend whom I had asked to be my sole companion for the "visit" there. As we stood before the gate that heralds "Arbeit macht frei," she could not go on. After we talked a while, I took her hand and walked her into the camp. Later in the day, after walking the hell that Auschwitz-Birkenau still is, I did not want to return to the main gate of that camp. She found a ditch with enough space under the fence for us to slip out. She went first. I felt too weak or ill to climb through, whereupon she gave me her hand and pulled me out. My friend is Jewish. I cannot fathom quite yet the symbolism of me, a German, taking her, a Jew, by the hand *into* Auschwitz and she, a Jew, holding me by the hand and getting me, a German, *out of* Auschwitz. I thank her to this day for that redeeming act, as I thank you now for your hospitality to me this night and for your gracious gift of attention.

Bibliography

Aly, Götz, and Susanne Heim. *Vordenker der Vernichtung. Auschwitz und die Pläne für eine neue europäische Ordnung.* Hamburg: Hoffmann und Campe, 1991.

Améry, Jean. *At the Mind's Limits: Contemplations by a Survivor on Auschwitz and its Realities.* Translated by Sidney and Stella Rosenfeld. Bloomington: Indiana University Press, 1980.

Améry, Jean. *Jenseits von Schuld und Sühne. Bewältigungsversuche eines Überwältigten.* Stuttgart: Klett-Cotta, 1977.

Améry, Jean. *On Suicide: A Discourse on Voluntary Death.* Bloomington and Indianapolis: Indiana University Press, 1999.

Barth Karl. *Letzte Zeugnisse.* Zurich: TVZ, 1969.

———. *Theologische Fragen und Antworten.* Zurich: TVZ, 1957.

———. "Die Not der evangelischen Kirche." *Zwischen den Zeiten,* vol. 9 (1931) 100.

———. "Evangelium und Sozialismus." *Karl Barth Gesamtausgabe,* vol. 22, *Vorträge und kleinere Arbeiten.* Edited by Hans-Anton Drewes and Hinrich Stoevesandt. Zurich: TVZ, 1993.

———. "The Christian Community and the Civil Community." In *Against the Stream: Shorter Post-War Writings 1946–1952.* Edited by Ronald Gregor Smith. Translated by Stanley Goodman. London: SCM, 1954.

———. *Der Götze wackelt. Zeitkritische Aufsätze, Reden und Briefe von 1930 bis 1960.* Edited by Karl Kupisch. Berlin: Käthe Vogt, 1961.

———. *Gotteserkenntnis und Gottesdienst nach reformatorischer Lehre.* Zurich: Verlag der Evangelischen Buchhandlung, 1938.

———. *The Knowledge of God and the Service of God According to the Teaching of the Reformation.* Translated by J. L. M. Haire and Ian Henderson. London: Hodder and Stoughton, 1938.

———. *Theological Existence Today. A Plea for Theological Freedom.* Translated by R. Birch Hoyle. London: Hodder and Stoughton, 1933.

Berenbaum, Michael, and Betty Rogers Rubenstein, eds. *What Kind of God? Essays in Honor of Richard L. Rubenstein.* Lanham, New York, London: University of America Press, 1995.

Bernstein, Victor H. *Final Judgment: The Story of Nuremberg.* New York: Boni & Gaer, Inc., 1947.

Bethge, Eberhard. "Der Weg vom 'Pazifismus' in den Widerstand. Gewaltlosigkeit und Gewalt im Tun und Denken Dietrich Bonhoeffers." In *Bekennen und Widerstehen,* 87. Munich: Chr. Kaiser, 1984.

Böll, Heinrich. *Frankfurter Vorlesungen*, 4. ed. Munich: Deutscher Taschenbuch Verlag, 1977.
Bonhoeffer, Dietrich. "Ethics as Formation." In *Ethics*. Dietrich Bonhoeffer Works in English, vol. 6, 81. Minneapolis: Fortress, 2005.
———. *Creation and Fall*. Dietrich Bonhoeffer Works in English, Vol. 3. Minneapolis: Fortress, 1997.
———. *Discipleship*. Dietrich Bonhoeffer Works in English, vol. 4. Minneapolis: Fortress, 2001.
———. *Ecumenical, Academic, and Pastoral Work: 1931–1932*, Dietrich Bonhoeffer Works in English, vol. 11. Minneapolis: Fortress, 2012.
———. *Letters and Papers from Prison*. Dietrich Bonhoeffer Works in English, vol. 8. Minneapolis: Fortress, 2009.
———. "On the Theological Foundation of the Work of the World Alliance." In *Ecumenical, Academic, and Pastoral Work:1931–1932*. Dietrich Bonhoeffer Works, vol. 11. Minneapolis: Fortress, 2012.
Bonin, Konrad von, ed. *Deutscher Evangelischer Kirchentag Ruhrgebiet 1991— Dokumente*. Munich: Chr. Kaiser, 1991).
Borchert, Heinrich and Georg Merz, eds. "Von der Freiheit eines Christenmenschen." *Martin Luther: Ausgewählte Werke*, vol. 2. Munich: Chr. Kaiser, 1962.
Borkin, Joseph. *The Crime and Punishment of I.G. Farben*. New York: The Free Press, 1978.
Brocke, Edna. "Seit Auschwitz muss jeder wissen, dass Schlimmeres als Krieg möglich ist," in *Kirche und Israel*, 6, no. 1 (1991) 64.
Buber, Martin. *Die Schrift. Verdeutscht von Martin Buber gemeinsam mit Franz Rosenzweig*. Gütersloh: Gütersloher Verlagshaus, 2007.
Busch, Eberhard. *Karl Barth: His life from letters and autobiographical Texts*. Philadelphia: Fortress, 1976.
Celan, Paul. *Gedichte in Auswahl*. Frankfurt am Main: S. Fischer Verlag, 1959.
Cohen, Arthur A. *The Tremendum: A Theological Interpretation of the Holocaust*. New York: Continuum, 1981, 1993.
Dramm, Sabine. *Dietrich Bonhoeffer and the Resistance*. Minneapolis: Fortress, 2009.
Fackenheim, Emil. *To Mend the World*. Bloomington: Indiana University Press, 1992.
Felstiner, John. *Paul Celan: Poet, Survivor, Jew*. New Haven, Conn., and London: Yale University Press, 1995.
Gerson, Jordie. "An American Jew in Poland: Grappling with a Tragic Living History." In *Harvard Divinity Bulletin*, 36, no. 3, 10–11.
Gniewoss, Ute, ed. *Störenfriedels Zeddelkasten: Geschenkpapiere zum 60. Geburtstag von Friedrich-Wilhelm Marquardt*. Berlin: Alektor, 1991.
Gollwitzer, Helmut. "Kingdom of God and Socialism in the Theology of Karl Barth." *Karl Barth and Radical Politics*. Edited and translated by George Hunsinger. Philadelphia: Westminster, 1976.
———. "Muss ein Christ Sozialist sein?" In *Umkehr und Revolution. Aufsätze zu christlichem Glauben und Marxismus*, vol. 2. Edited by Christian Keller. Munich: Chr. Kaiser, 1988.
———. "Reich Gottes und Sozialismus bei Karl Barth." *Auch das Denken darf dienen. Aufsätze zu Theologie und Geistesgeschichte*, vol. 1. Edited by Friedrich-Wilhelm Marquardt. Munich: Chr. Kaiser, 1988.

Greenberg, Irving. "Cloud of Smoke, Pillar of Fire: Judaism, Christianity, and Modernity After the Holocaust." In *Auschwitz: Beginning of a New Era? Reflections on the Holocaust,* Edited by Eva Fleischner, 23. New York: KTAV, 1977.
Gutierrez, Gustavo and Richard Shaull. *Liberation and Change.* Edited by Ronald H. Stone. Atlanta: John Knox, 1977.
Haas, Peter. *Morality After Auschwitz: The Radical Challenge of the Nazi Ethic.* Philadelphia: Fortress, 1988.
Hager, Thomas. *The Alchemy of Air.* New York: Broadway Books, 2008.
Hampl, Patricia. *A Romantic Education.* Boston: Houghton Mifflin, 1981.
Harris, Whitney R. *Tyranny on Trial: The Trial of Major German War Criminals at the End of World War II at Nuremberg, Germany, 1945–1946.* Dallas: Southern Methodist University Press, 1954.
Härtling, Peter. *Nachgetragene Liebe.* Darmstadt & Neuwied: Hermann Luchterhand Verlag, 1986.
Hegel, Georg Wilhelm Friedrich. *The Phenomenology of Mind.* Translated by J. W. B. Baillie. London: George Allen and Unwin, 1931.
Heidelberger-Leonard, Irene. *Jean Améry: Revolte in der Resignation.* Stuttgart: Klett-Cotta, 2004.
Heschel, Susannah. "Something Holy in a Profane Place." In *Christianity and Crisis* (Oct. 6. 1986) 391–92.
Hirschhorn, Simon, ed. *Tora, wer wird dich nun erheben? Religiöse Dichtungen der Juden aus dem mittelalterlichen Mainz.* Gerlangen: Verlag Lambert Schneider, 1995.
Hromádka, Josef L. *Der Geschichte ins Gesicht sehen. Evangelische und politische Interpretationen derWirklichkeit.* Edited by Martin Stöhr. Munich: Chr. Kaiser, 1977.
———. *Sprung über die Mauer.* Berlin: Käthe Vogt, 1961.
Hunsinger, George. *Karl Barth and Radical Politics.* Philadelphia: Westminster, 1976.
Hutchinson, Roger. "The Limits of Ethics in a Militarized World." An address delivered during the Project Ploughshares consultation. In *Defence Beyond Borders: A Consultation on Canada's Military Responsibilities in the Emerging World Order,* January 1993.
Junge Kirche, vol. 12 (1988) 683.
Kabitz, Ulrich and Friedrich-Wilhelm Marquardt, eds. *Begegnungen mit Helmut Gollwitzer,* Munich: Chr. Kaiser, 1984.
Kammerer, Gabriele. *In die Haare, in die Arme. 40 Jahre Arbeitsgemeinschaft "Juden und Christen beim Deutschen Evangelischen Kirchentag".* Munich-Gütersloh: Chr. Kaiser-Gütersloher, 2001.
Knight, Henry. *Celebrating Holy Week in a Post Holocaust World.* Louisville: Westminster-John Knox Press, 2005.
Kolitz, Zvi. *Yosl Rakover Talks to God.* New York: Vintage Books, 1999.
Krondorfer, Björn. "Ratner's Kosher Restaurant." In *Second Generation Voices: Reflections by Children of Holocaust Survivors and Perpetrators,* edited by Alan L. Berger and Naomi Berger, 263. Syracuse, N.Y.: Syracuse University Press, 2001.
Künneth, Walter and Helmut Schreiner. *Die Nation vor Gott.* Berlin: Wichern, 1933.
Levi, Primo. *Survival in Auschwitz.* New York: Macmillan, 1993.
Lukacs, Georg. *Von Nietzsche bis Hitler.* Frankfurt: Fischer Bücherei, 1966.
Marquardt, Friedrich-Wilhelm. "Christsein nach Auschwitz." In *Das Schweigen der Christen und die Menschlichkeit Gottes: Gläubige Existenz nach Auschwitz.* Edited

by Friedrich-Wilhelm Marquardt and Albert Friedlander. Munich: Chr. Kaiser, 1980.

———. *Eia, wärn wir da—eine theologische Utopie.* Gütersloh: Gütersloher Verlagshaus, 1997.

———. *Verwegenheiten. Theologische Stücke aus Berlin.* Munich: Chr. Kaiser, 1981.

———. *Von Elend und Heimsuchung der Theologie. Prolegomena zur Dogmatik.* Munich: Chr. Kaiser, 1988.

Meckel, Christoph. *Suchbild.* Frankfurt: Fischer Taschenbuch, 1987.

Mendes-Flohr, Paul. "Lament's Hope." In *Catastrophe and Meaning: The Holocaust and the Twentieth Century*, edited by Moishe Postone and Eric Santner, 253, 256. Chicago: University of Chicago Press, 2003.

Michel, Jean. *Dora.* New York: Holt, Rinehart and Winston.

Mitscherlich, Alexander and Margarete Mitscherlich. *Die Unfähigkeit zu trauern: Grundlagen kollektiven Verhaltens.* Munich: R. Piper & Co., 1967.

Mitscherlich, Alexander and Margarete Mitscherlich. *The Inability to Mourn: Principles of Collective Behavior.* Translated by Beverly R. Placzek. New York: Grove, 1975.

Mitscherlich, Margarete. *Erinnerungsarbeit. Zur Psychoanalyse der Unfähigkeit zu trauern.* Frankfurt am Main: Fischer Taschenbuch, 2006.

Naudé, Beyers and Dorothee Soelle. *Hope for Faith: A Conversation.* Grand Rapids and Geneva: Wm. B. Eerdmans and WCC, 1986.

Oren, Michael. *Six Days of War and the Making of the Modern Middle East.* New York: Oxford University Press, 2001.

Pangritz, Andreas and Paul S. Chung, eds. *Theological Audacities: Selected Essays.* Eugene, OR: Pickwick, 2010.

Pinnock, Sarah K., ed. *The Theology of Dorothee Soelle.* Harrisburg, PA: Trinity Press International, 2003.

Poelchau, Harald. *Die Ordnung der Bedrängten.* Munich and Hamburg: Siebenstern Taschenbuch, 1963.

Regehr, Ernie. "Culpable Nonviolence: The Moral Ambiguity of Pacifism." In *Voices Across Boundaries*, Vol.1. #1 (Summer 2003) 42.

Rogers, Barbara. "Facing a Wall of Silence." In *Second Generation Voices: Reflections by Children of Holocaust Survivors and Perpetrators*, edited by Alan L. Berger and Naomi Berger, 293–294. Syracuse, NY: Syracuse University Press, 2001.

Rohmann, Klaus. *Vollendung im Nichts?: Eine Dokumentation der amerikanischen Gott-ist-tot-Theologie.* Zurich: Benziger, 1977.

Rubenstein, Richard L. *The Cunning of History.* New York: Harper and Row, 1975.

———. *The Religious Imagination: A Study in Psychoanalysis and Jewish Theology.* Boston: Beacon Press, 1968.

———. "The Dean and the Chosen People" in Rubenstein, *After Auschwitz*, 2nd ed. Baltimore: Johns Hopkins University Press, 1992.

———. "God after the Death of God," in *Morality and Eros.* New York: McGraw Hill, 1970.

Ruh, Hans. "Josef L. Hromádka." *Tendenzen der Theologie im 20. Jahrhundert.* Edited by H. J. Schulz. Stuttgart: Kreuz Verlag, 1966.

Rumscheidt, H. Martin "Dying is the Inmate's Highest Duty." In *Studies in Religion/Sciences religieuses*, 14, no. 4 (1985) 487–96.

Rumscheidt, H. Martin, ed. *Adolf von Harnack. Liberal Theology at its Height.* London and San Francisco: HarperCollins, 1989.

———. *Revelation and Theology. An Analysis of the Barth-Harnack Correspondence of 1923*. Cambridge: Cambridge University Press, 1972.
———. *The Way of Theology in Karl Barth: Essays and Comments*. Allison Park, PA: Pickwick, 1986.
Sauter, Gerhard. "Wahrnehmung von Geschichte." In *Glauben und Lernen*, vol. V, no. 1. (1990) 5.
Sauvage, Pierre. *Weapons of the Spirit*. Pierre Sauvage Productions, 1987.
Schäfer, Hans Dieter. "Johannes Bobrowskis Anfänge im 'Inneren Reich.'" In *Almanach für Literatur und Theologie* vol. 4. Wuppertal: Peter Hammer Verlag, 1970.
Schellong, Dieter. "On Reading Karl Barth from the Left." *Karl Barth and Radical Politics*. Philadelphia: Westminster, 1976.
Schoeps, Julius H. *Ein Volk von Mördern: Die Dokumentation zur Goldhagen-Kontroverse um die Rolle der Deutschen im Holocaust*. Hamburg: Campe, 1996.
Scholem, Gershom. *Major Trends in Jewish Mysticism*, 2nd ed. New York; Schocken Books, 1946.
Sichrowsky, Peter. *Schuldig geboren*. Cologne: Verlag Kiepenheuer und Witsch, 1987.
———. *Born Guilty: Children of Nazi Families*. Translated by Jean Steinberg. New York: Basic Books, 1988.
Soelle, Dorothee, et al., eds. *Almanach für Literatur und Theologie*. Wuppertal: Peter Hammer, 1970.
Soelle, Dorothee. *Against the Wind: Memoir of a Radical Christian*. Translated by Barbara and Martin Rumscheidt. Minneapolis: Fortress, 1999.
———. *Den Rhythmus des Lebens spüren. Inspirierter Alltag*. Edited by Bettina Hertel and Birte Petersen. Freiburg, Basel, Vienna: Herder, 2001.
———. *Gegenwind. Erinnerungen*. Hamburg: Hoffmann und Campe, 1995.
———. *Mystik und Widerstand. Du stilles Geschrei*. Hamburg: Hoffmann und Campe, 1997.
———. *The Mystery of Death*. Minneapolis: Fortress Press, 2007.
———. *The Silent Cry: Mysticism and Resistance*. Translated by Barbara and Martin Rumscheidt. Minneapolis: Fortress, 2001.
———. *Thinking About God: An Introduction to Theology*. Translated by John Bowden. Philadelphia: Trinity Press International, 1990.
Stöhr, Martin. "Leben und Glauben nach dem Holocaust." In *Dreinreden: Essays, Vorträge, Thesen, Meditationen*. Wuppertal: Foedus, 1997.
Trials of War Criminals Before the Nuremberg Military Tribunals Under Control Law No. 10, vol. 7 Nuremberg (October 1946–April 1949) 1452. Washington, DC: United States Government Printing Office, 1953. 1452.
Villa-Vicencio, Charles and Carl Niehaus, eds. *Many Cultures, One Nation. Festschrift for Beyers Naudé*. Cape Town, Johannesburg, Pretoria: Human and Rousseau Ltd, 1995.
Wagner, Bernd C. *IG Auschwitz: Zwangsarbeit und Vernichtung von Häftlingen des Lagers Monowitz 1941–1945*. Munich: K. G. Saur.
Wagner, Gottfried. "To be German after the Holocaust: The Misused Concept of Identity." In *Second Generation Voices: Reflections by Children of Holocaust Survivors and Perpetrators*, edited by Alan L. Berger and Naomi Berger, 351. Syracuse, NY: Syracuse University Press, 2001.
Weissmark, Mona Sue. *Justice Matters: Legacies of the Holocaust and World War II*. Oxford: Oxford University Press, 2004.

Wiesel, Elie. *Night*. New York: Hill and Wang, 2006.
Winzeler, Peter. *Widerstehene Theologie: Karl Barth 1929–35*. Stuttgart: Alektor, 1982.
World Council of Churches. "Vulnerable Populations at Risk: Statement on the Responsibility to Protect." www.oikumene.org/gr/resources/documents/wcc-commissions/international-affairs/responsibility-to-protect/vulnerable-populations-at-risk